CONFESSIONS OF AN
OSU USHER

A Big Buckeye
Thank You
to all the food service workers and volunteer ushers at Ohio Stadium for your continued dedication to excellence.

Go Bucks!

THE
OHIO STATE
BUCKEYE USHER JOURNAL

CONFESSIONS OF AN
OSU USHER

by
TREVOR ZAHARA

foreword by
JACK PARK

Book Design & Production
Columbus Publishing Lab
www.ColumbusPublishingLab.com

LCCN 2014948134

Print ISBN 978-1-63337-008-1
E-book ISBN 978-1-63337-009-8

Printed in the United States of America
1 3 5 7 9 10 8 6 4 2

TABLE OF CONTENTS

For my loving wife Patti—
without her, none of this would have been possible!

FOREWORD

The Ohio State football program is steeped deeply in tradition. For 125 years it has provided incredible enjoyment and memorable experiences for fans of all ages—life-long friendships, incredible personal remembrances, national titles, thrilling victories, agonizing setbacks, abundant individual awards, and that noteworthy encounter each season with "that team up north."

Author Trevor Zahara, Ohio Stadium Portal Chief Section B-8, has created one of Ohio State Football's most distinctive publications. The Ohio Stadium Ushers are some of the Buckeyes' most committed people. Trevor reveals some of the most humorous, unusual, and captivating experiences of this very dedicated group. His long hours of research bring to light an abundance of fascinating stories.

I know Trevor Zahara personally, and look forward to talking with Trevor at Ohio Stadium prior to each game. This is a very unique Ohio State football book that will bring hours of enjoyment for Buckeye fans of all ages. Enjoy "Confessions of an OSU Usher!" You will be uplifted and feel a personal connection with many of these noteworthy happenings.

— **Jack Park**
Ohio State Football Analyst and Author
Commentator, Sports Radio 97.1 The Fan

PROLOGUE

Winners, I am convinced, imagine their dreams
first. They want it with all their heart and expect it to
come true. There is, I believe, no other way to live.
—**Joe Montana**

Those of us old enough to remember the 1958 TV show recall, "There are eight million stories in the Naked City." Well just as many stories have taken place at the Ohio Stadium. On game days this most famous of college football showplaces is transformed into a vibrant city of over 110,000 excited fans, security forces, tailgaters, vendors, Redcoats and the Ushers.

Having been an Usher at Ohio Stadium since 1997 I have listened to some funny, heartwarming, and a few downright incredible stories. The journal you are about to read includes some of the most entertaining of these stories in the Ushers' own words, so you can grasp the humor, the heartache and the hometown flavor of these tales.

It all started many years ago when, during the football off-season, I would have lunch with Jim Norris and some of the other Ushers. We listened for hours to all the great anecdotes and tales about fans, celebrities, and others who had the good fortune to attend OSU home games. It was disappointing to me that no one was documenting these tales.

Our good friend Jim Norris, and Head of the Ushers passed away on February 9, 2011 at the too-young age of 61. Therefore, I blame Jim for all the stories you are about to read. Knowing Jim, he would have wholeheartily approved this endeavor.

Jim was a 1967 graduate of Bexley High School. He received his B.A., B.S. and M.A., Education degrees from OSU. Jim was a 30+ year teacher with the Columbus Public Schools before his retirement in 2003. After his retirement, he taught at Otterbein College and advised student teachers. He penned supplemental textbooks and was an editor and co-author, as well. An avid Buckeye, Jim was an Usher at Ohio Stadium for over 40 years and served as Head of Ushers (1997-2011). Jim was a true renaissance man who enjoyed cooking, gardening, card-making, colloguing and was a master of trivia.

James A. Norris

THE
OHIO STATE
BUCKEYE USHER JOURNAL

1

THE JOURNEY BEGINS

When I began this journey I started getting all kinds of feedback from relatives, associates, executives, band members, the media, celebrities and other characters. It all started with, "Did you hear this one?" or wait until you hear what happened to me at the stadium or other Buckeye related events. Whether at a family gathering, business event, golf match or other social event, I soon realized that a lot of folks had a special interest in the Bucks and wanted to add to the journal.

I incorporated these stories and also took the liberty of detailing my own passionate path as a 1971 alumnus. I hope that you can see by the scope of my involvement with The Ohio State University and the passion I have for the university, it means more than attending a sporting event. I was amazed by the total number of my family, friends and co-workers who attended Ohio State and how equally passionate they were for the university.

ONCE UPON A TIME IN COLUMBUS...

I don't usually answer the telephone after 9:00 on a weeknight but I was expecting a call from my boss. An old colleague, Ron Friday, was on the line and after the usual back-and-forth banter my friend dropped the bomb: "We have an opening for an Usher at my portal—would you want to be an Usher?" Obviously I was thrilled to learn of this opportunity. The kicker was that I had to make up my mind that evening. Ron explained that an Usher at his portal had been offered a position in Kansas. I had subbed for this guy in the past and loved it. After conferring with my wife Patti I decided to accept Ron's offer.

How in the heck did Ron pull this off? It appears that the Head Usher was retiring and Ron had worked with this guy for many years, so Ron was allowed to hand pick his portal Ushers. The decision was made and now all I had to do was wait for my first football season to start.

2014 USHER/REDCOAT PROGRAM

529 Ushers ... that volunteer at home games, assisting in every stadium portal

185 Supervisors ... oversee the volunteer Ushers and manage stadium portal areas

475 Redcoats ... scan tickets, work in the club-seating areas and in the press box, among other duties

36 New Ushers ... for the 2014 season

50 Boy Scout Ushers

1953 ... year that the longest-serving Usher began

Ushers—In Their Own Words...

The spirit, the will to win, and the will to excel are the things that endure. These qualities are so much more important than the events that occur.

—Vince Lombardi

Mission Statement

Ushers are to provide quality guest service to all individuals who patronize The Ohio State University. The goal is to create and maintain a safe, enjoyable and entertaining atmosphere. This is achieved through four main concepts:

1. Service
2. Safety
3. Courtesy
4. Neat Appearance

The following stories are from my fellow Ushers at Ohio Stadium: These dedicated volunteers come from all walks of life, doctors, lawyers, business owners, factory workers, CEOs, retirees etc., each with a story to tell.

South Stadium

You Did What??

Jim Howard, portal chief South Stands, 35-37 AA-A –B, has been an

Usher since 1979. Jim played football for Woody Hayes in the 1950s. He weighed 215 pounds (now 155), tore up his knee and ended his football career. He joined the Navy and, with a firm push from Woody, went to flight school (Senator John McCain was in his flight class). After the Navy, he went back to OSU and graduated in 1968.

Alabama-Birmingham game- September 22, 2012. Jim was notified by one of the Ushers in B-35 that a lady in his section was extremely distressed and needed help. She was crying and between sobs blurted out that she had lost her purse and her husband, who was disabled, could not help her.

Jim consoled the lady and said that he could help her find her purse. She replied, "I didn't lose my purse — I dropped it into the Porta-Potty!" Evidently she had placed her purse on a shelf in the Porta-Potty and when she stood up she knocked the purse into the hole in the pot. The purse landed upside down with all the contents spilled into the mess below. Anyone who has ever used a Porta-Potty knows what is in the bottom of that nasty thing!

While silently wondering if this was in his job description Jim immediately decided that he had to help this lady. She said they had driven down from Michigan (that explains some of it), and all her money — $300 — credit cards, IDs and other important stuff was intermingled with all the human waste along with that thick blue liquid junk that is supposed to keep the smell down.

Jim told the lady to not let anyone else near the Porta-Potty, then went to the maintenance people and procured several pairs of rubber gloves, a bucket and a few boxes and returned to the scene of the crime. He put on the gloves, held his nose, reached his arm through the hole and fished out the purse and the contents that he could find in the mess. Next he gave a pair of gloves to the lady and told her to separate the critical items she wanted to keep and dispose of the rest of the saturated possessions into the bio-bag.

He took the valuables down to the men's restroom on A-Deck and proceeded to clean them in the sink. He returned the freshly cleansed items to the lady.

She thanked Jim profusely and offered to pay him a reward. Jim replied, "We are here to provide a service to our fans and would not accept any reward." He then questioned the lady: "Wouldn't you do the same for me?"

Without hesitation the lady replied, "Are you out of your mind?"

OSU won the game 29-15.

The next home game, his supervisor Larry Black presented Jim a plaque honoring his service above and beyond the call of duty with a certificate of the Grand Order of Porta-Potties emblazoned with a picture of a potty!

A winner never whines.

—**Paul Brown**

NEVER, EVER GIVE UP!

Ron Byrd, Usher for three years at 37-38 B South Stands:

I was at work when I noticed a fellow wearing an OSU Usher shirt collecting our aluminum cans for charity. We got into a conversation about how he became an Usher and how I could be one. He gave me all the information and after five long years I got the call from Jim Norris and one of my dreams finally came true. I was an Usher at Ohio Stadium!

Unfortunately, my good fortune was short-lived; while traveling on my Suzuki Savage 650 along Sunbury Road in Westerville, a 16-year-old driver plowed into me. After flying through the air, I landed with a thud. Before blacking out I really thought I had bought the farm. Waking up in the hospital I learned that the EMTs had to cut my helmet off (it saved my life), I lost a kidney and the doctor said my stomach looked like a bomb had gone off inside it. I was lucky that in addition to my great helmet, I had on a Kevlar vest and boots; this allowed me, after many months of rehabilitation, to return to my Ushering position during the fall. In fact, the powers that be must have thought I was one tough SOB, and made me a portal chief that year.

My hard head has also made me very stubborn. As a portal chief our directions are to check everyone's ticket as they enter the portal. Well, one fellow took exception to showing me his ticket, so I blocked his entrance with my arm on the steel railing. It became a battle of wills; neither of us would back down. This guy was going to charge me with assault! A police officer was summoned to the portal and listened attentively to both sides of our lively discussion. Because the game was starting the officer advised the guest to show his ticket, shake hands and enjoy the game. Cooler heads prevailed!

ROPE BURNS

Ed McCleaf has been an Usher since 1978 at various locations in C-Deck, South Stands and on the field. He is currently the South Stadium Superintendent:

One of the benefits of Ushering in the South Stands is having easy access to the field. Prior to the renovation to the stadium in 2001 one of our primary responsibilities was to "man the ropes" as the teams entered and exited the field. Sometimes this became quite difficult when only three Ushers tried to hold back dozens of fans trying to get a glimpse or even touch their heroes.

One time in particular, I believe it was the Iowa game in November 1979, the weather was nasty, wet and cold and it was difficult to grasp the rope, even with gloves. I lost hold of the rope and fell backwards, did a flip that would make a gymnast proud and ended up sitting in a mud puddle. Needless to say I was embarrassed. As I attempted to get to my feet a hand was extended to help. I found myself eye-to-eye with the Iowa Coach, Hayden Fry. After Coach Fry and a gigantic state highway patrolman helped me to my feet, he asked me if I was all right and chatted with me for a while before he resumed his coaching duties.

I learned that Coach Hayden was hired after the 1978 season to try to reverse Iowa's fortunes. After decades of losing, Fry revived the Iowa program. In 20 years at Iowa, he led the Hawks to 14 bowl games, three Big Ten titles and three Rose Bowl appearances. He retired in 1998.

Among the legends Fry left behind is the iconic pink visitor's locker room, as well as a statement he made the day he started as Iowa Head Coach that he would take the team to a bowl game within four years or he would step down. He would not only succeed in his boast, by sending Iowa to the 1982 Rose Bowl, he would do it in three years, coming in one year under his promise and compiling a career college football record of 232-178-10. He was inducted into the College Football Hall of Fame as a coach in 2003. I will always remember his kind act that day. And by the way, the Bucks won that day, 34-7!

As mentioned, it is a lot of fun being down on the field and provides many wonderful experiences. I especially enjoy it when I have the opportunity to see a youngster screaming his head off as they watch the team storm out of the locker room. They get very excited; eyes wide open and scream their "heads off." Their parents are always very thankful and say their kids will always fondly remember this day. It also gives me great satisfaction of a job well done!

South Stadium Crew

We have to be realistic. If we don't win, life will continue.

— **Hayden Fry**

Richard Leslie, Tim Miller, Dan Griffin, Matthew Hall
(Missing from the picture are Troy Embry and Ken Emerson)

A-DECK

A MIND READER

Dan Griffin has been an Usher and portal chief for 10 years in A-14-16. He grew up in Columbus and is probably one of the few Ushers/Redcoats who actually LIVED in the stadium. While attending Ohio State in the late 1970s, he lived in the Stadium Scholarship dorm. "We used to be able to go out on the field at night and we had our stadium intramural softball leagues in the stadium." He met his wife while attending Ohio State and his daughter also met her husband at OSU. Everyone knows he bleeds scarlet and gray! He writes:

One of my co-workers told me he was coming to the game and it turned out he would be sitting in my section with his brother who was visiting from Montana. I asked him if he wanted to have some fun with his brother when he came in, and he thought that would be great (it was his brother's first OSU game).

When my co-worker Todd and his brother entered my portal, I immediately stopped him and said that I was practicing my "mind reading skills" and wanted to see if I could try them on him.

He reluctantly said "ah...sure" and his brother looked confused but interested. I told Todd to hold one side of his ticket, and I would hold the other and I would read his mind through the ticket. I said that I was getting a decent strength signal from the ticket and asked him if his name was Tom or something like that.

His brother's eyes widened with surprise. I then said that it felt like he worked for the state of Ohio (he works for a state agency). Lastly I correctly guessed that he had two kids and "just missed" his kids' names.

Todd exclaimed, "Hey, you're pretty good — you want to try this on my brother?"

The brother was looking at me suspiciously at this point. I told him to hold his end of the ticket and I told him I had real strong signals emitting from his ticket. I told him it felt like this was his first OSU game and that I sensed that he was in from out of town— somewhere out west. I asked if he lived in Montana or Wyoming? I then correctly guessed his name. At this point I told the guys I had to go because there were some other folks coming up the aisle. His brother followed Todd to his seat and sat down but periodically kept looking back at me.

He told his brother, "Man, that Usher is freaking me out — how did he know all that?" Todd said he had heard of an Usher who likes to read minds of fans. For the next two quarters, I occasionally glanced up toward them and every time, his brother was looking at me as if I was a ghost.

Finally at halftime I couldn't take it, so I told him that I worked with Todd and he just started laughing hysterically.

A-Deck Crew

Catch That Thief!

Section 14-A ,typically has various local celebrities and state politicians hidden within the loyal season ticket holders. One memory that always makes me smile: I once saw three young co-eds ask an elderly gentleman if he would take their picture. One of the ladies gave him her camera and he immediately said "thanks" and pretended to head off into the exit portal. Shocked, the girls yelled "hey" and started to run after the man as he darted toward the exit. Little did they know they had just been duped by former Franklin County Sheriff Jim Karnes, who was not in uniform and attended every game with his wife in our section. The girls had no idea who he was until I introduced them. They had a great laugh and a memory for a lifetime! And yes, he did return the camera.

A Deck Crew

DREAM JOB

Dan Yoder, 28-30 AA, has been an Usher since 2008:

I often talked about my desire to be an Usher at OSU. I searched on the web until I finally dug up the name of Jim Norris who at the time was in charge of Redcoats and Ushers at OSU. So after numerous phone calls, I called him to talk to him about becoming an Usher.

This was early on in Jim Tressel's years, and I was told that there was a waiting list of four years or so, and because of that, it may be better to try to be a Redcoat, since I could start the following year. I told him no, I would rather wait it out and be an Usher.

As an Usher at Ohio Stadium, Dan Yoder, from Archbold, Ohio, helps an OSU fan find her seat at a Buckeyes football game in October. Yoder became an Usher this year after waiting six years to be called. One perk of the job? He gets to watch the Buckeyes play. Photo by Scott Schultz. For an Ohio State Buckeyes football fan, Dan Yoder has a dream job.

Mr. Norris explained how to go about becoming an Usher.

At the end of our discussion he said, "Now for the hard part. When I receive your application, I will put it at the back of the file, and when your application gets to the front, I will call you. It is going to take at least four, maybe five or more years, since the turnover has slowed down since the hiring of Mr. Tressel. You just need to trust that I will move yours up as the applications are taken out."

And so the wait began. Year five came and went, as did six, and seven. At the start of the eighth year Mr. Norris called and said, "Dan, are you still interested in being an Usher for OSU?" I of course said yes and was invited down for orientation and told to show up at the first game that year.

At the first game, like all the rest of the first time Ushers, I was told to sign in and move off to the side where we waited until our name was called and we were given an assignment. I happened to be the third person signed in, and overheard the first two, sent to a section in C-Deck, then waited until Mr. Norris called my name. He said, "Dan, do you know where 28-30-AA is?"

I said, "Sure."

He said, "They need extra people there this week, would you go help them?" I quickly left before he could change his mind! I felt so fortunate to be sent to 28-30-AA, which is where the team comes out of the tunnel.

Each week I would pick someone who had their little boy there for his first game and take him down the steps to the gate, close to where the team came out of the tunnel, and let him stand there while the team took the field. How fun it was to see the eyes of those little ones just light up when the team came out of the locker room to take the field. The parents' appreciation was nice, but the joy on the faces of those kids is something I will never forget.

I have made many friends, some of whom come to my new area just to say hey or chat a bit about our Bucks every time they are at a game. That has been the best part for me of being an Usher, making lasting friendships with the many fans I have come to know so well.

One of the best stories I can remember comes from the Nebraska game in 2012. I was at my portal when they announced the gates were open. In a few moments, a couple dressed in complete Cornhusker garb was standing next to me, one snapping pictures while the other was on the phone talking to friends about how much bigger the stadium was than the one in Nebraska and how nice a day it was and the like.

The longer the gentleman was on the phone, the more frustrated his wife appeared so I struck up a conversation with her and before long the guy was off the phone. I continued my con-

versation with the two of them and learned they stopped on their way home from vacation to see if they could get a ticket, which cost them $300 apiece from a scalper, who had been kind enough to escort them to the stadium since the gentleman was worried the ticket would be no good.

Since I have relatives from Nebraska, I thought I would see where the two were from. He smiled and said, "Well, you probably never heard of the town. It's called Beatrice." And I smiled, thinking to myself, this guy is going to know my relatives.

He chuckled and asked why I was smiling, and I said, "I do in fact know where Beatrice is. I have relatives who live there." He asked what their last name was and I said, "Their last name is WEIBE."

He smiled and said, "Sure it is." Then he asked, "What is your aunt's first name?"

I said, "It's Vera."

He said, "I do know her, she goes to the same church I do — in fact I took her, her daughter and son-in-law out for dinner before we left on vacation."

He gave me a business card, telling me his daughter works in the ticket office at the university, and that when the Bucks travel to Nebraska for the game there, to call him and he will get us a ticket, and we can stay at my cousin's house, go tailgate with him, go to the game and have a great day together. How fun!

LOTTERY TICKET ANYONE?

Mark Wise, a 1977 graduate of The Ohio State University with a BA in Journalism, has been an Usher in 25-A since 2006 (seven years):

In 1968 I was at the Ohio State vs. Purdue home game. I did not know at the time we would win the National Championship.

Mark Wise touring the stadium after an Usher Meeting-2013

This was back in the old days when the stadium held 84,000. I was sitting in the bleachers and the crowd was going wild. Confetti was coming down all over; I looked down and to my surprise a piece of confetti landed on my knee. I realized it was a ripped up phone book and to my surprise what landed on my knee was my own name, address and phone number.

After the game I went down to the end zone and grabbed a piece of pay dirt from the end zone. To this day I have the pay dirt and my name and address in a case on my mantle. I figured the odds were 84,000 people and 2,000,000 people in the Columbus phone book.

This was before they had the lottery...hmm!

THAT'S GOING TO LEAVE A MARK!

Phil Stidham, an Army veteran, has been an Usher since 2002 in 13-15 A:

Phil Stidham, Vicki Fritzen, Kevin Lloyd, Tom Henry, Don McVay

On October 26, 2002, #10-ranked Penn State came to the Shoe to play #2-ranked Ohio State. The pre-game fever was sky high as all the usual traditions were taking place. The flag-raising is one of those time-honored traditions; ROTC cadets march out in precision to take their positions in the ceremony. The huge flag is unfurled as cadets on both sides of the flag hold it in place while other cadets grab the ropes to start raising the flag up the 150-foot pole. When the flag reaches its pinnacle the last cadet holding the rope runs down the ramp to secure the ropes.

Unfortunately, it was a very windy day, the flag caught a draft and as the cadet was heading full speed down the ramp, that draft pulled the rope taut and the poor fellow rammed headfirst into the casement and lay groggy on the ground. You could hear the whole crowd groan at the same time. As he staggered to his feet, his unsympathetic sidekick was laughing his butt off while trying to gallantly hold his salute. As the cadet made his way back to his seat I heard a fan in the stands comment, "You might want to put some ice on that."

11-A, Mike Esch, Kathy and Bill Staber, Gerald and Mary Cole, portal chief David Culver
Coldest Game Ever! Indiana 2013

UNDER COVER OF B-DECK

The difference between a successful person and others is not a lack of strength, not a lack of knowledge, but rather a lack of will.

—Vince Lombardi

PASSION AND LOYALTY

Ron Friday. When you talk about passion and loyalty, my mentor, Ron Friday and his dad Paul had a total of 94 years as Ushers in section B-8. They both traveled from Cincinnati for every game — between the two they logged over 150,000 miles getting to the games. Known to his friends as "Rjay," he was an all-around athlete from Barnesville High School who played football for two years at Ohio University until he injured his right shoulder and realized he liked frat parties better than getting beat up as a back-up tackle. After four years of Air Force ROTC, he graduated from OU and entered the military as a 2nd Lieutenant; he went to Pilot Training and flew the F-86 until they were phased out in 1961. After eight years in the Air Force, he resigned his commission as Captain in 1967:

My dad worked in 8-B from 1939 until his death in 1996. He missed only two games: the snow game in 1950, I think, and when I got married in 1959. He gave up being portal chief when he turned 70. I took over then.

RUN OF THE STADIUM

As a youngster, in the late 40s early 50s, I loved going to the games with my dad. He would walk me right into the games, along with all the other Ushers. This was in a more trusting time, before 9/11 and all of the added security.

When my dad got busy with his duties, it was great having the run of the stadium. I would find all kinds of mischief to keep me busy — from visiting the cop on top of the columns on the north end of the stadium to bumming soda from the concession stand.

Dad did not have a lot of patience with some of our customers in 8-B if they did not follow the rules. I had to calm him down at times. If anyone dared stand anywhere in the portal, he reminded them in no uncertain words, to MOVE.

I remember that often he made anyone who wore a nasty t-shirt turn it inside out. If they gave him any grief he would have us find a cop. That was usually all it took for the offender to abide by Dad's rules!

TRAGEDY ON B-DECK

It was the second game of the 2001 season, the crowd was just settling in to watch the Bucks tear up the Toledo Rockets when we heard someone in the crowd scream, "This man needs help! Call the squad!"

I looked up and about eight rows back I saw a man crumpled over and people gathered around him. I had all my Ushers rush to his aid and help carry him out. He was a rather large man and it took six of us to get him down the ramp. The medical personnel arrived and started CPR trying to revive him. They worked frantically to save his life, but unfortunately he passed away.

At the next home game against the Colorado Buffaloes, I noticed the deceased man's wife was in attendance, so after giving her my heartfelt condolences the lady said this was the way her husband would have preferred to leave this earth — he was a passionate Ohio State fan and loved the Buckeyes! She attended the remainder of the games that year to honor her husband.

Trevor Zahara, Perry Jones. Bob Vargo, Gary Snyder. Merry Christmas! Indiana Game 2013

Squeeze In

The Michigan game in 2004 was the coldest of the year and as usual the stadium was sold out. As the fans poured into the stands, all the Ushers were frantically trying to seat the last of the stragglers. On these freezing days the fans often stay at the bars, restaurants and tailgates until the last minute, creating a mad rush minutes before kickoff.

A middle-aged lady approached me, complaining that she had no seat — there must be someone taking her spot. I accompanied her to her section in row 17. Her seat was 23. I looked down the row and immediately understood the situation. There in the middle of the row were four of the largest gentlemen I have ever seen. Tressel would have loved to have these guys on the offensive line! They looked like sumo wrestlers in their winter coats.

I thought to myself, "Oh, crap we have a problem." Being the Michigan game, I realized that relocating the lady would be tough, but I noticed a couple of empty box seats. So I moved the couple to some much better seats.

Everyone was happy and OSU beat that team up north. 37-21!

Don't give up at half-time. Concentrate on winning the second half.

—Paul Bear Bryant

$10,000 Bet

Perry Jones has been an Usher since 1989 in section B-8. Perry and his buddy Bob drive 125 miles from his hometown in St. Clairsville to Columbus for every game:

I was very excited to attend my first Michigan game as an Usher; both teams were rated in AP's top 20. It was a hard fought first half with OSU on top 10-6 at halftime.

As is tradition, the visiting band takes the field first for their halftime show and all was going well until a streaker ran out onto the field and started doing cartwheels through the Michigan band. This fellow, who was later identified as former Eastern Michigan football player Matt Swank, 27, of Canton, Ohio, wore only maize and blue paint as he ran the length of the field in front of 100,000 fans.

When he reached the end zone the Columbus Police were there to wrap him in a trench coat. All he had in his possession was an ID he had clenched in his teeth!

According to the Ann Arbor Journal, Swank said he did it on a $10,000 bet, pleaded no contest to a charge of being disorderly involving obscene conduct. Before accepting the plea, District Judge Timothy P. Connors questioned Swank about his November 25 dash. "Now I want you to tell me how much this bet was you made. And I know the answer and I want to see if you'll tell me the truth," Connors said.

Swank took a breath and said, "Well, it was $10,000."

He faced a $100 fine and 90 days in jail at his January 26 sentencing. Swank's lawyer, Ronald Egnor, said the $10,000 bet is probably uncollectable. "This was a prank, pure and simple," Egnor said. I never did find out if Swank was convicted, but OSU got whipped 16-13 by the team up north, darn it!

Pain heals. Chicks dig scars. Glory lasts forever.

—Vince McKewin,
from the movie The Replacements

Hot Ticket

The Akron game, September 3, 2011, had to be the hottest game I can recall in my 24 years as an Usher in section B-8. B-Deck provides shelter from the rain, even though the "legend of Woody Hayes" prevents rain from falling on game day at the Shoe. It can also be stifling hot during the early games in late August and early September. When the new addition was built in 2001 the outer shell of the stadium completely surrounded the length of B-Deck in the enclosed part of the stadium, which makes it difficult for air to circulate in the higher rows.

The weatherman said it was over 90 degrees in Columbus, but for the people packed shoulder to shoulder on the bench seats high up in B-Deck it had to be over 100 degrees. People were noticeably drenched in sweat with bright red faces. They had to be true die-hard fans to endure that heat. There were more calls for first aid during that game than any other in history. One fellow in my section collapsed and the medical personnel showed up in minutes. They finally revived the poor guy and wheeled him to the first aid station. He was back in his seat for the second half cheering the Buckeyes on to their victory over Akron.

Water Monsters

After the learning experience of that sweltering Akron game in 2011, an action plan was established for future early season games. According to James Ericson, Assistant Director, Event Management, "To alleviate what happened in September 2011, all concession stands offer free courtesy cups of water and we purchased multiple Water Monsters (huge stand-alone vats) that are strategically placed around the stadium."

Usher Judith Hensel, who ran one of the monster water stations, said, "The fans were very grateful at the 2013 opening game against Buffalo on August 31. The temperature soared to near 90 degrees as the sweaty fans lined up to accept the free water."

Greg First, Red Cross volunteer, said this was a typical opening-game day, with over 160 heat related incidents. The American Red Cross has provided first aid during Ohio State games for decades, with over 50 volunteers dispatched across the six first aid stations inside the stadium. First commented, "Heat-related games are not my most favorite games. It's a lose-lose situation as an onslaught of overheated fans arrived at the first aid station."

The real glory is being knocked to your knees and then coming back. That's real glory.

—Vince Lombardi

Great to Be an American

Jason Overly has been an Usher for five years:

The Ushers have to enter the stadium three hours before game time, so I set my alarm for 4 a.m., eat breakfast, shower and gather all my Usher gear, then head out to meet my carpool buddies, Bob and Perry, for 1½-hour drive to the stadium. We arrive at the Lane Ave. parking garage, walk across the street and take the bus to the stadium. Perry has a disability parking pass due to an injury that prevents him from walking great distances. We check in at gate A-8 and head up to our work area at portal B-8.

As soon as his supervisor's meeting is over, our portal chief, Trevor Zahara gave us our briefing. Trevor told us The Ohio State University and its Athletics Department would be honoring the men and women serving in the U.S. armed forces with a variety of activities and recognitions before and during the football game. The events had been planned as part of the Veteran's Day celebration. The Illinois game, November 10, 2007 was designated as Military Appreciation Day; the stadium announcer asked for a moment of silence before the National Anthem,

then there was a fly-over of F-16s. The crowd went wild as the jets flew over the stadium. My heart skipped a beat and the hair on the back of my neck stood on end and I felt a flush of pride. The crowd cheered as if the Bucks had scored a touchdown!

Ohio State's request for football events usually are a high priority for the pilots. After the fly-over they are invited to watch the game and are introduced at halftime. With the average speed of 300 knots (about 350 mph), the planes are visible for only a few seconds, but Col. Zane Brown, director of operations for the Ohio Air National Guard, knows well the time and energy that goes into each pass: "With every plane you see flying in these things, there's a lot going on behind the scenes. Everyone takes these seriously. It takes a lot of planning." The planning is as extensive as mission preparation, he said, and requires timing almost as precise.

"First we define the route and the timing, take a look at what we're trying to see and look at the hazards. In Afghanistan, it might be small-arms fire. In Ohio Stadium, it is civilian traffic, coordinating with local air-traffic control, banner tows and things like that. Such hazards must be frequently assessed on the fly be-

cause of smaller aircraft that might not be in contact with any control tower or other aircraft. With such obstacles, coupled with the height, speed and direction calculations, pilots have plenty to worry about while in the air.

"Upon arriving at the predetermined position calculated by how long the jets need to reach their target, the planes begin looping around the area. In contact with someone on the ground at the event, the pilots often have to try to adjust the flyover to the ending of the National Anthem, giving them only seconds to time the pass, which explains the occasional gap between the final note and the aircraft flying over the stadium."

The military celebrations went on during the first quarter break and all the Ushers that served in the military would be honored on the field at halftime. I was among the many Ushers to be recognized for service in the United States Armed Forces. The OSU band's halftime show would honor all the armed forces; Air Force, Army, Coast Guard, Marines and Navy.

This was an exciting time for me, an ex-Marine sergeant. This was especially rewarding to me because I served during the Vietnam conflict, an unpopular war that split the nation, consequently not a very good time to be in the Marines. I remember coming

home to very little fanfare for my fellow servicemen and women. A lot of us didn't even wear our uniforms when we returned from overseas. So it was nice to hear the cheers of the crowd for those that served so gallantly over the years. We all huddled under the goalposts in the north end of the field, taking each other's pictures and reveling in all the band's activities. It made me proud to be a Marine, Semper Fi!

Every generation of Americans must be expected to do their part to maintain freedom for their country and freedom for those associated with it...there is no final victory in a difficult and dangerous world.

—John F. Kennedy

THE JOKER

Bob Zadrozny started Ushering in 1969 as an Usher at 22-C, moved to track security and is presently the B-East Superintendent responsible for the supervision of all portal chiefs and Ushers on the east side of B-Deck. He has missed only one game during this time and is currently serving on the advisory board to make recommendations for the betterment of the Usher program. His day job was working as a teacher and administrator for the Columbus City Schools for 44 years. He reports that he is currently retired — "sort of":

Several years ago, as I was making my rounds and taking attendance, I stopped at one portal and told a joke I had heard the previous day. The joke was a hit and so I retold it at the next portal. The joke was well received there as well, and I figured I might be on to something.

Ever since, I have made it a B-Deck tradition to tell a joke to each portal as I visit to take attendance. It seems that the "joke of the day" is now expected and I am quickly reminded if I move on without telling one. As part of the tradition I always have one week of the season where each portal must come up with a joke to tell me the following week.

It isn't everyone who gets to hear 14 bad jokes in a single day.

JOKE OF THE DAY

A 6-year-old and a 4-year-old are raking the yard.

The 6-year-old asks, "You know what? I think it's about time we started learning to cuss." The 4-year-old nods his head in approval.

The 6-year-old continues, "When we go in for breakfast, I'm gonna say something with hell and you say something with ass." The 4-year-old agrees with enthusiasm.

When the mother walks into the kitchen and asks the 6-year-old what he wants for breakfast, he replies, "Aw, hell, Mom, I guess I'll have some Cheerios." WHACK!

He flies out of his chair, tumbles across the kitchen floor, gets up and runs upstairs crying his eyes out, with his mother in hot pursuit, slapping his rear with every step. His mom locks him in his room and shouts, "You can stay there until I let you out!"

She then comes back downstairs, looks at the 4-year-old and asks with a stern voice, "And what do YOU want for breakfast, young man?"

"I don't know," he blubbers, "but you can bet your fat ass it won't be Cheerios!"

TRIPLE OVERTIME THRILLER

The most exciting game I remember is when the North Carolina State Wolfpack visited Ohio Stadium in 2003. The Bucks were on a 16-game winning streak and fans were thrilled by the first overtime game in the history of the stadium as well as the longest game ever for OSU, lasting 4 hours and 17 minutes.

The Bucks held what seemed to be a comfortable 24-7 lead in the 4th quarter before Wolfpack quarterback Philip Rivers ignited a comeback. Rivers threw for a pair of touchdowns and NC State added a field goal in the final minutes of regulation to tie the game at 24.

Then things got really interesting. Buckeye quarterback Craig Krenzel ran for a 6-yard touchdown in the first overtime period before Rivers tossed his fourth touchdown pass of the game to send the action into a second overtime, where the teams traded touchdowns again, setting up the third overtime!

Krenzel threw a 7-yard touchdown pass to Michael Jenkins but then misfired on the 2-point conversion, leaving the Wolfpack with a chance at victory. But on 4th-and-goal at the 1-yard line, OSU defenders A.J. Hawk and Will Allen stopped NC State tailback T.J. McLendon just short of the goal line to preserve the win for the Bucks, 44-38.

It's not whether you get knocked down; it's whether you get back up.

—Vince Lombardi

Iowa Game, October 19, 2013: Gary Snyder,
Trevor Zahara, E.Gordon Gee, Perry Jones and Bob Vargo

HERE COMES THE (FORMER) PRESIDENT!

Bob Zadrozny is a member of the advisory board that makes suggestions for the betterment of the Usher program, so we are constantly coming up with ideas. One of the ideas was for former OSU President E. Gordon Gee to be an Honorary Usher for the Iowa game in 2013.

President Gee showed up at portal B-8 at 2:50 p.m. and immediately gave me a big hug and told me what a great honor it was to be selected as the 2nd Honorary Usher at Ohio Stadium (Anne Hayes was the first in 1989). He apologized for being five minutes late. I looked at Gary, a fellow Usher, and said, "Let's give him five demerits." We all laughed.

I introduced him to Bob and Perry, the other Ushers who work the upper ramp, and then I explained to Dr. Gee his Usher duties. He then immediately started "working the crowd" and once people realized who was at our portal, out came their cameras and photo requests.

Dr. Gee was most gracious and posed with fans of all ages. Even though I didn't get much work out of Dr. Gee, his presence was well received. Many fans came up to me remarking how cool it was to have Dr. Gee mingle with the crowd.

Dr. Gee left after about 40 minutes saying what an honor and joy it was to be selected as an Honorary Usher and that he would cherish his Usher jacket. He said to pass on to all the other Ushers what a wonderful job they are doing to make The Ohio State University the best place in the country to attend a football game. "GO BUCKS!"

Bob Zadonzny, Dr.E Gordon Gee

You Meet Some Great People

Bob Vargo, 83, has been an Usher at B-8 for 24 years and travels from St. Clairsville with his buddy Perry for every game. Bob has missed only one game in 24 years; his granddaughter got married during the Michigan game a few years ago. Bob quipped, "Did I tell you she's no longer in my will?" Bob has a great sense of humor and is one of the friendliest and good-natured Ushers in the stadium.

Bob always greets the fans with a huge smile. He says "welcome to the stadium" and slaps hands with all the little kids, after which he crinkles his fingers — like the little fellow just destroyed his hand with that massive slap. Then they both burst out laughing!

He and Perry are stationed at the top of the ramp in our portal, giving Bob the ability to see who is walking up the ramp. When a husband and wife walk up together he points out the location of their seats to the husband then says, "Welcome sir, is this your daughter with you?" The wife walks to her seat with a big smile on her face! If he spots a fan with the opposition as they walk up the ramp he shouts, "Sorry we are all sold out!" Everyone has a good laugh. You can really tell when someone enjoys their job:

> *One of the benefits of being an Usher for so many years is that you get to meet some great people. Every year we get to welcome back the season ticket holders that retain their same seats in our*

Michelle Harcha, Howard Harcha, Bob Vargo

section. A family, the Harchas, have the box seats positioned right next to the column where I stand during the game. Over the years I have enjoyed sharing laughs, football stories and learning details of the lives of Howard, a retired attorney, his wife Mary Lee and their children. I would meet the couple at the bottom of the ramp and assist Mary Lee to her seat; for years she would show up at the games with her walker. After storing her walker, I would get updates on the family and share our thoughts on the game.

I noticed at one of the games that Mary Lee was not as cheerful and talkative as usual. She shared with us that she was battling cancer. The next season Howard walked up the ramp with his daughter at his side; Howard informed us that Mary Lee had lost her battle with cancer. Needless to say we were all very sad for the family, but we were heartened to see Howard show up for every game, either with his daughter, Michelle, a veterinarian who works at the OSU College of Veterinary Medicine or his son, Scioto County Judge Howard "Hank" Harcha, III. His triplet grandsons often stopped by to see their Grandpa during the game. What a wonderful family!

The Buckeye Leaf

I was informed by my portal chief that during the supervisor's meeting held four hours before the start of the game, it is tradition to award a "Buckeye Leaf" for outstanding deeds performed by Ushers during the previous game. I had been nominated and received the Buckeye Leaf Badge for the October 2, 2010 Purdue game. The honor was detailed in my hometown newspaper, the St. Clairsville, Times Leader:

November 26, 2010
Vargo Receives Buckeye Leaf Badge

A

BUCKEYE Leaf Badge recently was presented to Bob Vargo, an Usher at Ohio State's football games, for his service. With Vargo are the other Ushers who also work at portal 8B at the Shoe. From left are Perry Jones, Gary Snyder, portal chief Trevor Zahara, Vargo and Jason Overly

A ST. CLAIRSVILLE man, who is an Usher at football games at The Ohio State University, recently was honored with a Buckeye Leaf Badge from his portal chief for "service above and beyond."

Bob Vargo, who was given this special honor, said the others working with him, also should receive badges, because they work "as a neat team." Presenting the badge to the St. Clairsville resident was portal chief Trevor Zahara.

Vargo referred to himself and the other Ushers working at portal 8B at the Horseshoe as a "band of brothers." Included are Perry Jones, also of St. Clairsville; Zahara and Gary Snyder, who reside in the Columbus area; and Jason Overly from the Canton area. Overly is an ex-Marine.

"What is nice about this 'job' is that you become friends with some great regular fans," added Vargo. He mentioned former attorney Howard Harcha as being one in particular. Harcha, whose wife died of cancer a few years ago, now attends games with his

son, Howard III, and daughter, Michelle.

Vargo, a Martins Ferry native, added that he learned that two former Ferrians, Eddie McGlumphy and Chad Hirth, also work at the stadium.

The badge honorees younger brother, Kenneth, was co-captain of the 1955 Buckeye team, and his nephew, Bo Delande, is a junior running back on this year's team.

He spoke two words regarding the Ohio State team: "Go Bucks."

Let's face it, you have to have a slightly recessive gene that has a little something to do with the brain to go out on the football field and beat your head against other human beings on a daily basis.

—**Tim Green**

Bob Vargo detailed this story about his little brother Ken, who was co-captain of the 1955 Buckeye team and visits him whenever he attends a Captain's meeting at the stadium.

Ken recently related this quip during the Captain's meeting at the 2012 Nebraska game. The first Heisman Trophy winner, Les Horvath, discussing his success with a reporter, said that he couldn't have gained the Big Ten record number of yards that pushed him into winning the trophy without the help and support of his 1944 teammates. He was so grateful to the seven living teammates that he bought them all Rolex watches.

Ken, sitting next to 1955 Heisman winner, Hopalong Cassidy, questioned Hop about getting their watches. Hop fired back, "You'll get your watches when there are seven of you characters alive!"

Dylan Baxter, Homecoming Court, Kayla Francis

HOMECOMING IOWA 2013

Dylan Baxter and Kayla Francis, on the 2013 Homecoming court, visited our portal during the Iowa game and commented, "Thanks to all the Ushers for being so kind to the Homecoming Court. We were able to visit our friends and family in different sections of the stadium. The entire experience created so many memories in its entirety! I will never watch a Buckeye game the same after being on the field and seeing the stadium from so many different views."

WATCHFUL EYES

Bob Maibach, portal chief, B-24:

I have the responsibility for all the folks in my section, especially the little ones. I was very watchful of two young fans who were cheering their hearts out for the Bucks during the 2012 game

---

with the Miami Redhawks. Mike, our portal chief noticed that there were no adults close to the kids providing adult supervision. He found this a little strange so he approached the youngsters and asked if their parents were around. The 7-year-olds responded, "Nah, they are back at the tailgate partying with their friends!" Mike kept a watchful eye on them the rest of the game and in the fourth quarter had the boys call their parents on their cell phones — how thoughtful of the parents to provide them with means to contact them!

After the Bucks destroyed Miami 56-10, Mike escorted the boys to meet their parents at the gate, Mike's job was done. All in a day's work for an observant supervisor!

Proud To Be A Buckeye

Dave Gustin, portal chief and Usher for 10 years.

I decided to share with you what it means to me to be a portal chief and a Buckeye and why. It goes back to a decision my wife Carol, who is an Usher with me at 26-B, and I made to go to Africa with our three daughters where we worked with CMF International as Field Administrators in Kenya, and Benin, and with Food for the Hungry International during the Ethiopian famine relief effort of 1988. We left for overseas with a four-year commitment and ended up serving six years. When we left for Tanzania in January, 1988 we flew out of Columbus after saying tearful goodbyes to family, some of whom were elderly so goodbye was truly goodbye. The last thing we saw of Ohio was the Shoe. Having been a Buckeye all my life I looked down as we flew by and imagined Archie and Woody, Rex, Jack and many more. I swallowed the lump in my throat and remembered Marines are supposed to be tough — missionaries too.

Nearly seven years later we had been through the mill. We had had all our belongings confiscated by a rogue Tanzanian government, and had all suffered for years with malaria and had stuck it out, doing our best. Finally the doctors ordered us off the field for the sake of Carol's health.

As we flew back I thought of the family we would see and felt some pain as I thought about those who had passed while we were away and that we would not be seeing again. I smiled at the idea of Skyline Chili and a Wendy's hamburger. Then as we circled to land I looked down and saw it again: The Shoe. She was gleaming and huge and beckoning and the lump returned to my throat and this time I didn't care. I looked at Carol, and she was feeling the same. We were home. World travelers that lived in four countries in seven years, yet we knew we would always be one thing and one thing only — Buckeyes. It is still hard to sing Carmen Ohio and not tear up, to watch TBDBITL marching down the field and witness game day and not get the lump in the throat. But after the years of working the portal at 26-B, I am never prouder or more at home than at the stadium, cheering on the team and high-fiving the fans. Go Bucks!

Lou Ranft, Pat Giamarco, 2nd row, John Bindas, Sharon Samuelson, and Craig Charleston.
Craig Charleston has been an Usher in B-10 since 1984 (28 yrs).

C-DECK

There's no substitute for guts.

—Paul Bear Bryant

DEDICATED DRINKER

Rick Sellers, portal chief, C-12 has been an Usher for 33 years, and has many stories to share:

About 10 years ago, a woman came down to the portal quite upset. She said a man was drinking heavily in the row in front of her and using foul language. Her husband would not say anything to the guy but she needed to say something. She returned to her seat and we kept an eye on the guy but did not observe anything.

She returned to the portal and said she was not going back up until the police took care of it. The man was continuing to swear and he was sneaking drinks of beer. I accompanied the police officer to the row in question and we asked the man thought to be drinking to come down to the portal.

We asked him several questions and he denied drinking and swearing, and we were at a point of almost believing him when a beer can fell to the ground from under his trench coat. The officer then opened up his trench coat to show pockets sewn on the inside of his coat and approximately 18 beers in the pockets. The police officer and I looked at each other and had to laugh. The officer then escorted the man to a trash can where he drained all the beer cans and then he escorted him to the exit.

Over the years, we have had many drinking incidents but this was the most memorable.

GOOD MEMORIES

I started Ushering 33 years ago after selling programs for 15 years, 48 years in total coming to OSU football games. When I started, my father, my three older brothers, and my brother-in-law all Ushered. All six of us would meet at the Big Bear on Lane Avenue where we would have breakfast at 10:00 a.m. At that time all the games started at 1:30 p.m. and Ushers had to be in the gate two hours before kickoff.

After breakfast, we would cross Lane Avenue and walk through the RV lot at St. John and we would occasionally attend the OSU band Skull Session in St. John. We would then mosey over to the stadium to arrive right before 11:30 a.m. and the gates opened to the public at 12 noon. Since then, my father and oldest brother have passed away and we are left with four of us Ushering.

Baseball players are smarter than football players. How often do you see a baseball team penalized for too many men on the field?

—Jim Bouton

WOMEN'S RIGHTS

Before the stadium was remodeled and bathrooms were added in C-Deck, we had to go to B-Deck to find a men's room. On one occasion, Ray Roberts, the portal chief at the time, and I went to B-Deck to the men's room and found a rather long line. We waited our turn and talked. We noticed the line was not moving and in fact the door was shut on the bathroom. In looking further, we saw a short young lady "guarding" the door and arguing with the men *at the front of the line.*

Finally a man in the front said, "I am tired of catering to women's rights, get out of my way." Not knowing what was really going on, we followed the line into the near empty men's room where we found three young ladies sitting on toilets doing their business. The line stopped with Ray and I standing right in front of the three ladies. Even though the ladies were done doing what they needed to do, they would not stand up to pull their clothes back up. As they sat there embarrassed with us laughing, we decided to be gentlemen and turn our backs to them. They pulled their clothes back up and left the men's room as 15-20 men laughed and gave them a verbal whipping for taking over our restroom.

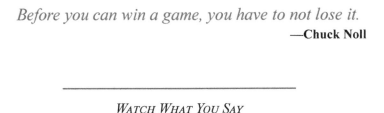

Before you can win a game, you have to not lose it.
—**Chuck Noll**

WATCH WHAT YOU SAY

A few years ago when the "F*** Michigan" t-shirts were real popular and we had students in our section, we had to keep our eyes open for people wearing the shirts. On one occasion, an attractive young lady came in wearing a "F*** Michigan" shirt. I stopped her and explained that the university finds these shirts offensive and she either needed to take it off or turn it inside out.

Before I could say another word, she ripped off the shirt and handed it to me. All she had on was a bra and she proceeded to leave the portal and head to her seat. At that time, I repeated to her that she was supposed to go to the restroom to turn it inside out or put another shirt on. She reluctantly put the shirt back on inside-out, and proceeded to her seat.

When you win, nothing hurts.

—**Joe Namath**

WATCH WHERE YOU PARK

About 10-12 years ago when Ray Roberts was still portal chief in 12-C, I used to pick Ray up close to the stadium and bring him with me because I had a parking pass closer to the stadium. Ray had back problems and could not walk the long distances to the stadium from where Ushers had to park. I would drop Ray off about 100 feet from the stadium then he would use the elevator. This allowed Ray to continue Ushering.

One time we met at University City shopping center on Olentangy River Road. Ray left his car there. Neither one of us noticed the sign that said no parking unless shopping there otherwise you would be towed. Upon our return after the game, Ray's car was gone. We noticed multiple people walking around looking for cars and we figured out they had all been towed.

I drove Ray to the tow lot which was in the southeast part of Franklin County in an industrial area. Upon arriving, Ray was told it would be $120 to get his car back but he did not have the money. They would only accept cash. Fortunately, I did have enough cash so we were able to get Ray's car back.

Some people not having $120 in cash had to walk 1.5 miles to an ATM, so Ray and I shuttled 6-8 people back and forth to the ATM. Ray tried to pay me back all $120 but I insisted he only give me $60 because it was my idea to park where he parked.

Unfortunately, Ray had to give up Ushering two years later because his back problems were too severe.

Photo left to right, Don (Weatherby) Dave In front
(Albrecht) Kevin (Girton) Fred (Freytag) Claudia (Berry)

*I learned that if you want to make it bad enough, no
matter how bad it is; you can make it.*

—Gale Sayers

Dave Albrecht has been an Usher since 1976 (38 years).

*I am still a rookie compared to my brother-in-law Don Weath-
erby, who has perfect attendance for home games since 1968 (46
years). Together, we have a combined 84 years in the same portal
C5.*

INTERCEPTED PASS

*We have a lot of students in our section and even though they
are a lot of fun they get to be pretty rowdy sometimes, mostly because they are having a good time. I remember the Wisconsin game
in 2013, it was a night game and our section was jam packed. One*

of our responsibilities is to walk up the aisles during time outs and between quarters just to assure the fans we are there for their safety and well-being. Well the aisle was especially crowded, so I sat down in an empty seat while people passed by me. At the same time a flask was being passed from person to person to take a "hit" of the alcoholic content. The guy beside me took a big swig and turned to give it to his buddy (who had left for a bio break) and handed me the flask.

He realized his mistake when he saw my uniform and tried to grab it back. I hated to be a party pooper, but booze is not allowed in the stadium, so I had to confiscate the contraband.

My second story was about too many people in a row. I have a reputation for standing the entire row up and requesting that each person put their ticket on their forehead. Then I can go down the row quickly to determine who doesn't belong and who is in the incorrect seat. Over the years it must have become a legend. I had a male student tell me that his parents told him that I did the same thing when they attended a game; boy did I feel old but, that is what I get for 37 seasons.

The Berlin Wall

James Decker, C-15, born and bred in Central Ohio has been an Usher for 50 years:

Growing up in Central Ohio everyone was exposed to Ohio State football, even though it wasn't on TV and didn't have as much media coverage as today's teams do. Like many other young boys in our neighborhood I was a Buckeye Fan. When we played sand lot football everyone wanted to be Vic Janowitz or Hop Cassidy.

My real understanding of what OSU football meant was at

the age of 14 when I signed up to play freshman basketball at Mifflin High School. Joe Trivisonno, a fullback on the 1957 National Championship Team, was our coach. I am sure that being coached by Coach Trivisonno was like being coached by Coach Hayes himself.

After graduating from high school in 1961, I enlisted in the military. Upon completing six months of training I was sent to Berlin as part of the European troop build-up associated with the Berlin Crisis of 1961. After several months I was transferred to southern Germany where I met a fellow Buckeye, Bill Breehl. Bill's brother Ed had played on the 1957 team along with Coach Trivisonno. For the duration of our tour in Germany we read everything available and shared info from home pertaining to the Buckeyes.

My Ushering experience started after I was discharged in 1964, a month before football season. While looking for a full-time job, I was working part-time for a gentleman who knew Dr. McClintock, at that time the supervisor of stadium Ushers. I had never been to a game before and indicated my desire to attend one. Tickets as well as cash were scarce, and my boss offered to call Dr. McClintock if I was interested in becoming an Usher. I agreed and soon after that received an invitation to be one. The only stipulation was that I would complete the full year. My first game was SMU in 1964 and I have just completed my 49th year. Although it is somewhat tattered and torn, I still have my original stadium cap.

The National Championship Team of 1957 is very special to me. In addition to Coach Trivisonno and sharing many experiences with Ed Breehl's brother Bill, I was privileged to meet Frank Kremblas, the quarterback on that team. Before Frank's death several years ago we were members of the same golf club. We spent many days playing golf, socializing in the clubhouse, and discussing Ohio State football. One of Frank's favorite topics was passing; he averaged around five passes per game!

One of the most interesting events I experienced as an Usher is when I was transferred to the 15-C portal. The first day, I introduced myself to the other Ushers. One of the Ushers was Jim Chuck. After working the games with Jim for several years, my wife and I were invited to his birthday party at the Buckeye Lake VFW. Before entering the hall all visitors had to be a guest of a member and then sign in. We stated that we were the guest of Jim Chuck and were informed that they had no record of a member named Jim Chuck.

As we were preparing to leave, another couple who had overheard our conversation asked if we didn't mean Jim Wright. That's when we discovered Jim Chuck was actually Jim Wright. Story goes, Jim Wright's half-brother, Chuck Smith, a Michigan fan, had given his acceptance letter to be an Usher at Ohio Stadium to Jim. The application to be an Usher was submitted by Chuck's co-workers as a prank because of him being a Michigan fan.

Jim Wright had been signing in as Chuck Smith for a number of years. All the other Ushers on the portal knew the situation and had nicknamed him Jim Chuck and that is how I was introduced.

I thought it best to set the record straight. Jim Wright bled scarlet and gray, was a very dependable Usher and deserved to have his real identity known. A friend of mine, also an Usher, knew Dick Weber, at that time the supervisor of Ushers. My friend volunteered to ask Dick to straighten out the record. Dick issued a Proclamation on Ohio State University letterhead stating that from that day forward Jim Chuck would be known as Jim Wright, his real name. We framed it and presented it to Jim. He was overwhelmed. Jim retired from Ushering in 2005. I bet the Proclamation is still hanging on his living room wall.

Of all the great games I have seen at Ohio Stadium, the one that sticks out in my mind is the Purdue Game in 1968. A lot of great games come down to one or two good plays but every play of that Purdue game had me on the edge of my seat. Purdue was #1 with a veteran team and OSU was #4 with a young team. OSU was not expected to win. However, as we all know, we did win 13-0! And how about the 50-14 win in 1968 over the #4-ranked team from up north? Then the 1968 Rose Bowl win against #4-ranked USC. The 1968 National Championship Team was one of my favorites.

I can't forget to mention how much I enjoy Senior Day at the stadium. It is difficult to describe the emotion I feel when the players are introduced, the Coach meeting them on the field, and then joining their parents. How great is that??

I hope to be Ushering for many more years. GO BUCKS!!!!!!!!!!

The price of success is hard work, dedication to the job at hand, and the determination that whether we win or lose, we have applied the best of ourselves to the task at hand.

—**Vince Lombardi**

How It Came To Be

Patrick O'Leary, 20-C, 10 years as an Usher:

I became an Usher the season after the Buckeyes won the National Championship in 2002. I was told that I would be a reserve Usher and fill in for any permanent Ushers around the stadium who had called in sick, or were out for a wedding, funeral, etc.

I was excited! I figured some games I'd probably get to work in what were considered premium areas of the stadium — the 50 yard line, VIP seating or on the field! There would no doubt be weeks I might get some less desirable assignments too. (I once had to guard a stairwell in the north end of B-Deck to make sure fire code wasn't broken by people blocking the stairs. You'd probably be quite surprised at how much of an issue this turned out to be.) But overall I was just thrilled to be in the Shoe on football Saturdays as part of the Ohio State Buckeye game day stadium crew!

After my second or third game I was asked to go up to 20-C. One of the Ushers from that section had broken both ankles over the past summer so they were sending Reserves to fill in his spot each week. It was a great group. Each member of that crew had an enthusiasm for the Buckeyes that matched my own, as well as a genuine desire to make the experience of every person who walked through their portal the most enjoyable one of their life. They knew the season ticket holders by name. They treated the first-timers as if they were the most important people in the stadium. They welcomed and joked with the visiting fans in a way that made them feel good about their visit to Ohio Stadium whether their team won or lost.

After a couple of games working in 20-C I was asked if I would want to fill in for their missing crew member the rest of the season. I was more than glad to stay, even if it would only be for the rest of that season. It was a great group!

Anyone can support a team that is winning—it takes no courage. But to stand behind a team to defend a team when it is down and really needs you, that takes a lot of courage.

—Bart Starr

THE TOWEL MAN

One of the Ushers in section 20-C was named Larry. Larry had been an Usher for quite some time and was more than a few years older than me. Over the years I've met several Ushers with *the same love and dedication to the Buckeyes and the fans in their portals that Larry had, serving 25, 40 even 60 years as Ushers. But few, myself included, could match the energy Larry had on game day.*

Larry was known to many as "The Towel Man." He had his Ohio State towel (full beach towel size) with him each game. And after each touchdown, when we needed a big defensive stop or just when the crowd needed that extra little bit of motivation, Larry The Towel Man would run up the portal stairs, all the way to the top, waving his towel in the air, cheering and giving high fives to the fans of 20-C!

I became an Usher the season after our last National Championship. I attended several Ohio State functions and got autographs and pictures taken with various coaches and players. It wasn't too many games into the season that Larry bought a new, full size Ohio State National Champions beach towel. I asked him if he would want me to bring it with me to one of the events I went to and have it signed by some of the team? Larry thought that was a great idea, but didn't want his towel signed by the coaches or players. Instead he borrowed one of my sharpies and started having fans sign his giant "rally towel." He loved the Buckeyes, but he was there for the fans.

Larry passed away a few years ago, but for the next couple of seasons we had fans coming through our section asking about The Towel Man. The fans he cheered with, the people he worked with and the friends he made all appreciate the life and energy he brought to our section each game day Saturday. He, along with the rest of the "team" in Ohio Stadium section 20-C helped teach me how we can do more than just show someone to their seat or point the way to the nearest bathroom. We have the ability to share smiles and high-fives and moments with people they will never forget—moments I will never forget, because of people like Larry.

WATCH YOUR STEP

Tom Dole has been an Usher for 32 years and is currently a portal chief in 20-C Deck:

> *I am a little biased, but I believe that C-Deck affords one of the best viewing areas of the stadium. Over the past several years, some of the fans have told me that their visits to the Shoe on home Saturday football games have been made special by the Ushers in 20-C (my assigned portal). Undoubtedly, the Ushers work hard for the opportunity to view a Buckeye football game from this area of the stadium.*

O-H...

3C—Mike Davis (portal chief), Ruth Cline, David Tracht, Adam Eberhart

...I-O

I can recall this humorous story: the wife of a fellow OSU Usher, Larry Clarkson was walking to her seat in our section on a hot September Saturday with a hot dog in one hand and a Coke in the other. She lost her balance and tumbled down the stairs from row 5. All we could do was watch in horror as she finally stopped just short of row 1. Her Coke was history but she did save that dog with only an embarrassed look and smile on her face!

Guess the Major

Ed Evans has been an Usher since 1993:

I was born in 1930 in Bellefontaine. My father went to OSU. He was there when the Horseshoe was built and gave a small amount of money to the building fund, so you might say I have a family investment interest in the stadium!

I went to my first game at the age of seven. The ticket cost $3 and OSU played Indiana. Thirty thousand people attended that game. I have been a fan ever since.

I graduated from West Mansfield High School in 1948. There were only seven in my class. I went to Ohio Wesleyan University for three years. The Korean War came and I was drafted, and I joined the US Marines (once a Marine always a Marine). My last duty station was in San Francisco and too late to return to OWU. I was accepted at Stanford University, Palo Alto, California and graduated with a degree in economics.

I came back to West Mansfield. We did not farm, but owned farmland and had people farm for us. I have managed the land since my father died. I got a real estate license in the early 80s and sold real estate, but don't do much of that now. I take it easier in West Mansfield, a village of 800 people, where I was mayor for eight years. As Woody used to say, "You have to pay forward."

You might say that it is my wife's fault that I became an Usher, because my portal chief, Tom Dole, and my wife were co-workers. Tom is the fine gentleman that introduced me to being a part of the Usher team nearly 20 years ago!

Since I started working in 5-C I have had some wonderful memories and experiences. In 2001, when the track was removed and the playing field was lowered by 14.5 feet to add seating closer to the field, I was assigned as a supervisor behind the OSU team. This was a tremendous vantage point to see these student athletes up close and personal. You realize what this game is all about when you look into their young hopeful faces and see the enthusiasm pouring out onto the field. The players I was closest to and had many conversations with were the ones that would see little or no action and none of the glory, but it never dampened their spirits. They would stand on the benches and wave their towels to get the crowd fired up when the team needed it most!

MAIZE & BLUE

While I supervised down on the field I noticed a fellow, dressed in a bright blue blazer with a yellow tie, (you know-Michigan colors) trying to make his way down to the Buckeye bench. He had the total access credentials hanging around his neck, near that yellow tie, meaning that he was allowed on the field. But I wasn't about to let this guy get away Scott free without messing with him about his choice of colors. I walked over to him and said, "Sir you are not permitted on the field-" He was just about to start arguing with me - when I said - "with that maize & blue uniform." He looked me in the eye and we both started laughing. Bret Mussberger, ABC TV Broadcast Analyst then went back to the press box to prepare for the game.

I was then assigned to C-7 with a great bunch of guys who are fun to work with. In fact, the last home game of the year we have our own tailgate inside the stadium with my old teammates in C-5. Lots of good food and fellowship.

The students are what keep things interesting. Their antics during the game and the conversations on various topics make me feel young. One Saturday I asked a group, "Are you all studying the same thing?"

They replied, "Yes, tell us what we are studying."

I said, "Nursing or school teachers."

They said, "Yes, which one?"

I said, "Nursing."

They all laughed and said, "School teachers." This is one of the many experiences I had had with these wonderful students. We all should be very proud of all of our students.

The thing I enjoy most about being an Usher is meeting people, the customer service we provide and the lasting memories and friendships that I will keep for the rest of my life. GO BUCKS!

MOTHER WARNED US TO HAVE CLEAN UNDIES

The Akron game in 2012 was the hottest day inside the stadium I can remember. C-Deck is in direct sunlight, so the heat can be unbearable on a cloudless day. We heard a commotion a few rows above us and someone yelled for us to get medical help for a lady who had passed out. We finally got the Red Cross paramedic to help the poor lady. She was lodged in between the rows and it was difficult to administer help for her in that position, so they placed cold towels under her head and supported her back on a stretcher, then lifted her legs up on the seat. They were then able to check her blood pressure and determine the next steps to aid her.

Ben Tarqunio, Tony Tarqunio, Don Armstrong, Ed Evans, Jim Rosser

While all this was happening, a couple of ladies were scream-ing at us to please cover her up. Little did we know that this lady had zero undergarments under her dress! She obviously wanted to stay cool on this hot day, but did not expect to be in this embar-rassing situation. Thankfully she was okay once she cooled off in the Red Cross area, but she never did return to her seat.

Speaking of hot days, back about 15 years ago, when we had Boy Scouts assigned to C-Deck, a young scout was near the top row of our section when the heat got to him. He blacked out and began rolling down the steps until some of the other fans stopped his fall. He was immediately revived after drinking some water, but sat out the rest of the game at a lower level in the shade of B-deck!

POPULAR LADY

Quinn Carter, Usher on C-Deck before moving to B-6 as portal chief:

I noticed a lot of attention being paid to a very pregnant lady in their section of C-Deck. How very considerate that all these people were especially interested in this yet-to-be born OSU fan! All during the first half a steady stream of boisterous fans continued to congregate around this young lady.

After a long while Quinn finally discovered the real reason that this lady had garnered so much attention. Under her poncho was strapped a pony keg of beer. No wonder she was so popular with the fans in section C. And, thanks for leaving the empty keg!

D-DECK
THE UNKNOWN DECK

Greg Wolfe has been an Usher for 38 years starting in 15-A. He became a portal chief in 1978, working Standing Room for Jim Miller, then C-East Asst. Supervisor under Bill Coldren and is now the D-Deck Superintendent: Most people don't realize there is a D-Deck in the stadium. D-Deck has 11 rows plus box seats located between the press box and C-Deck. It is accessed by taking stairs up from C-Deck or the press box elevators if you have a green sticker on your ticket. We are perhaps best known for our annual year-end potluck which started off-site during the 2002 Illinois game; this is a tradition that has grown every year. We have a great staff of Ushers who are dedicated to insuring our guests have a safe and great game day experience.

MYSTERY MAN

The stadium was packed on November 14, 2009 anticipating

the match-up between #15-ranked Iowa and #10-ranked Ohio State. We noticed a fan in our section without a proper ticket that kept showing up and sitting in the folding chairs in the front row of D-Deck. He had been approached by our Ushers three times in different sections of D-Deck and removed without incident. I had been involved in the last one and recognized him from other sections in D-Deck. I asked the Ushers if they had checked his ticket; he did not have a valid seat assignment in our section, so he was removed from the portal.

Fast forward, late in the night setting, I was walking the sections when I saw the same man — mid 50s, white hair, and shorts— sitting in yet another D-Deck front row chair. When I approached him and asked for his ticket, he became belligerent and started shouting that he had a right to be there. I told him he had a right to sit in his assigned seat in C-Deck for which he had a ticket; but, as he had been told previously, could not sit in D-Deck. He escalated his level of shouting. I looked for a police officer, but they had cleared at the beginning of the fourth quarter to take their positions on traffic duty.

All of a sudden the crowd erupted to loud cheers. The Buck-

eyes had scored a field goal and won the game. Game over! Confrontation over! The mystery man disappeared into the crowd. I have looked for him every game since, it still haunts me.

A Fan's Perspective

Love being in the D-Deck. You are up there — right under the press box, sheltered from the sun and the rain/sleet/snow. Great sight lines, short restroom lines. We love it!

Anonymous Fan

Good Luck Charm

Marianne Wenger, Columbus born and bred, an OSU alumna, retired teacher now working as an IT professional, has been an Usher for three years at D-13:

My most unusual event occurred at the Purdue 2012 game. I walk up and down the aisle between quarters or time-outs and chat with folks. It got to be a joke that I did that, because on the next play or so, the Bucks would score.

During this game we were not doing so well, we had just been scored upon by Purdue. I did the usual walk and the comment was made that it was about time I came up because we really needed a touchdown. Sure enough, I returned to the portal and the Bucks scored.

One of the fans came rushing down the stairs and planted a big kiss on my cheek. I never saw it coming! Too funny—or at least I thought so.

Game Day is Pay Enough

Leo Oberting, a Columbus Steelworker, has been an Usher since 2006.

I feel like I hit the lottery, when my number finally came up in the summer of 2006, after four years of waiting. According to my conversation with Jim Norris, Superintendent of Ushers, "That length of wait is typical for what may be the most-coveted volunteer post in Central Ohio. One of three things happens when I call; applicants have moved, forgotten they applied or they break out in tears (of joy)."

I thanked Jim for selecting me as one of 50 rookies in 2006 (among the 700 Ushers who staff each game). I happily paid $50 for my uniform—a cap, polo shirt and black jacket with "USHER" emblazoned in white on the back.

Quickies

Over the course of compiling these stories from the Ushers, every now and then an Usher will start to tell a story, then stop and say, "Please don't use my name or I'll get fired." These are the stories from some of the anonymous Ushers:

Last Request

A man walked over to me as I was stationed in the field area of the stadium. He whispered to me, "I have a big favor to ask of you. My best friend died this year and one of his last requests was to have some of his ashes scattered on the field during a Buckeyes *game." He started to hand me $20 to let him onto the field. (Ushers or Redcoats are not allowed to take tips from fans.) I said I could not accept the money, but I did understand his passion to honor his friend's last request, so I escorted him down to field level and let him scatter his buddy's ashes. He turned to me with tears in his eyes, shook my hand and shouted a heartfelt thank you, as the Buckeyes played on in the background.*

Serve with Pride

A lady mentioned to me that her son had just returned from a tour of duty in Afghanistan and was going to propose to his girlfriend before he had to return to active duty. She asked if we could escort them down onto the field under the premise that they were getting their photo taken. Knowing that only people with proper credentials were allowed on the field, I went to my supervisor to ask his opinion. We both confirmed that this would be a great exception to the rule and guided the happy couple down the ramp to get their photo taken. As they approached the bottom of the ramp, the young Marine turned to his girlfriend, got down on one knee, reached into his pocket and presented the ring with his heartfelt proposal. She screamed with delight, accepted the proposal with a wholehearted YES. They now have a wonderful story to share with their children and grandchildren!

Hit 'Em Long and Straight

We were busy at the portal showing people to their seats when one of our Ushers, who happened to be a golfing fan, noticed that a professional golfer was attempting to enter our section. The only problem was that he could not find his ticket, but managed to slip past the busy Ushers and took a seat. After the game started and the section filled up, a disgruntled fan walked down and complained that she had no place to sit because their row was too crowded. The portal chief checked tickets, one at a time, until he came to the professional golfer, who got up and left the row, obviously a little embarrassed. And then there was plenty of space, because two of his friends left with him!

WAH! WAH! WAH!

Fans come to the stadium in all shapes and sizes, young and old. I have helped elderly fans who could barely make it to their seats who, as true Buckeye fans, never missed a game. The one fan that still baffles me did not walk into the stadium and didn't seem to have the slightest idea where he was. A baby, maybe three or four months old, was carried into the stadium by his parents. Around the baby's neck was a game ticket.

Now, I understand that the parents are dyed-in-the-wool OSU fans, but paying $70 for a newborn to sit in a crowded, noisy stadium for four hours! Are you nuts? Anyway, the game was a blowout for the Bucks, so the young parents, with their offspring in tow, left after the third quarter — maybe the youngster had a blowout too!

After they left, some other fans asked me if the baby had to have a ticket. An official's response: The Ohio State University follows the Big Ten policy of requiring a ticket for everyone, regardless of age, including infants for football, men's and women's basketball and men's ice hockey. For all other regular season OSU athletic events children age 6 and under are free.

WHEEL CHAIR USHER

From long-time Usher, **Steve Houck**:

One of the first things I ask a customer is, "Where are you from?"

As I was assisting an older lady, her son is tagging along. She first tells me that she graduated from OSU and this is the first game she has attended since graduating — 50 years ago!

So I asked the usual, "Where you all from?" and she responds that she is from Newark, which happens to be my hometown. So we have a pleasant trip all the way to D-Deck talking about "Nerk." After the game, I had the privilege of wheeling her back out and she didn't even recognize me when I told her that I was the guy who took her up. Turned out it was the fact I had my sunglasses off. They told me they had a great time and thanked me several times.

Another time I began wheeling another couple from D-Deck that I had wheeled up before the game. It was the Purdue game and everybody was leaving early because Baxter had been knocked out of the game and we were not having much luck with the backup.

I had the older gentleman in the chair while his wife was following slowly from behind using his walker. We tried to get her in a chair too, but she refused. It was a slow ride from the west side to gate 22.

We are about to gate 14 when a roar came from the field, so we pushed over to a monitor to see that the Bucks had scored with a few seconds left! We wheeled down to the next monitor and watched the 2 point conversion attempt, which they made.

I looked at my customers and said, "You don't want to leave now, do you?" They said no. So I started to wheel him back up to the wheelchair deck nearby. Turns out many people were rushing back in for overtime and the wheelchair deck was full of standing fans. So I turned to the other Ushers and told them I wanted to seat this couple for overtime. They cleared the deck and we got them seated.

1950s

The past is never dead. It's not even past.

—William Faulkner

COST OF LIVING IN 1957
Annual USA inflation rate - 3.34%
Average cost of new house - $12,220
Average monthly rent - $90
Average yearly wages - $4,550
Cost of a gallon of gas - 24¢
Bacon per pound - 60¢
Eggs per dozen - 28¢
Children's shoes - $5.95

I was 9 years old in 1957. Things that occurred in that time period: the continued growth of bigger, taller tail fins, more lights, bigger, more powerful engines on new cars. An average new car sold for $2,749. The Soviet Union launched the first space satellite Sputnik 1. Movies included Twelve Angry Men and The Bridge over the River Kwai, and TV aired Perry Mason and Maverick. Rock and roll music was on the rise. Slinkys and Hula Hoops were the popular toys. The continued growth of the use of credit was shown by the fact that 2/3 of all new cars were being bought on credit. Some of the situations that would eventually escalate were beginning—South Vietnam is attacked by Viet Cong Guerrillas and troops were sent to Arkansas to enforce anti-segregation laws.

The President of the United States was Dwight D. Eisenhower and Woody Hayes was Coach for The Ohio State University.

THE NEWBIE

Another important event happened in 1957: **Glen Abel** was discharged from the US Army and attended his first OSU football game. One year later he became an Usher working at the visitors' gate on the field, where he stayed for 30 years. He told Dick Weber, head of the Usher program, that he had "served his time in purgatory." Consequently he was moved to various locations on A and B-Decks. He is now a portal chief at 21-D-Deck.

Glenn Abel, 80, attended University of Illinois from 1950-55 and graduated with a degree in Architecture. He worked at JBA Architects for 40 years starting on the ground floor and ending as CEO. Shortly after he became an Usher he had to return to the Army and missed his first game. Since then he has only missed three other games in 55 years as an Usher:

I would describe my first year as an Usher in one word — magical. The Buckeyes were coming off a national championship year and had some of the best college players returning to the team. I had a front row view from the field. I was in heaven when I walked down to my position at the visitors' gate and the #20-ranked SMU Mustangs trotted onto the field to do battle with the #1-rated Buckeyes. The Bucks prevailed 23-20, and I was hooked on OSU football. The other two games I recall from that season were with #13-ranked Wisconsin and #8-rated Purdue and had the dubious distinction of both games ending in ties — the former 7-7 and the latter 14-14. This, of course, would not happen today due to the new tie breaker rules implemented by the NCAA.

The last game of the season was with the hated rivals from up north. It was a hard-fought game with the Bucks winning 20-14.

These games will always hold a special meaning for me because I had the honor of meeting Michigan Coach Bo Schembechler. Of all the coaching match-ups in the long Michigan-Ohio State rivalry, none has been more intense and at times bitter than that between Woody Hayes and Bo Schembechler. For 10 years the two dominated the "Big 2 and Little 8," splitting 10 conference titles and finishing second eight times. Hayes supposedly could not bring himself to speak the name of that school up north, and Schembechler, who played for Hayes at Miami of Ohio and was an Ohio State assistant coach, savored nothing more than putting it to his old mentor. After a decade of memorable on-field strata-gems, sideline antics, and locker room psychological ploys, the two coaches came out almost dead-even, Schembechler holding a slim 5-4-1 advantage. But the thing that I will always remember about Bo was his down-to-earth personality.

The Bucks finished the season 6-1-2. Believe it or not, the one loss was an away game at Northwestern. Even with this record (by today's standards this could cost a coach his job) Woody had some outstanding players — four of whom stand out to me: Don Clark and Dan James, #1 draft choices went on to play in the pro football league; and two of my all-time favorites, Dick Schafrath and Dick LeBeau went on to play with the Cleveland Browns! I will always remember my first season as an Usher!

I fondly remember the coaches, players, band members and fans that walked down the ramp to the field, but sometimes my job required me to be a vigilant. People often thought they had the right to walk onto the track without the proper credentials. One guy in particular showed me his FBI badge, but I told him he still needed an on field credential to enter the field. He was none too happy, but my supervisor backed me up, and the FBI guy walked back into the stands.

Always be prepared to start.

—Joe Montana

ACTS OF KINDNESS

Once during my third season I heard someone scream, "Help! Get a doctor!" I turned around just in time to see an elderly woman who was walking from the stands fall to the ground. She had passed out and was lying on the cold ground. Another fan gave me her blanket and I covered her until the squad arrived to assist her. They took her from the field on a stretcher, blanket and all. I apologized to the Good Samaritan for losing her blanket, but she was more concerned for the elderly lady.

I didn't think anything of it until the next game, when a fellow walked up and thanked me for taking good care of his wife, who was recovering nicely, then handed me the blanket — cleaned and folded in a plastic wrap!

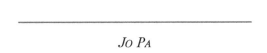

JO PA

On October 5, 1996, #4-ranked Penn State came to the Shoe for a much anticipated game with the #3-ranked Buckeyes. Ushers are required to be at their assigned areas three hours before game time, so we are on the field as the visiting team enters the stadium for a walk through before they change into their uniforms for the game. I was impressed by the size of the Penn State players and how well dressed they were, when none other than Joe Paterno, long-time coach of the Nittany Lions, walked by me and stopped while his players observed the stadium. Not knowing what to say I blurted out, "Coach how do you get the players to dress up so nice?"

Joe's response: "I don't say a thing to them. The players set their own dress standards." That was my one and only contact with the storied coach.

OSU won 38-7. Rest in peace, Jo Pa.

SMILE FOR THE CAMERA

Early on in my life as an Usher I had a strong back and was willing to work for food. Most fans don't realize there is a camera deck. It is located on D-Deck and has electric heat in the ceiling. So I would "cozy up" to the media crew that broadcast the game for the day. During the 1950s and 60s the TV cameras were big and bulky and mostly made of metal, so I would help manhandle them in place with my good buddies the cameramen. The pay-off: I would be assured hot dogs and other goodies from the press box and a nice warm spot to hang out on those cold winter game days.

One especially cold day I was working on the camera deck with the cameraman. His associate on the field would let us know 15 seconds before the end of a commercial and the start of the next play. Because the camera was made of metal and the cameraman could not wear gloves due to the delicate nature of working the device, his hands would be nearly frozen. So I directed him to the ceiling panels where he would stand on a chair and warm his hands on the heating vents. When his buddy on the field signaled that the next play was within seconds, I would alert the cameraman to get back to his camera — with his hands nice and warm. I did not think anything of it again until the next year when I received a nice letter from the cameraman thanking me for getting him through that frigid football Saturday. I still have that letter in my OSU memorabilia!

FLASHBACK: OHIO STATE VS. USC, 1990

One of my most memorable games at the Shoe came against USC in 1990, the last time the USC Trojans came to Ohio Stadium. As a portal chief we are trained to be prepared for any possibility, including the weather. It was a game that most OSU fans of the day will remember, although not fondly.

The game started out badly for the Bucks. USC blocked an OSU punt and returned it for a touchdown to quickly go up 7-0. Then the USC ground game got going. USC ran sweep after sweep with Ricky Ervins carrying 28 times for 199 yards and his back-up Mazio Royster carrying 7 times for 70 yards. OSU had no answer for the USC stampede and they trailed 14-0 after the first quarter.

Things didn't get a lot better in the second quarter — OSU trailed 21-10 at halftime. But Ohio State fans were not about to leave the stadium. After all, this was basically the same team that had come back from a huge deficit at Minnesota the previous year. Greg Frey was still the quarterback and he still had wide receivers Bobby Olive and Jeff Graham at his disposal. And the addition of stud freshman running back Robert Smith made the attack even more lethal. Playing at home before a partisan crowd that hated USC every bit as much as they did, the team was sure to rally all of their resources for a comeback.

Indeed, in the second half Frey got going and led the team back after USC upped the lead to 28-10. But just as the comeback was beginning, a massive thunderstorm arrived bringing a torrent of rain and some spectacular lightning to the stadium. The rain only seemed to inspire the Buckeyes as they scored and converted on the 2-point attempt. USC scored again on the ground, but then Frey and the OSU offense went back to work on a 50-yard drive for another touchdown. This time Raymont Harris plunged in from one yard out, and Frey passed to Jeff Graham for the 2-point conversion. All of a sudden it was 35-26 with 2:38 left on the clock, and Frey was thinking about another comeback. That's

---

when OSU fans got a bitter taste of the unexpected.

*The lightning had increased and referee Ron Winter was be-
ginning to get concerned about the safety of players and fans.
He conferred with both coaches about suspending the game. Of
course, Larry Smith was all for it since he had the lead. But somehow John Cooper went along with it on the condition that if his
team could successfully recover an onside kick they would play
on. Suffice it to say that they did not recover and the game was
suspended. USC players were elated, but the same cannot be said
for the Buckeyes.*

*In the post-game interview room, Cooper said, "I told him
(Winter) we were going to try an onside kick. I told him if USC
gets it, it's all over." Indeed, it was all over. Ironically, the weather
calmed down as soon as the fans left the stadium. But the fans' an-
ger at Cooper's decision never did. Despite the glorious triumphs
of the mid- to late-1990s, he never lived down the decision to sus-
pend the game with time left on the clock.*

The star of the show

*I want to be remembered as the guy who gave his all
whenever he was on the field.*

—Walter Payton

Hooked on OSU Football in the 1940s

Dick Windle had been an Usher and portal chief at 18-B for 58 years:

My first real taste of OSU football was when I was a 13-14 year old teenager. My parents, with my uncle and aunt, took me to see the WWII Buckeyes and Ollie Cline play. We sat in C-Deck in the closed end of the stadium. That was all general admission seating. Uncle Roy McKinley had coached Ollie at little Fredericktown High School in Knox County, Ohio. Ollie was a great running back at OSU and Uncle Roy's pride and joy. Ollie went on to lead the Big Ten in ground gaining in 1945 and was voted the Big Ten's most valuable player.

From that day on, I was hooked on OSU football. Although I didn't attend many games in person, I listened to play-by-play broadcasts on the radio.

OSU Football Player Perks

I was fullback and linebacker on the Hilliard High School football team that won the Franklin County league championship in both my junior and senior years.

I walked on at OSU as a freshman in 1949. Wes Fesler was head coach. I earned a freshman letter as a defensive/offensive end.

A perk for freshman football players to earn money was to put up the flags and pennants on C-Deck the morning before each home game (all games began at 1:30). We would then take them down about the middle of the fourth quarter to prevent them from being stolen. I did the west half of the stadium and received $10/

game x 5 games, or $50/season.

My, how times have changed. Who does this now and how much they are paid, I don't know, but the flags and pennants are still flying every home game in the Horseshoe.

MY FIRST YEAR AS AN OSU USHER

After the Army, I got my first full time job at Jeffrey Mfg. Co. The next year, five or six of us went to the stadium to get hired on as Redcoats to take tickets at the gates. Two of us didn't get hired and were told to wait another year.

In the meantime, Barney Atkinson, a co-worker said, "You don't want to work the gates when you can be an Usher like I am and see all of every game." Redcoats had to stay at the gates through the end of the first quarter and were in a lottery to work under the stadium one full game a season.

Barney lived in Upper Arlington near Mr. McClintock who was portal superintendent at the time. He wrote a recommenda-tion letter and in 1957 I was put on 18-B with him. Clark Coffman from Dublin was portal chief. The next year our portal chief was Lowell Dean. I succeeded him in 1996 until my son, Doug, took over in 2008.

SNOW BOWL ROMANCE

Barney was an Usher before I knew there were Ushers. In 1950, at portal 18-B during the OSU/Michigan Snow Bowl game, a nice looking young OSU female student was wrapped up in a blanket on the first row of B-Deck right beside the portal. At half-time she invited Barney to sit and share her blanket because it was so cold. A few years later they became husband and wife.

SPECIAL DAYS

November 3, 2007 - Ushers with 50+ years at OSU were recognized on the field and acknowledged on the scoreboard. I was among the 12 that were introduced in the north end zone.

November 10, 2007 - I was among many Ushers honored on the field recognized for their service in the United States Armed Forces.

DEDICATION TO A GREAT VOLUNTEER JOB

Three of my rules:
- *Be on time*
- *Treat others as you would like to be treated*
- *Never leave a game until it's over*

IN 56 YEARS I MISSED ONLY 5 GAMES:

1. *I was in Mt. Carmel East Hospital having a ½-inch piece of rusty fence wire removed from my left foot instep. The wire kicked out the back of a powered push lawn mower.*

2. *Took my wife and mother-in-law to the annual Swiss festival in Sugarcreek, Ohio, Amish country.*

3. *My daughter got married on alumni game day the first game of*

September in 1990.

4. The flu got me the last game of the 2008 Michigan game with afternoon temperatures below freezing.

5. I attended my Hilliard High School 60th class reunion in 2009.

MOST COMMONLY ASKED QUESTIONS AT THE SHOE

Where is 17-B or 19-B? Sad to say odd number sections are straight across the field from 18-B. A long walk around, but you can stay on B deck without going back downstairs.

*Where is the smoking area? There are **NONE** inside the stadium anymore.*

ODDITY

You used to walk in through portal 18-B and you were directly in line with the 50 yard line. After a stadium renovation in 2001 when the field was dug down (lowered) you now walk in looking at the 40 yard line. The playing field was shifted 10 yards south.

STILL A THRILL

When TBDBITL marches onto the field from the north ramp about 20 minutes before game time.

When TBDBITL performs Script Ohio with a senior tuba player dotting the "i ". Why? In the past it included my brother

Bob in 1960 and my son Doug on New Year's Day at the Rose Bowl in 1980.

MY MOST REMEMBERED OSU HOME GAME

It took place my first year as Usher in 1957 against Iowa between two undefeated teams vying for the Big Ten Championship. In the last quarter OSU needed a score to go ahead and win the game. With less than eight minutes to play we got the ball with about 80 yards to go.

Fullback Bob White carried the ball seven of eight plays to score the winning touchdown. The Iowa defense knew what was happening but couldn't stop it. OSU went on to defeat Michigan and win the Big Ten Championship.

That one man show, keeping the ball on the ground with good blocking and ball carrying no doubt reinforced Woody's "three yards and a cloud of dust" thinking.

COLUMBUS MAYOR

When Buck Rinehart was Mayor of Columbus he came to an early-season game escorted by two Columbus police plainclothes detective body guards. Columbus mayors always had seats on the 50 yard line directly below our portal entrance at the top of A-deck, but had never had bodyguard protection.

One of the bodyguards was sitting on the steps next to the mayor's row and the other one kept getting in the way standing in the aisle entrance to the B-box seats. Our portal chief finally got frustrated with them being in the way of other fans. Lowell told them they had to stand out of the way either in or outside the por-

tal. I overheard him say that he had been a portal chief or Usher at 18-B for many years and, "We haven't lost a mayor yet!" In other words — were they really necessary?

They did stay out of the way the rest of the game and were never a problem the rest of the season. Buck evidently thought he needed them to be there in the immediate vicinity for his safety and well-being.

DON'T CALL ME A "SENIOR"!

GLENN
AGE

November 3, 2007 - Ushers with 50+ years at OSU were recognized on the field and acknowledged on the scoreboard. These are the 12 that were recognized.

YOU ONLY LIVE ONCE

I have received dozens of letters and emails for Ushers over the years, but this has stuck with me: For those who understand, no explanation is needed. For those who do not understand, no explanation is possible:

One day I had lunch with some friends. Jim, a short, balding, golfer type about 80 years old, came along with them — all in all, a pleasant bunch. When the menus were presented, we ordered salads, sandwiches, and soups, except for Jim who said, "Ice cream, please. Two scoops, chocolate."

I wasn't sure my ears heard right, and the others were aghast. "Along with heated apple pie," Jim added, completely unabashed. We tried to act nonchalant, as if people did this all the time. But when our orders were brought out, I didn't enjoy mine. I couldn't take my eyes off Jim as his pie a-la-Mode went down. The other guys couldn't believe it. They ate their lunches silently and grinned.

The next time I went out to eat, I called and invited Jim. I lunched on white meat tuna. He ordered a parfait. I smiled. He asked if he amused me. I answered, "Yes, you do, but also you confuse me. How come you order rich desserts, while I feel I must be sensible?"

He laughed and said, "I'm tasting all that is possible. I try to eat the food I need, and do the things I should. But life's so short, my friend, I hate missing out on something good. This year I realized how old I was." (He grinned.) "I haven't been this old before. So, before I die, I've got to try those things that for years I had ignored. I haven't smelled all the flowers yet. There are too many trout streams I haven't fished. There are more fudge sundaes to wolf down and kites to be flown overhead.

"There are too many golf courses I haven't played. I've not laughed at all the jokes. I've missed a lot of sporting events and potato chips and Cokes.

"I want to wade again in water and feel ocean spray on my face. I want to sit in a country church once more and thank God for His grace.

"I want peanut butter every day spread on my morning toast. I want un-timed long distance calls to the folks I love the most.

"I haven't cried at all the movies yet, or walked in the morning rain. I need to feel wind on my face. I want to be in love again.

"So, if I choose to have dessert, instead of having dinner, then should I die before nightfall, I'd say I died a winner, because I missed out on nothing. I filled my heart's desire. I had that final chocolate mousse before my life expired."

With that, I called the waitress over. "I've changed my mind," I said. "I want what he is having; only add some more whipped cream!"

REDCOATS

You have to perform at a consistently higher level than others. That's the mark of a true professional.
—*Joe Paterno*

THE REDCOATS ARE COMING

A lot of fans associate the term "Redcoats" with all the Ushers in the stadium, in reference to the bright red coats that all the Ushers used to wear. There is a distinction between the actual Redcoats — those who check the tickets at the gates — and the Ushers who show fans to their seats. Of the estimated 3,000 service people who work every football game at Ohio Stadium, at least 450 are dedicated Redcoats who come from across Ohio and the nation. Some Redcoats have even come from Florida and New York to serve fans on game days. "Redcoats are people who love Ohio State," said Mike Penner, Assistant Athletic Director of Events Management. "And they love to provide a valuable service to fans." Penner said the term Redcoat arose after workers agreed to wear scarlet blazers to events they attended. After the construction of St. John Arena in 1956, the Redcoats became a staple at many athletic events on campus.

Redcoats work throughout the year at many sporting events. Some sign up to work for lacrosse or baseball games, others for women's ice hockey or basketball games. For 10 months of the year, many work with the people and the university they love, Penner said. Present at every home football game, the Redcoats are responsible for scanning tickets, working the press box, checking in the media, enforcing rules and helping fans in need.

"You welcome people in and try to make them feel comfortable," said Ann Baca, a 10-year Redcoat. "OSU fans, visiting fans, whoever it is that comes through those gates, you want to make them feel welcome." A Redcoat's responsibility can also include collecting tickets at gates, helping fans with questions or patrolling the stadium or arena, but his or her main objective is to make fans' experiences safe and enjoyable.

Becky Rich, a 15-year Redcoat veteran, agreed. "We are an extension of the eyes and ears of the university," Rich said. "We protect the guests and try to make them happy at the same time." As ambassadors of OSU's athletic program, Redcoats are hourly-paid university employees. The position is considered part-time and the hours vary.

"It all depends on the season and the sport," said Jon Yake, a supervisor for the Redcoats. "If it's just football you might only work about eight hours a week, but if you work multiple sports at a time or the sport has a busy week, it's more." Yake, a 37-year Redcoat, said he worked about 30 hours per week during an OSU baseball team's recent 10-game home stand.

Redcoats make minimum wage while 25 supervisors make up to $10 per hour. The yearly Redcoat staff usually consists of about 400 employees, and students can also apply for the positions. Rich and Yake said Redcoats are expected to work at least two sports — football and something else. "That's the big one," Yake said. "Of the 450 or so Redcoats we have, the majority of them work during football games."

Other events aren't as big in numbers, he said. For example, an OSU baseball game may have as few as 17 Redcoats in attendance — but because every gate in the stadium must be manned before, during and after the game, the number of Redcoats at football games is far greater than other sports. Many Redcoats work more than the required two sports. Yake said he works football, baseball, men's and women's basketball and football and lacrosse summer camps. "We're kind of expected to work when called upon," he said.

Rich also works more than two sports. She works baseball, football and wrestling, in addition to being a full-time medical bill review nurse. At one point, she said she was offered a nursing position at the Wexner Medical Center at OSU but turned it down because of her Redcoat position. Because she was already an hourly-paid employee of the university, she was not able to accept the salary-paid nursing position without turning in her red blazer.

"I loved my Redcoat job too much," she said. "I couldn't give it up." Rich, 59, said that if she were younger, she is not sure she would be able to hold a full-time position and be a Redcoat. "Young people don't necessarily have the time," she said. The time issue is also why she said she believes most Redcoats are generally older and considers herself one of the younger Redcoats. "Most other Redcoats I know are older than I am," she said. "If I were to guess the average age of a Redcoat, I'd say it's in the mid-50s, maybe higher."

Yake, 73, agreed with her about the average age of a Redcoat. "If they were to set an age limit, they would have a big turnover, that's for sure," he said with a smile.

One of the perks for the Redcoats is attending and watching OSU games when they're not busy with assigned duties, Baca said. "We cheer and get into it like the fans do," said 16-year Redcoat Rich Rinker. "We just have to watch what we say."

Yake said the fans like to see the Redcoats enjoy the action. "When we get into the games, I think it gets the fans excited seeing us like that." The opportunity to be in the stadium and be present as a fan while working is the main reason Yake became a Redcoat. He said he used to acquire football tickets through his boss at work, but when he left the company, "I still wanted to be a part of it and come and see the games," he said. "I didn't want to have to give that up." Learning about the Redcoat position from his wife's hairdresser, he said the application process was simpler in 1975, his first year as a Redcoat. "Back then, all you had to do was show up at the year's first meeting and put your name in a hat. They drew names and if you got your name drawn, you were a Redcoat."

Yake said he has enjoyed the past 37 years with no regrets and will

Jon Yake stands at the gates of Bill Davis Stadium waiting for fans to begin entering the stadium. OSU Lantern photo

continue to be an ambassador for the university and its athletic program. "I'll continue (to be a Redcoat) as long as I'm enjoying it and having fun," he said. "When the day comes that I'm not—whatever the reason may be — I'm done."

While the games might have enticed them to become Redcoats, Yake and Rich said they get more out of the job than free entry into football or basketball games. "It's not only about going to the games," Yake said. "You get to talk to a whole lot of people. They get to know you and you get to know them. You create friendships."

The Redcoats are stationed at various gates surrounding the stadium and miss a large part of the game; some can go into stands and watch the game after their gate closes, but all agree there is never a dull moment when they man the gates.

Fans unable to obtain tickets to Ohio State games sometimes resort to devious methods of entry. Some have tried slipping through the north gates with the marching band, others have tried the emergency exits inside the Stadium Scholarship Dormitories, and a brazen few have scaled the gates.

ENTERPRISING YOUNG GATE CRASHER

From the book, "Ohio State Football: The Great Tradition": by Jack Park:

> *Frank Buffington, supervisor of gates, remembers a clever incident back in the early 1970s. A young boy, about 11, approached gate 10 carrying a bag of ice on each shoulder. He explained that a concession manager had sent him out to obtain the ice. The ticket takers were somewhat suspicious of the boy's story but finally let him through. Buffington recalls one of the gatemen saying, "Now let's see what he does."*
>
> *`After walking approximately 60 feet inside the stadium, the youngster suddenly dropped both sacks of ice and took off running at full speed. Buffington laughingly remarks, "What an enterprising young gate crasher! Just think, this youngster engineered his way inside Ohio Stadium for the cost of two 25-cent bags of ice!"*

EXPERIENCE SCARLET AND GRAY

Jeff Bordner has been a Redcoat at Ohio Stadium since 1979:

> *I recall my first days working at Ohio Stadium as a Redcoat in 1979. Back before the buzz of scanners approved tickets, I stood at the gates, snug in my red blazer and greeted people from every*

Superintendent of Red Coats Dan Milligan (left) and Assistant of Redcoats Jeff Bordner in the press box at The Shoe. Photo by Matthew Hashiguchi

walk of life. Just 11 years earlier, I sold programs at the Horseshoe as a teenager and watched Woody Hayes' run to a perfect season.

While many other Redcoats work until the end of the first quarter at the gates of Ohio Stadium, I can work as long as 14 hours a day in the Club and press box level. I have the responsibility of conducting tours throughout Ohio Stadium, sometimes juggling three or four stadium tours a day in between overseeing women's ice hockey and incoming conventions in St. John Arena.

I retired from the Grandview Heights Police Department after 24 years, and have worked for the university at many events including commencement. Nestled between stories of past athletic events and crazy moments with fans, I have watched both of our daughters graduate from OSU. Our daughters "grew up" at St. John Arena as ball girls for the women's basketball team and helped me greet guests. Seeing them graduate from the university I love was a proud moment in my life.

I have had the privilege of acquiring tickets to watch my beloved Buckeyes win a National Championship in Tempe, Arizona. I also attend away games, including the Michigan State game with four other Redcoats with whom I have become friends over the years. We always proudly wear our scarlet and gray. And I must say, we have been treated well at our foes' stadiums, just as we would treat them at the Shoe.

Each year, one of my other responsibilities is to invite a varying number of future Redcoats to train, go over the handbook and become an official Redcoat. Many times people are waitlisted and train by working at Skull Sessions before working a football game,

As I describe to the new guys, the Redcoats are many things to many people, among the most important duties we perform for fans is that of being a friend! People get to know you and expect to see you. You get to be friends with them. People are the reason we are here.

The height of human desire is what wins, whether it's on Normandy Beach or in Ohio Stadium.
—**Woody Hayes**

NOSMO KING AT THE STADIUM

Bill Lobuzzetta is from Niagara Falls, NY, and grew up three blocks from the thundering of the falls. After serving four years in the USAF, he graduated from Duquesne University. He married Donna in 1973 and moved to Columbus in 1974. They have two sons. Bill recently retired as the Recreation Supervisor in charge of adult sport leagues and special events for the City of Hilliard. He joined the Redcoats in 1988 and has missed only one home game in the 25 years of working the gates of the football games:

I currently scan tickets at gate 11 and like to have fun interacting with the fans. When a guest aged 10 or younger comes to

1930 - Stadium ticket-take

the game I say to them, "Just in case your parents didn't tell you, there is no smoking in the stadium." This usually brings out a smile from the child and the parent.

I have a great story of a gate crasher. It happened about 23 years ago. If I recall correctly, he was a pharmacist from a small Ohio town. The crasher had his picture in the Dispatch and was bragging how he had gate crashed the Michigan game multiple times in various ways including as a band member, a photographer, concession worker, Usher, etc.

Frank Buffington, who was in charge of the Redcoats, said during our pregame meeting that he wanted us to be especially on the lookout for this person. On that day I was working at Gate 1, which is at the north main entrance of the stadium. I recognized the so-called crasher because he had on the same unusual hat he was wearing in the newspaper picture. He was pulling a wagon with boxes of booklets and claimed he was supposed to take them to the press box. I immediately got my supervisor Joe Jones to deal with him. After not being let in, he pulled a ticket out of his pocket and gave it to Jones to tear and he proceeded in, leaving his goods at our check-in area. The next day the Columbus Dispatch ran an article stating he had again successfully gate crashed using the delivery to the press box story. Upon reading this I became furious knowing that he did not sneak in.

I called the Dispatch and spoke to the writer of the article and asked him how he got his information. He said the crasher told him to meet him where his family was sitting and he would tell him how he managed to get in. I told him that the crasher's story was totally bogus then told him what really happened, advising him to verify my story with Joe Jones. The writer did verify it and the next day the Dispatch ran a story with the heading "Lobuzzetta catches gate crashers." It told what really happened. The next day the gate crasher was quoted in another brief article claiming that we were mistaken, but that he had decided not to gate-crash anymore.

Bill Lobuzzetta

O, we

don't give a damn for the whole state of Michigan
The whole state of Michigan,
the whole state of Michigan
We don't give a damn for the whole state of Michigan, we're from Ohio

We're from Ohio...O-H
We're from Ohio...I-O

O, we don't give a damn for the whole state of Michigan,
The whole state of Michigan, the whole state of Michigan
We don't give a damn for the whole state of Michigan, we're from

Ohio

GERMAN ONE OF MANY REDCOATS AT OSU

From The Daily Jeffersonian, October 1, 2005-Cambridge, Ohio:

When Paul German began doing volunteer work at the WOSU-TV station in Columbus back in 1998, he never thought it would lead to being a Redcoat at Ohio Stadium during Ohio State football games. German became a volunteer at the TV station because his son Tom was working there as an employee and suggested that Paul give some of his spare time to help the station. German had helped answer phones during the fund raiser telethons, which is what led to his current gig at OSU. According to Paul, some volunteers were asked to hand out programs at the open house of the rebirth of The Horseshoe and while he was there, he chatted with one of the female Redcoats and inquired about becoming a Redcoat himself. The lady told German to talk to Jan Reinhard a supervisor of approximately 80 Redcoats who was also in charge of the Skull Sessions at St. John Arena where the OSU band practices prior to each home game. Reinhard told German she needed a few new Redcoats and after a meeting, Paul was hired and has been on the job since the 2000 season. The hiring is never advertised, German stated, but only by word of mouth by current Redcoats. Otherwise, many people would be interested in holding that position. Redcoats under Reinhard report to St. John Arena five hours prior to kick-off of each game and then are assigned to an area in the arena. German usually watches Ramp 4-A on the northwest side of the arena. After the Skull Session is over, German and other Redcoats escort the band from St. John to Ohio Stadium by forming a human chain to allow the band and cheerleaders to get into the stadium. When German reaches Ohio Stadium, he reports to another supervisor and then heads off to Section 37 to watch the Buckeyes warm up and the band's pre-game tunes. With about two to three minutes left in the first quarter, German reports back to Gate 10 for gate watch through the second and third quarters. Once the gate is opened by an OSU stadium employee during the fourth quarter, German and others can either leave or find a seat inside the stadium to watch the rest of the game. I usually head to the 50-yard line to watch the rest of the game, German stated. That is always my choice. German said Redcoats are employees of the OSU Athletic Department and are paid on an hourly basis. Paul usually receives eight hours of pay and free parking; and gets to see at least half of each game. As far as being a Redcoat, German said it is indeed an honor and is just as exciting each and every Saturday. One of the big thrills is to hear the band practice session that includes some invited high school bands as well as visiting bands, Paul noted. Once at the stadium, it is a great feeling to see the OSU band come out of the tunnel and down the ramp to perform on the field. Along with that, just being there with 104,000-plus fans each game is a special treat.

PRIDE OF A REDCOAT

Gary Hensley has been a Redcoat since 2004:

I've always been an Ohio State fan. Our son was a physical therapist in Columbus. A patient came in one day, and her boy-friend was the one who hired the Redcoats. In the conversation, my son said I was a big Ohio State fan. After talking to her boy-friend, I was asked to contact him, I did, and he hired me.

I make sure the opposing team gets ready to face the Buck-eyes, serving as the escort for the visiting team and officials as they come to the stadium.

My day begins 4½ hours before kickoff, meaning that I will be in Ohio Stadium around 11 a.m. for a 3:30 p.m. start, helping the visiting team's pre-game personnel get to where they need to be. When the team arrives, I make sure those who have the pass to get to the locker room and field are pointed in the right direction and those needing to get to the press box make it there. Other duties, such as procuring carts to move equipment and people, and occasionally getting beverages for the staff, keep the two hours before kickoff busy.

I make sure the visiting team gets to and from their locker room. Then I coordinate the delivery of the post-game meal for the team. When the team gets loaded up and on the road 90 minutes or so after the final play, I head home.

There's a lot of pride in being a Redcoat. When the visiting team comes into the stadium, we want them to feel welcome and leave feeling they were well-treated. We've had a lot of good comments from visiting teams on how they were treated.

Over my five years of work at the stadium, I have conversed with a number of coaches. Among those that stick out is longtime Penn State coach Joe Paterno, especially a moment when Paterno had to leave the field due to illness several years ago. He's just a quality gentleman. When he went into the locker room after falling ill, he said in 60 years he's never left the field early while playing or coaching. He will stand and visit with me 10-15 minutes when he arrives or gets ready to leave. He's just a regular guy.

Another memorable conversation involves the late Northwestern coach Randy Walker. I immediately found a topic to bond with Walker in former Celina quarterback Mike Bath, whom Walker coached at Miami.

But it was about another topic closer to the heart that I remember most. He talked to me about a half hour before the game. One of the best stories was about how his son wanted to get into coaching. He explained to his son the type of life it was. To see if he really wanted to work in coaching, he made him work without pay for six months. I believe he's still on the staff at Northwestern.

Although I have been a Redcoat for many years these three games stick out: The night games with Texas and Southern Cali-

Hensley enjoys his
work as a Redcoat

fornia, and the 2006 game with Michigan when OSU was top-ranked and the Wolverines second. That was exciting to be there. I only hope to keep working with the team. As long as I can walk I will do it. I would also like to get the chance to work the Ohio State side in the future.

FELLOWSHIP

Carrol Schwien has been a Redcoat since 2006:

I am a fledgling compared to most of the people I have worked with. At the urging of a friend I attended one of our August meetings and that is basically how I become a Redcoat. I served one year of being assigned to supervisors that needed additional help.

My post on game day

This is the North Rotunda, or the front entrance to the stadium at Ohio State

Since then I have been on the North Rotunda Gate.

I was born in 1930 and raised in Kansas, finished some college before being drafted into the Army; served 1951-1952 in Korea.

I have enjoyed the fellowship of other Redcoats as well as the whole football atmosphere. I find that greeting and working with patrons and their young children is the most rewarding part of being a Redcoat.

My biggest pleasure about being a Redcoat at the Rotunda gate is greeting families bringing their children for the first time. When you ask if this is their first time to attend a game, either their eyes light up and a big smile comes across their face, or they appear apprehensive that this IS their first game. The parents so much appreciate the interest that we express to their children. That means a lot to me.

WILL CALL

Jon Weller and his wife **Beth** have been Redcoats since 2007. They've

---

been working at Player Will-Call/Customer Service since 2008. Jon, now 58, is originally from Mason, Ohio and currently living in Hamilton. He's a 1977 graduate of Ohio State, and retired from Delphi/General Motors in 2007. Prior to becoming Redcoats, they attended most home games. They currently go to most away games and bowl games. They have also been Cincinnati Bengal season ticket holders since 1981:

This happened in 2009 at the USC home game. I was working at the home player's Will Call/Customer Service door as a Redcoat. A gentleman who had just finished talking to a ticket rep came to our door and starting giving me his story about getting stuck with counterfeit tickets. He was in his 60s and had purchased three tickets through eBay for $450 each for his three sons who had come to the game from Alabama, Texas and Missouri. The ticket rep had told him that since the tickets were purchased through an outside vendor, there was nothing they could do about it and that there were no tickets to be purchased. He said that he would do or pay any amount to get his sons in to see the game.

After listening to his story, I knew there were some tickets available at the ticket office due to ticket exchanges for handicapped seating. I got the attention of the ticket office supervisor and told her the guy's story. She got the guy to the window and said that though she couldn't give him replacement tickets, she could sell him 3 tickets, although not together, at face value. I thought the fellow was going to have a heart attack—he started jumping up and down in celebration.

Then he said that he had to run and find his sons who were somewhere outside the stadium. He started to run but then realized he couldn't leave the window without paying. He reached in his vest pocket and pulled out an envelope that was stuffed with $50 bills. There had to be a couple thousand there. He stuffed the envelope into MY HAND and said pay them whatever they want and started to run off. After a couple of steps, he stopped, ran back to me and gave me his wallet which was also stuffed with cash. He said, *"Just in case"* and ran off into the crowd. About 3 minutes later he came running back. I gave him the envelope and wallet back and told him the tickets were just about ready and he could pay the lady himself.

After he paid, he shook my hand and said I was a gem and ran off with the tickets to find his sons. Always good to help someone out.

The will to win is important, but the will to prepare is vital.

—Joe Paterno

THE ROOKIE

Gene Menning became a Redcoat in 2012.

I am a rookie; the 2012 season was my first. My assignment was the North Rotunda where I could peer out over the people entering the stadium. The best part of that post is that it provides a great view of the band when it enters the stadium just before kick-off. Guests begin forming in the rotunda balcony an hour before the band marches in, just to see the TBDBITL up close. Visitors from out of town, including people from the visiting team, stand and wait to see the band. This is a great opportunity for a Redcoat to be friendly and welcoming to guests.

I spent four years in the Air Force, 36 months of it overseas. I was an enlisted man, trained as an aircraft and engine mechanic in the US Air Force during the Korean conflict. The Air Force thought I was needed more in Europe so for 13 months I was assigned to England from 1951-52. I always wanted to attend Ohio State, but I grew up and graduated from high school in Toledo.

A photo of Gene Menning with his granddaughter who is a graduate of OSU.

My parents sent me to the University of Toledo; they wanted to see how I would do and said if I made good grades they would consider sending me to Ohio State. Unfortunately, my father died after two years and I had to leave school.

After my discharge in 1954 I could not afford to attend Ohio State and I returned to the University of Toledo. I worked nights in a factory while I attended school. In 1957 I graduated, married a girl I was dating from Ohio State, and then went to work in Toledo at the Champion Spark Plug Company. In 1969 I received a master's degree from the University of Toledo.

My wife and I had four children and I was able to send all four of them to Ohio State, even though I was never able to afford to go myself. My children married OSU graduates or Columbus residents, and we have two grandchildren who have graduated from

Ohio State, plus another who is a senior there, and we have three more grandchildren who are entering Ohio State as freshmen.

I guess I really kind of did make it to Ohio State University.

MY START AS AN OSU REDCOAT BY GENE MENNING

The 2012 season was my first as a newly minted Redcoat. It turned out to be a daunting experience particularly because I am new to Columbus. My wife and I moved here from Coldwater Lake, Michigan to be closer to our children. For 17 years of our retirement we lived on an inland lake in Michigan where we became spoiled driving on two lane roads with few traffic lights — none at all if we took the right route to town. Suddenly we found ourselves in Columbus living in a condo and driving in unfamiliar territory on Daytona 500 expressways.

A granddaughter who attends Ohio State and works in the Events Planning Department told me that I should volunteer to be a Redcoat for football games in Ohio Stadium. She said I'd meet all kinds of retirees like myself and would be able to get into home games. How could I say no to that!? So I interviewed and was hired. At that point I had it made. What I didn't consider in my enthusiasm was my inexperience driving on expressways and side streets or anywhere at all in Columbus, especially around the university.

I attempted to find my way to the stadium for the first game with much difficulty. Even my GPS unit got lost and had a nervous breakdown in the process. There were certain parking areas where I was supposed to deposit my car, but I didn't know where they were. When I tried to enter a lot, I was rejected. I tried to explain that I was a new Redcoat and I did not know where to park and I was going to be late reporting to my post. It became obvious that the police didn't know where I was supposed to park, only where I WASN'T supposed to park. Even though I had left home a couple of hours early to accommodate my navigational dyslexia it was obvious I was running out of time. Not a good way to start a new job.

Then the parking god shown down upon me and lo and behold there appeared a parking lot with plenty of empty spaces. I thought: this is odd and maybe this relatively empty parking area is open for a reason, and maybe that reason does not include me parking here. But with time running out I pulled in, parked, and ran to my reporting gate, late but not too late. I explained that I was late because I didn't know where to park, to which I was asked, "Where did you park?" I explained how I had driven aimlessly all around the stadium never knowing exactly where I was and suddenly found this strange parking lot that was nearly empty. Oh, there, I was told, that's reserved for VIPs who would be attending games, and that my car would probably be towed, which would cost me lots and lots of money.

At first I thought I would deal with the situation after the game, or at least when I was off duty, but the more I thought about it I came to the conclusion, this gig isn't for me. I told my supervisor that I had evaluated my situation and decided to quit, and promptly ran off to find my car, which was also a challenge because I really wasn't sure where I had parked. As luck would have it, I eventually found my car, which was fortunately still there. I got in the car, hooked up the GPS (I needed it to get home) and drove out of the parking lot before they caught me and put me in solitary.

On the way somewhere, I didn't know where because my GPS unit didn't engage with the satellite for a long time, as I was wandering aimlessly down strange, narrow side streets waiting to engage with the satellite, I suddenly encountered a caravan of huge buses turning in front of me accompanied by police cars with flashing lights. I had to pull off the road next to a tree to avoid having the front end of my car amputated by one of these massive buses. Then I recalled that the Republican candidate for Vice President, Paul Ryan, was coming to the stadium for an appearance during the game. This would have been a major faux pas to be in an accident with that bus. I could see the news: "Redcoat collides with VP candidate's bus as he arrives at opening day game: major embarrassment to university and Redcoat organization." The bus caravan zipped by, leaving me shaken, with my bumper up against a tree. Then my GPS caught the satellite and a feminine voice said, "If possible make a U-turn."

Eventually I was able to get home before the end of the game which I viewed from the comfort of my big couch and my large screen TV with high definition while enjoying a low definition adult beverage as a sedative.

Ah, the safety of home. That might have been the end of the story, but fortunately it wasn't. That evening I received a phone call from my supervisor, Judi Murphy. Judi was very kind, and asked me in greater detail what had happened, and moreover, did I really, really want to quit the Redcoats? She said that it is a great organization with wonderful people associated with the best university in the land and that I would really regret it if I were to quit. She said that she understood the situation considering I was new to Columbus. Judi asked me to give it another try. She suggested I study the route to the stadium and the approved parking lots and try again.

I did reconsider, and even though I still had difficulty finding a suitable legal parking area I gradually overcame my navigational deficiencies and had a truly enjoyable first year as a Redcoat. Maybe it is like basic training — you become a better person for having gone through it. Now I am very proud to be a Redcoat and am looking forward to next season.

FLASHBACK!

Don't Blame Me!

The Ohio Stadium Recruiting Room is in the southeast tower of the stadium, near Gate 32, but that does not mean that any recruit can just walk in the gate. Back in 1988, Raymont Harris, a prize recruit from Lorain, Ohio, making his first trek to Columbus to see a game, was not ready for such a massive structure and went to the wrong gate. He was turned away, despite receiving an invitation from the coaching staff. Meanwhile the crowd inside was going crazy, the Buckeyes had staged a sensational comeback and defeated LSU.

"I was pissed," Harris recalled. "I remember saying, 'I'm never going to Ohio State.'"

But Harris did return for a visit and once he saw the Horseshoe from the inside, his feelings changed fast. He committed to the Buckeyes and won the Silver Football Award as MVP of the Big Ten in 1993.

4

RUDY

A great feel good movie about the dreams of a regular guy is Rudy, a 1993 American sports film directed by David Anspaugh. For those who do not know the plot here is an overview from Wikipedia:

> *Rudy is an account of the life of Daniel "Rudy" Ruettiger, who harbored dreams of playing football at the University of Notre Dame despite significant obstacles. It was the first movie that the Notre Dame administration allowed to be shot on campus since Knute Rockne, All American in 1940. Daniel Eugene "Rudy" Ruettiger grows up in Joliet, Illinois dreaming of playing college football at the University of Notre Dame. Though he is achieving some success with his local high school team (Joliet Catholic), he lacks the grades and money necessary to attend Notre Dame, as well as talent and physical stature. Ruettiger takes a job at a local steel mill like his father Daniel Sr., who is also a Notre Dame fan. He prepares to settle down, but when his best friend Pete is killed in an explosion at the mill, Rudy decides to follow his dream of attending Notre Dame and playing for the Fighting Irish. He perseveres to do everything he can to get into the football powerhouse.*
>
> *After numerous rejections, Rudy is finally admitted to Notre Dame during his final semester of transfer eligibility. He rushes home to tell his family, and his father announces the news to his*

steel mill workers over the loudspeaker. After walking on as a non-scholarship player for the football team, Ruettiger convinces coach Ara Parseghian to give him a spot on the practice squad. An assistant coach warns the players that 35 scholarship players won't make the "dress roster" of players who take the field during the games but also notices that Ruettiger exhibits more drive than many of his scholarship teammates.

Coach Parseghian agrees to Rudy's request to suit up for one home game in his senior year so his family and friends can see him as a member of the team. However, Parseghian steps down as coach following the 1974 season. Dan Devine succeeds him in 1975 and honors Parseghian's promise only after a player protest. Led by senior team captain and All-American Roland Steele, the other seniors rise to his defense and lay their jerseys on Devine's desk, each requesting that Rudy be allowed to dress in their place. In response, Devine lets Ruettiger appear for the final home game against Georgia Tech.

At the final home game, Steele invites Ruettiger to lead the team out of the tunnel onto the playing field. As the game comes to an end, and Notre Dame is ahead, Devine sends all the seniors to the field, but refuses to let Rudy play, despite the pleas from Steele and the assistant coaches. As a "Rudy!" chant spreads from the Notre Dame bench into the stadium, and the offensive team, led by tailback Jamie O'Hare, overrules Devine's call for victory formation and they score another touchdown instead. Devine finally lets Rudy enter the field with the defensive team on the final kickoff. He stays in for the final play of the game, sacks the Georgia Tech quarterback, and to cheers from the stadium, is carried off the field on the shoulders of his teammates.

So, what does this feel good movie have to do with OSU and the Usher program? The player who agreed to come out of the game to allow Rudy his dream was none other than **Gene Smith**, Athletic Director of The Ohio State University. Actually, according to Gene Smith, he and another defensive end "came out at the same time."

Gene Smith starts his tenth year in March 2014 as director of athletics at The Ohio State University. He is widely recognized among the leaders of his profession and has been named "one of the most powerful people in collegiate sports." Smith was named to the post in March 2005. In January 2014 athletic director Gene Smith takes on more responsibility with the university as part of a four-year contract extension announced by the school; includes a salary increase, promotion to vice president and extension until June 30, 2020.

Gene has responsibility for the entire athletic program, including the Usher program. In the scheme of things, we are only a small part of the program, but every year, Gene never fails to address our whole group and express his gratitude for this largely volunteer group:

During my tenure as Athletic Director at The Ohio State University I have had the pleasure of meeting thousands of Buckeyes

Gene Smith — Nebraska Game, 2012

all around the world — great people who love being Buckeyes and supporting the university in various ways. The pride many have in the athletic program is the direct result of the great work the coaches and student athletes do.

Without the Usher program we would not be able to create the environment necessary for coaches and student athletes to do what they do, thus creating that deep pride Buckeyes have. Our job is to facilitate remarkable experiences for our Buckeyes and other guests. Be it a baseball, soccer, football, or basketball game or special events, thousands of fans are welcomed by the Ushers. That friendly and warm encounter is a hallmark of the remarkable experience beyond the event. Whether a person needs direction or just has a simple question about anything, their engagement with an Usher is always an enjoyable experience.

Over my eight-plus years here I have received several complaints about different things, but never one about an Usher. NEVER!!!! That speaks volumes to the customer service approach that is embedded in the good nature of the Usher program.

Lastly, I love the diversity that is represented within the group. The true definition of team—a group of people with diverse backgrounds coming together to achieve one common goal. The Usher program is truly representative of what our student athletes are all about.

THE BUCKEYE ICON

Another unofficial survey from the Usher/Redcoat ranks the all-time favorite Buckeyes:

 # 1- Archie Griffin (of course)
#2- Chris Spielman
#3- Eddie George
#4- Rex Kern
#5-Troy Smith

Archie, winner by a landslide, the only two-time Heisman Trophy recipient and President and Chief Executive Officer of the OSU Alumni Association, was a natural selection. In an era when the shelf life of athletes is short and fame can be fleeting, Griffin, 59, has maintained a blue-chip rating with the public for nearly four decades. While others sometimes struggle with the demands of celebrity, Griffin — aided by his pleasant demeanor and genuine fondness for people — makes the effort look easy. Archie was quoted in a Columbus Dispatch article:

"I'm not going to say that I never get tired of being recognized or going to alumni events, after working an adoring banquet crowd for about an hour. But once I get there, I feel blessed and energized. I never thought that people would remember me after this long."

Thirty-five years after making history with his second Heisman, No. 45 continues to embody all that is good — even revered — about Ohio State football. Archie had another laurel laid at his feet on January 1, 2014 when he was named the Rose Bowl's All-Century Player; The first player to start in four straight Rose Bowls.

"I'm extremely honored," Archie said. "We only won one of the four Rose Bowls that I was in, so it was surprising to me!"

The brainchild of ex-OSU quarterback Rex Kern and former Director of Athletics Andy Geiger, the Tunnel of Pride actually started in 1995, when Notre Dame visited Ohio Stadium for the first meeting between the two teams in nearly 50 years. In an effort to generate even more emotion,

excitement and enthusiasm than already existed, Kern and Geiger reached out to former Buckeye football players who were attending the game and asked them to form a tunnel for the team to run through as it came onto the field. Thus a tradition was born, which is now continued every other year when Michigan visits Ohio Stadium.

Archie also speaks proudly of the Usher Program:

Saturday in "the Shoe" wouldn't be complete without the support of over 1,275 Ushers and Redcoats. These two groups of dedicated people are a pivotal part of the game day experience. A lot of people probably don't know that they volunteer their time and work long hours which at times includes enduring inclement weather. They are often the first impression perceived by the thousands of fans as they enter Ohio Stadium. From assisting with ticket taking to showing fans to their seats they all have one thing in common; their true love for the Buckeyes. I would like to thank every Usher and Redcoat for all that they provide in making a football Saturday in Ohio Stadium such a special place to be.

To succeed, you need to find something to hold on to, something to motivate you, something to inspire you.
—**Tony Dorsett**

Archie Griffin –one of the fans at Tunnel of Pride

BOY SCOUTS

One thing I've found particularly interesting was the tremendous loyalty and allegiance to the university by the other Ushers — the Boy Scouts of America. A total of 50 Boy Scouts per game, from all across the Buckeye District and beyond, enjoy the excellent opportunity to attend select OSU football games at no cost in exchange for providing pre-game support to the regular Ushers at Ohio Stadium.

For several decades, the Ohio State University and the Boy Scouts of America have partnered in this civil service project which benefits the university and also provides the BSA with a highly visible profile at Buckeye games. Due to this high visibility, all participants must present the best image of Scouting possible and meet uniform requirements to participate. Participants must also agree to meet pre-defined standards of conduct prior to and during the game and provide a written acknowledgment of that agreement prior to each game they participate in.

Participants arrive at Ohio Stadium and register no later than 9 a.m. on game days and bring a light meal or snack with them to eat prior to the game. Participants are expected to be on their feet for several hours prior to game time and during the game as well.

Mike also mentions the tremendous support the Boy Scouts receive from the coaches, staff and Ushers. When his oldest son was becoming an Eagle Scout, one of the requirements was to send out letters of recommendation to some of the people they look up to for leadership roles. He sent his request to Coach John Cooper. Coach Cooper responded with an eloquent response that was very special to Ryan.

A year later, Mike attended a wedding in Upper Arlington. Knowing that the church was close to Coach Cooper's residence, he stopped by his house and saw Coach Cooper in his front yard. Mike jumped out of his car and ran up to the Coach. Coach Cooper was startled at first, but when

According to Mike Munsch, Boy Scout Supervisor for game day at the stadium, the scouts gather at the South Stands for the traditional "High Five" from Coach Urban Meyer and the team. Then they disperse around the stadium for their Usher assignments.

Mike caught his breath, he told the coach how special the letter was to his son and wanted to personally thank Mr. Cooper for taking the time to write the letter.

*Former OSU President **E. Gordon Gee** was an Eagle Scout.*

Boy Scouts With Big Nut

Three Boy Scouts Ushers with Jon "Big Nut" Peters. The three Ushers are Travis Gulling, Nick Linkenhoker, and Mike Munsch. Both Nick and Mike are OSU grads.

The Boy Scouts of America have been a mainstay at the Buckeye game for many years and have brought many memorable moments to those impressionable youths. These are some of the "Those Ohio State Moments" from the Official Buckeye Website:

I was born and raised in Columbus. As a grade-schooler, I played football on Ohio Field in pre-game activity. As a Boy Scout, I Ushered during the 1930s when the stadium would be half-filled with spectators. As a student, I attended all the home games. As a graduate and resident of Upper Arlington, I attended all the home games. The most memorable was the Blizzard Bowl against Michigan. I could park the car next to the stadium and sat on the fifty-yard line. It was a kicking game from start to finish, with the winner going to the Rose Bowl. Michigan won that time. No one who was there would ever forget that game.

-Charles B., Cocoa Beach, Florida.

It was the 1968-1970 seasons when OSU fielded maybe the most awesome collegiate teams ever with players such as Tatum, Mayes, Foley, Otis, Stillwagon, Provost, Zelina, Sensibaugh, Debevec, Kern, Brockington and many others. The weather always seemed to be rainy and cold, but being able to see my beloved Buckeyes more than made up for having to arrive hours before the game and standing in my red parka, often near the top of the stadium, through the wind and rain. Seeing Woody and his boys take the field, plus downing a few hot dogs and hot chocolates, was all it took to keep me warm in the big Horseshoe. The highlight for me was witnessing the 50-14 whupping the Bucks gave that team from up North in 1968.

-Scott L. MHA, Plano, Texa.

WHERE'S ROY?

The Ohio Stadium grounds crew had an almost impossible task removing the canvas from the frozen surface so that the 1950 Snow Bowl game between Ohio State and Michigan could begin. Many spectators, including several Boy Scouts, came down out of the stands to help clear the field.

Soon after the game started, a rumor spread that one of the Scouts had been caught and errantly wrapped in the canvas as it *was being rolled from the field. The boy in question was Roy Case of Columbus, who had fallen on the icy surface. Fortunately, the story proved to be false. After falling, Case rolled to the side and avoided being caught in the moving tarp.*

JOB OF A LIFETIME

While working out at the Westerville Recreation Center I overheard a conversation between two gentlemen concerning their younger days at OSU and when one mentioned he was a Boy Scout Usher, my ears perked up. Being nosy, I questioned him about his experience. After a few minutes of listening to William Joseph, 77, a lifelong resident of central Ohio, tell me his fascinating history and connections with Ohio State, we agreed to meet at the Westerville Panera Bread restaurant so he could fill me in on the details of his life.

Bill Joseph, a long-time dentist in central Ohio, graduated from OSU Dental School in 1960 and entered in the Navy as an Ensign in 1961:

> *I was very excited when my Scoutmaster informed me that I was chosen to be a Boy Scout Usher at Ohio Stadium in August of 1947. This was one of the happiest days of my life. I was assigned to a section near the end zone, but no matter, I was in a position to watch my favorite football team, the Ohio State Buckeyes! I*

continued to Usher over the next two years while I earned the distinction of becoming the youngest Eagle Scout in central Ohio. With that honor came the benefit of moving to the 50 yard line on the visitor's side of the stadium. Wow! I was in heaven. I was told by my fellow official Ushers that I was one of the best Scouts ever assigned to their section.

After I was no longer eligible to be a Boy Scout Usher I helped my dad sell the official programs in the stadium from 1950 through 1953. I suspect that my dad was awarded the program sales through his affiliation with Battelle Memorial Institute. My dad had all kinds of contacts with the world of football dating back to the time he was a "Leatherneck" in the old Professional Football league from 1926-28.

I don't think Mom ever cared for Dad playing that rough sport, coming home all bruised and bleeding, because in 1928 they moved to Newcomerstown and opened a new-fangled bowling alley with three lanes and a couple of billiards tables. Dad was quite a celebrity in town and played pool with the locals as well as some shady characters because this was a stop-off point for some of the notorious gangsters driving through town.

One of the locals that dad played pool with happened to be the superintendent of the local schools. Because the local high school football team was getting their butts beat on a regular basis, he asked dad, due to his pro football experience, to help coach the team. Dad accepted and coached the team for a few years. The center for that football team was none other than the future coach of Ohio State — Woody Hayes.

Later my parents moved to Worthington to work for Battelle and I was born in 1935. Dad was gone a lot, but I remember one day coming home from school and seeing Dad in the living room with the most distressed look on his face. Mom admonished me to just "let him be." I didn't realize the reason for his torment until Dad showed us the front page of the Columbus Citizen Journal a few months later. Two atomic bombs had been dropped on

Hiroshima and Nagasaki. Dad had worked on the atomic bomb project for Battelle for many months and never could share his heavy heart.

I was a scrappy little guy in high school who loved all sports. I played football for Worthington High School where I mostly got beat up due to my small stature. The highlight of my football career came at the football banquet of my senior year. The keynote speaker that night was the new OSU Football Coach, Woody Hayes. I was sitting in the back of the room with the other second stringers when Coach Hayes stopped his speech and asked everyone in the room, "Do you all know that your teammate, Bill Joseph's father was my coach in high school?" I was as proud as could be that evening, even though I received no awards. I can still remember another of Coach Hayes' comments, "If people don't criticize me, there's something wrong with them. Hell, I passed in front of a mirror this morning and almost took a swing at myself." I will always love and admire that man!

I mentioned that I liked all sports and my favorite was track. During the summer I worked for a company in downtown Columbus called Frecker's Ice Cream. They were famous for the "Yummy Bar" ice cream and had coolers on the back of a bicycle. I would ride my bike downtown; exchange that for one of the Yummy Bar bikes and pedal all over northern Columbus selling them. When I ran out I would pedal back downtown for more bars, then at the end of the day I would bike back to Worthington.

I used to train all year long. So I had the opportunity to train with Les Eisenhart, the world record holder for the 5000 meter, Earle Bruce, Future OSU Coach and Mel Whitfield. I competed against Earle in the 60 yard dash. This was great fun, but the crowning achievement of my track career was to compete in the state track meet inside Ohio Stadium. (The track was removed during the renovation of the stadium.) My track coach wondered why I was always in such great shape and was not bothered when my whole track team had to run gassers. Thanks again for Yummy

Bars and the OSU Indoor Track.

When I graduated from Worthington High School, my mom questioned my life's ambitions and said I should go out and see the world. I took her up on that challenge and went out West to become a ski bum. I got a job as bell hop at Sun Valley Ski Resort in Idaho and spent a lot of time on night duty at the resort. I became familiar with a lot of the regulars and provided room service and delivered drinks. One late evening I dropped off a few bottles of liquor for a customer and was invited to stay and have a drink. I ended up having an in-depth conversation, until sunrise, with Ernest Hemingway! Another regular that I will never forget is Gary Cooper. He was a great tipper.

When I returned home to Worthington and told my hometown buddies of my wonderful adventures, they always asked, "How did you get that great job?" I would tell them how I sold football programs at Ohio Stadium from 1950-1952, and back then the railroad would drop off fans from all over Ohio at the terminal right outside the stadium. There used to be railroad tracks running outside the stadium and I sold a lot of programs to the fans exiting the trains. I especially liked the Michigan games because the fans would be all liquored up and tip me big-time for the programs. Not as many people owned automobiles and lots of people rode the trains. I became good friends with the trainmaster who knew the manager of the Sun Valley resort and that's how I got that job of a lifetime.

Another memorable moment working with my dad selling programs came during the "Snow Bowl" game against Michigan. In those days the women dressed "to the nines" in the stadium, wearing high heels and stockings, so the few women who braved the blizzard and showed up for the game needed a place to get warm. Dad always parked his big Buick right next to the stadium so that we could unload all those heavy programs. He would keep his car running and those freezing young ladies would line up to get warm in dad's car. Way to go dad!

Freedom Train Traveling Outside Ohio Stadium-1948

In 1953 I returned to reality and attended Miami University from 1953-5, graduated and then headed back to OSU for dental school. While there, I also joined the Navy under a new government program that allowed me to attend school and be in the Navy at the same time. I had to stay in shape, so I joined the OSU weightlifting club with my good buddies, Dr. Nick Hoston, president and founder of the club and Dr. John Polscamp, who participated in the Rome Olympics.

The club moved from St. John Arena to the Bell Tower in Ohio Stadium. This allowed us to have heavy duty Olympic style weights and equipment. This was many years before the many public gyms like Universal and others sprung up all over Columbus. The club was home for some of the more serious athletes and bodybuilders in the area, including visits by Lou Ferrigno, better known as the Incredible Hulk. Because of the heavy weights and all the grunting going on, Woody and others at the stadium would often complain about the noise.

While in school I met the most wonderful young lady who became my wife. She had her heart set on joining the OSU Marching Band, but in those days it was a "boys only" organization. In fact, the only girls allowed on the field were the cheerleaders, so my wife and some other enterprising young ladies formed the first OSU Drill Team — "The Scarlett Steppers." They were the first females allowed on the stadium field and also marched in the Rose Bowl. Never underestimate the powers of a woman scorned!

I will forever remember with fondness and gratitude for my time at OSU!

OHIO STATE AND THE BOY SCOUTS

In 2006 the decision was made that, for safety reasons, the Boy Scouts would not be Ushering in the stadium. For years, Scouts had been helping Ushers at the stadium in exchange for free tickets. The Scouts didn't get seats but were permitted to watch the game while Ushering.

After much discussion and tremendous support for the Scouts, the decision was reversed and the Scouts were back in the stadium for the next game.

According to a Columbus Dispatch article, Associate Athletic Director Steve Snapp said, "We're not sure what their functioning is going to be. They are certainly back for this game and I think for the foreseeable future. We need to ensure their safety first and foremost."

University officials met with local Scout leaders to help determine an appropriate job for the group, which consists of boys ages 11 or older. The decision was reversed and they decided Scout Ushering worked well and was well-received by fans. According to the Simon Kenton Scouts spokesman, "It was expected and part of the lesson we wanted to teach. We wanted to earn our way," he said. "Many Ushers started as Scouts."

The Boy Scouts returned to Ohio Stadium during the next game and have every game since!

5

GAME DAY

---

*"Playing football in the morning is like eating cab-
bage for breakfast."*

—author unknown

FOOTBALL SATURDAY

The sounds of Sunny 95 awake me to football Saturday in Columbus;
nothing like knowing that in a matter of hours the scarlet and gray will
battle another opponent in the Shoe. A typical game day starts at 5:30 a.m.
for a noon start. Supervisors have to be in the stadium 4 hours prior to the
start of the game so I usually have breakfast, shower and shave, then I'm
on my way.

*I suit up for the game — Ushers have to purchase their own
uniforms consisting of a white polo bearing the OSU Usher crest
($19), OSU baseball cap ($12) and for colder weather, a light
weight fall windbreaker ($32) or a heavier coat ($39.00); long
pants have to be gray or black, no jeans. The dress code for all the
Ushers was updated when Coach Tressel was hired and he suggested that there should be uniformity and pride in all aspects of
OSU football. Each Usher is issued a named 4" x 6" laminated
credential that allows free parking in any of the official game day
parking lots.*

Typical portal chief uniform: black ball cap (portal chief), polo shirt, credentials & atypical pom pom!

THERE'S A HURRICANE COMING

Ken Bemauer has been a Redcoat since 2003; he worked the Skull Session at St. John Arena for a year then moved to stadium gates 24 and 34. Ken is presently working the field tunnel for recruiting and media access. He has also been a Special Usher for events at Value City Arena since the Schottenstein Center opened in 1998. He works full-time for the Department of Defense, currently serving as a Value Engineering Analyst. He says that next to raising a family, working OSU events has been the most interesting part of his life:

In 2010, the year we played the Miami Hurricanes, I was walking by the tailgate of an acquaintance where I was shocked to see a Heisman Trophy on display! It belonged to Gino Torretta, the 1992 winner. Torretta, who played for the University of Miami, was one of the large contingents of U of M alumni on hand for the much anticipated return match-up of the 2003 National Championship game.

I met him and was able to get a picture with the trophy, even though there was much bantering back and forth about the game. The #12-ranked University of Miami Hurricanes were underdogs against the #2-ranked Ohio State — the Buckeyes won 36-24. Yea Bucks!

Athletic competition clearly defines the unique power of our attitude.

—Bart Starr

Lucky Buckeye

Ken Bemauer pictured with the Gino Torretta Heisman

One of the most satisfying things about being a Redcoat is greeting the first-time guests and kids. I try to make their visit to the Shoe a little more meaningful by giving them buckeyes from the tree in my backyard. I write the year on the buckeyes so they have a lasting memento of the game.

I have made many friendships working as a Redcoat. Former students and guests have kept in touch via e-mail and Facebook, sharing their milestones in life, wedding photos, the births of their children and updates on their daily lives. Obviously, being a Redcoat means much more than taking a ticket or showing a person to their seats. It is a passion I will enjoy as long as OSU will let me!

THE MOST AMAZING MOMENT OF MY YOUNG, BUCKEYE-OBSESSED LIFE

Josh Selway, Ohio State Intern:

I am a lifelong Ohio State fan and I have tons of great Buckeye memories. The first real memory I have is watching Ohio State play Arizona State in the 1997 Rose Bowl. For those who don't remember, it was a tight game throughout. ASU took the lead late on a Jake Plummer touchdown run.

I'm not ashamed to say that when that happened, I ran out of the room crying — I was only six, okay? My dad came after me, saying, "They still have time." He was right. Joe Germaine drove the Buckeyes down the field, capping the drive off with a touchdown pass to David Boston with 19 seconds left.

TAILGATING WITH MY COUSINS BACK IN THE DAY

Another memory that sticks out for me is the 2003 Fiesta Bowl. I watched at my house as Ohio State seemingly won the game, then lost it, only to win it again. Even as an Ohio State fan, I was concerned about our chances, so beating a Miami team like that was exhilarating.

*But all my other memories pale in comparison to the "Game of the Century" — the #1-ranked Wolverines vs. the #2-ranked Buckeyes in 2006. That day had everything, that **year** had everything (ahem, besides a championship). You could just feel the build-up, it was destiny. Sports fans saw the possibility weeks in advance. Then, the game day arrived.*

That November night, my family and I made the three-hour trip from Salem, Ohio, to Columbus. Our mission: tailgate, be loud, make burgers and cheer on the Buckeyes as they made history by beating Michigan. We woke up the next morning around 5 a.m. We made the trip from the hotel to the parking lot between the Longaberger Alumni House and Fawcett Center, our usual spot. We put up our tent, got out the charcoal, hooked up the TVs, and prepared for what would be an unforgettable day.

Initially, none of us had plans to attend the game. We figured

that tickets were just too expensive. Instead we enjoyed the food, watched the early games and chanted O-H-I-O! Now, I may have thrown out a few hints to my dad about getting to see the game in person, but I never thought he'd pull the trigger. "They're too expensive, bud," he would say in a somber tone. I understood. I was fine with watching the game on TV.

As the day progressed, I would go from watching whatever game was on TV, to throwing the football with my cousins, to just enjoying the game day atmosphere. It was probably around 1 p.m. when my dad told me he was going to see if he could find some tickets. I tried to compose myself but it was nearly impossible. I couldn't even imagine getting to see a game like that. I sat patiently at our tailgate, waiting for my dad to get back. People had been throwing out astronomical numbers for ticket prices, some asking for over $1,500. So, hearing things like that, I wasn't expecting to go to the game. But just when I thought I'd be sitting in the parking lot all day, my dad came back, two tickets in hand: "Three-hundred bucks each, C-Deck seating, though."

I smiled, "I don't care!" Couldn't believe my old man came through.

He still wanted to get one for my mom, though. So they both went out looking for one more ticket, and that's when things got interesting. They found a guy with a few tickets. My dad said he was wary of the guy as soon as they started talking, but he was offering a good price for the ticket. The stub even looked a little funny, but with the rush of game day and the hope of getting my mom in the game, my dad bought it. As soon as my parents turned around to walk away, however, they thought about something the guy had said: "You'll be sitting next to me; we'll have a beer together." That sounds great, except Ohio Stadium doesn't sell beer. It appeared my parents had been scammed.

My dad was furious, probably just as much at himself for buying the ticket as he was at the guy who sold it to him. My dad is a guy that works hard for his money, is a great saver, and is par-

My sister, Mom, and me.

ticular about how he spends it. Suffice it to say, when he realized he shelled out a few hundred bucks for a fake ticket, he wasn't very happy, and went looking for the guy. He looked and looked and looked, almost making us late for the game. Finally, he conceded defeat. Some people told my mom just to try the ticket, that maybe it wasn't counterfeit after all. She was too uncomfortable and didn't want any part of it. My friend Aaron decided to give it a shot.

My dad, Aaron and I made the walk to the Shoe, hoping that Aaron's ticket would work. Our plan was for Aaron to go in first, that way it didn't seem like we were all together if he got in trouble. Sorry, Aaron.

The ticket didn't work. Security grabbed Aaron and pulled him aside, asking him question after question. We told Aaron just to tell the guy the truth and to say that my dad was his dad (which of course isn't the truth but close enough) and he had bought the ticket, yada yada yada. They eventually let Aaron go but kept the phony ticket.

When all that was settled, my dad and I made our way to our seats. He was still upset about what had happened, but did his best to enjoy the game. And what a game it was.

Back and forth the teams went, one touchdown after another. Not until Antonio Pittman's first down run in the 4th quarter did I know the game was over. Ohio State was going to the BCS National Championship. I had just witnessed history.

What I hadn't considered was the storming of the field. If it had been with a friend instead of my dad, I would have been down there in a second. I looked at him as people made their way onto the field and all he said was, "Let's go."

We hurdled barriers and pushed down small children (exaggeration, don't worry), finally making our way onto the field. It was madness. We did our best to snap some pictures and grab some turf, and then followed the push of the crowd as thousands made their way out of the north end of the stadium. The best part? Walking past the members of the Michigan band, who sat there dejected and helpless.

Cheers of O-H-I-O followed us back to the tailgate site as Buckeye fans rejoiced. All there was left to do was celebrate. What an amazing day.

PRE-GAME ROUTINE

I park at the Cannon Drive Lot and walk to the stadium. Sometimes it is still dark at 7:30 AM and when I approach the soccer field I hear The Best Damn Band In The Land practicing their routine for the game. The band is required to assemble at the stadium for game day five hours before the start of the game in the Band room. They dress for the weather of the day then head over to the practice fields south of the stadium. There is an eerie pall over the field. The band leader is above the crowd on an elevated stand, hollering at the poor band member who makes a misstep. "Mister or Miss, if you make a bonehead move like that in the stadium every fan in the stands will see it! Get it together!"

There is a small crowd of onlookers, mostly parents, out-of-towners and other stadium workers watching the band practice, as I walk by and head down Buckeye Grove Lane. I have this lump in my throat and sense of pride as I view all the names of the All- Americans who played on this field.

THE BUCKEYE GROVE

In 1929, 11 buckeye trees were planted in the Buckeye All-American Arbor at the northeast corner of 17th Avenue and Tuttle Park Place to represent the first starters of the Ohio State football team. The Arbor, later re-named Buckeye Grove, was planted by the Scarlet Key, a non-profit group of student athletic managers dedicated to serving the OSU community and the athletic program. Every year since, a tree has been dedicated to honor each football All-American, totaling 134 trees. Ohio Staters, Inc., a student service organization committed to promoting the welfare and traditions of the Ohio State University, has also played an important role in the history of Buckeye Grove. In 1955 Staters assumed the responsibilities for planting new buckeye trees and preparing a ceremony to honor All-Americans

during Homecoming Week; during this event, coaches, players, and Buckeye fans come together to commemorate this prestigious accomplishment. While the Player/Honoree, returning to Ohio Stadium, customarily tosses the first pile of dirt on the newly planted buckeye tree.

Once I reach the stadium there is the hustle and bustle of vendors checking into the stadium and security readying their staff. I walk by armored cars and troopers with camouflage uniforms getting out of vans and police cars. Band members zoom by me in golf carts with last minute supplies for their ongoing practice. It takes a small army of workers to service a crowd of over 100,000 on game day. The stadium seating capacity is 102,329 so when they announce a crowd larger than that, it includes everyone else — vendors, Ushers, players, press, security and anyone else who enters the stadium.

When I arrive at Gate 14, the security people check my bag, I sign in twice, and scan my BuckID — security is really tight. Promptly at 8:00 a.m. all the supervisors for the Ushers, Redcoats and CSC meet in the band room, named for Joan Zieg Steinbrenner, OSU alum and wife of the late George M. Steinbrenner III. The Band Center, located on the lower level of B-Deck on the east side of the stadium, first opened its doors for the 2001 Band Season, welcoming TBDBITL to the newest and best Band Center in the country. The previous band room was under the northeast corner of the stadium, but was forced to move when the stadium was reconstructed.

This facility is truly state-of-the-art and houses all components of the Marching and Athletic Bands. When first walking into the Band Center, one is greeted by murals spanning the two story staircase featuring all instruments in the band, the Drum Major, and Ohio Stadium, as well as the official crest of the OSUMB, embossed upon the wall. One then reaches the foyer of the Band Center — a horseshoe-shaped room filled with display cases documenting the history of the band from its beginnings in 1878 with artifacts, articles and pictures. The ceiling is adorned with the words to the alma mater, Carmen Ohio.

The 2013 supervisor meetings were chaired by James Ericson, Assistant Director-Event Management, Ohio State Athletics, and usually last about 45 minutes. After the meeting we head to our prospective portals.

As we head out, the band members head in from their rehearsal. Outside the band room, a pre-game box lunch awaits the band members and they adjourn and disperse to their favorite spots throughout the stadium and devour their well-earned meals.

By the time I reach my portal, there are usually two groups of band people sitting under cover, chatting and eating. All of a sudden the stadium scoreboard erupts with loud blasting music. A few of the band members put down their hot dogs and start dancing — some jump up on the wall between the box seats and the bleachers and gyrate to the sounds! The Ushers ordinarily don't condone this type of behavior, but this is TBDBITL and they are about to perform in front of 100,000+ fans. They deserve to let their hair down and have a little fun — after all, they are college kids!

After they finish their meals the band meets back on the track on the east side of the field, they form ranks and play music as they exit the stadium via the north ramp. This is an added benefit to the Ushers who get to view this precision movement.

There is a precise time that the band members are supposed to be in place to join their ranks. One game during the 2012 season, as the band formation started to move, there were late members running full speed

Senior band member shows off his Buckeye Leaves
awarded for outstanding performance!

to join their comrades. Some were leaping over the wall, dragging their instruments behind them, others were on a 100 yard dash from the South Stands till they were able to fill in their spots and take up the correct steps to assemble into that precision marching force. Kids will be kids, but I would hate to listen to that stern lecture they received about being on time! The band then heads over to St. John Arena for the Skull Session.

SKULL SESSION

Should you make it to only one game, be sure to take in a Skull Session. The Ohio State Marching Band Skull Session starts two hours before kickoff of every home football game. Held in St. John Arena, the Skull Session is a popular concert/pep rally, attended by more than 10,000 fans. The event is free, with seating on a first-come, first-served basis. Doors open four hours prior to kickoff. Attendees should anticipate security checkpoints at the arena before entering.

During the Skull Session fans are treated to a variety of activities. Each week the band's "cheer groups" perform a song to go along with the football team's opponent of the week. The cheer groups are selected from their respective sections: Trumpet Cheers (the oldest cheer group), Trombone Cheers, Horn Cheers, Baritone Cheers, Stadium Brass (an instrument from every part of the band except percussion), Percussion Cheers and the Tuba-Fours.

At some point after the cheer group performances, the football team enters to the sounds of "Fanfare for a New Era." Immediately after their entrance a pre-selected senior football player speaks to the band and fans amassed in St. John Arena followed by the Head Coach.

Upon the football team's exit, the band commences with the traditions associated with the Skull Session. This includes a performance of "Fight the Team Across the Field," first softly and slowly, then well beyond the normal volume and tempo on the repeat of the chorus. The band is also known for performing Eternal Father, Strong to Save (otherwise known as The Navy Hymn), to formally begin every Skull Session concert. If a visiting band is in attendance they will perform their pre-game and halftime show, followed by the OSUMB's performance of pre-game and halftime.

There's something special about the Skull Session atmosphere that makes it a unique experience. There have been some concerns that Urban Meyer won't continue the tradition, but it doesn't seem totally off the table, at least not yet. The 2012, senior captain Zach Boren seems to think it could stick around: "I think he is trying to implement some of his own traditions, but at the same time, he's not going to do anything too drastic compared to what we've done before," Boren said. "There are some things that we love, like the Skull Session before games and stuff like that. We for sure wanted that to stay, but it hasn't really come up yet."

BRIEFING THE USHER TEAM

Before I arrive at the stadium I stop at Panera Bread Restaurant and get snacks for the Ushers in my portal. All four of them drive time between 1 and 2 hours on game days, so we have these snacks during our pre-game meeting, where I hand out meal tickets (Ushers get 50% off a one- time purchase at the concession stand). We also discuss information from the supervisors' meeting, such as, weather related issues, security, stadium events of the day and anything pertinent to providing a safe and enjoyable day for the fans. After we finish our snacks the Deck Superintendent, Bob Zadrozny stops by our portal to take attendance, tells a joke and moves on.

Then, approximately two hours before kickoff, all heck breaks loose when Coach Meyer leads his team into the stadium. Ear-splitting music selected especially for the team erupts from the huge scoreboard and the 600+ appreciative Ushers give the team a heartfelt welcome! "Go Bucks!" comes down from the stands! Previous coaches, upon entering the stadium walking down the north ramp, would lead the team along the east side of the field walking on the track; But Coach Meyer started his own tradition by marching straight down the field. This caused great pandemonium among the small crowd of Ushers, and other staff members, cheering

Ohio State coach Urban Meyer on the walk to
Ohio Stadium on Saturday, Oct. 6, 2012.
Players slapped hands with fans the whole way.

wildly from the stands. We knew we were witnessing a new era in Ohio State history!

Fans ask why Ushers have to be at the stadium four hours before the game and the time of certain traditional events. The following is my unofficial schedule. Please check with the Ohio State University website for Official times and events.

THE PRE-KICKOFF SCHEDULE SUMMARIZED

* 6 hours before kickoff: Day-of-game campus parking lots open.
* 5 hours before kickoff (approximately): OSU Marching Band public uniform inspection and rehearsal, field directly south of Ohio Stadium.
* 4 hours before kickoff: St. John Arena doors open for Skull Session.
* 3 hours before kickoff: Skull Session with OSU Marching Band at St. John Arena, team appearance followed by band's march to Ohio Stadium.
* 2 hours and 10 minutes before kickoff: Team led by Urban Meyer enters Ohio Stadium.
* 2 hours before kickoff: Ohio Stadium gates open.
* 23 minutes before kickoff: "Quick Cals" pregame routine with team and fan participation.
* 6:36 before kick-off: Band enters from the north ramp
* 3 minutes before kick-off: Alma Mater played by band
* National Anthem played by band and American flag raising
* Coin toss by Captains and kick off — time varies according to TV broadcast

THE BEST DAMN BAND IN THE LAND (TBDBITL)

Former band director Dr. Jon Woods claims, "Supposedly at a pep rally one year, Woody Hayes stood up after the band played a song and said, 'That's the best damn band in the land!' That's all it took. When Woody says something, it's law!"

UNCHANGED TRADITION

Unchanged since its inception in 1928, the ramp entrance precedes every home pre-game in Ohio Stadium. After Skull Session, the band march-es across Woody Hayes Drive toward the main stadium entrance. When the band reaches the rotunda, the percussion cadences increase speed and the band bursts through the gates, thundering down the ramp, and break-ing off into their assigned rows to gather at their respective positions on or around the ramp.

When the drum cadences cease, a lone sousaphone player initiates the singing of "I Wanna Go Back," quickly joined by the crowd of fans gathered under the stadium. With the call of "Two minutes!" left on the stadium clock before pre-game, the percussion leader at the bottom of the ramp sets the tempo of 180 beats per minute and yells "Drums on the side," to his section. Together they march onto the field to nothing but a chant of "O-H-I-O."

Once the percussion section is in place the announcer exclaims, "La-dies and gentlemen, The Pride of the Buckeyes, The Ohio State University Marching Band!" The percussion breaks into full cadence and the band files down the ramp, into the block position, with impeccable military pre-cision. Once the band is in place, the drum major struts down the ramp through the block to the front of the band to perform a back bend. As the plume touches the turf, cheers explode from the stands and the band storms down the field to "Buckeye Battle Cry." In front of the South Stands, the drum major tosses the staff over the goal post — it's bad luck if the drum major drops the staff in the end zone! — before the band performs an about-face maneuver to await the raising of the flag in the north end zone.

Your Ohio Stadium Moment: a Fan's Perspective

Timothy B, Bexley, Ohio:

I grew up in west-central Ohio listening to the "Pride of the Buckeyes" and to the football games on the radio with my mother, who was a huge fan of Ohio State football and the marching band.

In the 1950s whenever she and my father were able to get last-minute tickets from friends they would drive to Columbus and always stay after the game to see the band's postgame show. When she got home, she would excitedly report back to me how great the band performance was; she inspired me.

So several years later in the fall of 1965, my first year in the marching band, I was about to make my first pre-game ramp entrance. I remember the thrill that surged through my body when they yelled, "The drummers are out!" That meant the horns — meaning me! — were next. I nearly broke into tears, there I was about to make my first "ramp entrance" onto the field, that emerald patch of earth nearest to heaven known as the Shoe, or the house that Woody built and that Coach Tressel finished.

As I worked my way toward the light at the end of the tunnel and broke onto the red track that surrounded the field, the roar of the crowd was so deafening it literally sucked the air out of my chest. For a second I was dazed by the moment, then I was next to make the flourish turn toward the sideline and finish the block band formation. By the time I completed playing the introduction to "Fight the Team" I was already out of breath, but somehow I floated down the field to play the "Star Spangled Banner."

It was such an exciting moment that as a member of TBDBITL, I return each year to "do it one more time" on Alumni Band Day. But that first time gave me such a rush that I still feel it today every time I drive past the Shoe. It's great to be an alumnus of The Ohio State University and a life-long Buckeye!

KEEPING IT IN THE FAMILY

Contributor **Doug Windle's** family is well-represented at The Ohio State University. His father, Dick Windle was a walk-on for the football team in 1949 and has been an Usher (B-18) for 56 years. His uncle Bob

Windle was in the marching band from 1957-1960 and an "i- dotter" for Script Ohio in 1960. Doug was in the marching band from 1976-1980 and was an "i-dotter" for Script Ohio in the 1980 Rose Bowl. Doug has served as an Usher with his dad at portal B-18 since 1988 — that's a total of 81 years as Ushers for both father and son!

PLAY OR GO HOME!

One of my most vivid memories is 1978. I was a third year member of the marching band sousaphone section. It was a home game that was to be Woody Hayes' last OSU vs. Michigan game. In the first quarter with OSU leading 3-0 on a Bob Atha field goal, the Michigan band director had been persistently getting the jump on OSU director, Dr. Paul Droste at every break with the Michigan band playing "Hail to the Victors" until play resumed. Dr. Droste was simply observing band etiquette of not "playing over" the visiting band.

My location was in a folding chair on the stadium running track on the OSU sideline near the five yard line. During a game break I witnessed what I describe as The Parting of the Scarlet Sea. With OSU players standing on the sideline, Woody stormed through the players toward the OSU band. Just a few feet from me and my fellow sousaphone players he stopped and yelled at us that all he's hearing is that Michigan band every time there's a break in the game. "NOW DAMMIT, PLAY OR GO HOME!"

Just as quickly as Woody appeared, he disappeared back into the scarlet sea of players and the sideline. Dr. Droste saw Woody but couldn't hear what he said over the stadium noise so he came to us and asked what Woody had said. When we told him we just got chewed out by Woody for not playing enough, Dr. Droste struck "Across the Field" every chance he got whether the Michigan band was playing or not. We wore out the song and our chops the rest of the game.

What I found most interesting about this incident was that in the heat of battle — in The Game — with OSU leading, Woody was cognizant of the fact that he was hearing the fight song of that team up north, which he despised, way too often and decided to correct the problem himself. The 10-year war he fought was on all levels.

OSU lost that day 14-3 and went 7-4-1 for the season.

THE INCOMPARABLE SCRIPT OHIO

Script Ohio is the signature formation of The Ohio State University Marching Band. It is the most identifiable trademark associated with OSU football and the marching band. Script Ohio was first performed by the band on October 10, 1936 at the Ohio State vs. Pittsburgh football game.

The formation was devised by band director Eugene J. Weigel, who based the looped design on the marquee of the Loew's Ohio Theatre in downtown Columbus. The script is an integrated series of evolutions and formations. The band begins from a triple Block O formation, then slowly unwinds to form the famous letters while playing Robert Planquette's Le Régiment de Sambre et Meuse. The drum major leads the outside O into a peel-off movement around the curves of the script, every musician in continuous motion. Slowly the three blocks unfold into a long singular line which loops around, spelling out Ohio in script.

Each time the drill is performed, a different fourth- or fifth-year sousaphone player is chosen to "dot in the 'i'." Because the Script Ohio formation was one of many new formations included by director Weigel, originally no special emphasis was placed on the dotting.

An E-flat cornet player, John Brungart, was the first "i-dotter." In the fall of 1937, Weigel turned to Glen Johnson, a sousaphone player, and shouted, "Hey, you! Switch places with the trumpet player in the dot." A year later, when a drum major arrived at the top of the "i" several measures too early, Johnson turned and bowed to the crowd to use up the rest of the music. The crowd roared, and the bow has been part of the show

Jack Nicklaus dotting "i" in Script Ohio at 2006 Minnesota game

since then. Glen thus became the first sousaphone player to dot the "i" on October 23, 1937. Since then, a sousaphone player has dotted the "i" over 800 times.

Today, toward the end of the formation, the drum major and the "i"-dotter high-five each other. With 16 measures remaining in the song, they strut to the top of the "i." When they arrive, the drum major points to the spot and the "i"-dotter turns and bows deeply to both sides of the stadium.

Only members who have served in KL-Row for at least four years are granted the honor of dotting the i. Honorary "i-dotters" are reserved exclusively for those who have given selflessly toward the betterment of the band, university, or nation. In the 75 years of Script Ohio, the only honorary i-dotters have been: Bob Hope, Woody Hayes, Buster Douglas, Dr. E. Gordon Gee, Novice and Marjorie Fawcett, Jack Nicklaus, Jack and Carol Evans, Paul and Anne Droste, John and Annie Glenn, Les Wexner, and most recently, retired marching band Director Dr. Jon R. Woods.

ROW TRADITIONS

Traditions include the playing of the solos for *I Wanna Go Back to Ohio State* and the world-famous *Round on the Ends and High in the Middle*. Sousaphone players also are responsible for signaling to the rest of the band for the beginning of the chorus of *Buckeye Battle Cry* in their traditional ramp entrance.

ROW MASCOT

The mascot of KL-Row is the Chiquita Banana, a tradition begun by members of K-Row in the late 1960s. Often fans can see a 4th- or 5th-year member of KL-Row brandishing their beloved plush Chiquita banana in the end zone after a scoring drive for the Buckeyes. The plush is emblazoned with the immortal truth of "BEAT BLUE" and is to be handled with the utmost care.

HE'S NOT HEAVY — HE'S MY BROTHER

Judy Malone, a Redcoat at North Gate since 2005, moved to Columbus in 1950 from Galion, Ohio where her father was a physician who passed away in 1948. After her brother graduated from high school, they moved to W. Woodruff Avenue where they ran a rooming house for 15 students; they also had a rooming house on Michigan Avenue for medical students. She graduated from North High School in 1957 and started to attend OSU. Her mother got cancer and she had to take over the management of the rooming houses at age 17. They moved to Grandview in 1960 and have lived there for over 50 years. She is now a retired medical billing clerk and enjoys working as a Redcoat at the stadium and Schottenstein Center:

> *After their first Rose Bowl appearance in 1920, OSU would not make another bowl appearance until 1949. My brother was in the OSU marching band for that game. I also had a 16-year-old younger brother who announced that he was going to the Rose Bowl. He proclaimed, "If my brother is going to the Rose Bowl, then I am going too!"*
>
> *We did not have the money to send him to California, but the people of Galion got together and managed to get him rides from different people. When he got there, he had no place to stay and no ticket. The OSU band let him stay with them. He was able to see the Rose Parade and somehow got into see the game. He hitch-hiked back to Columbus with 35 cents in his pocket. He stayed at my brother's rooming house and we came to get him the next day. The Buckeyes, coached by Wes Fesler, beat the California Golden Bears 17-14.*

FIRING UP THE FANS IN THE STANDS

A favorite of the fans are the cheerleaders and band members who move throughout the stadium and play the Fight Song and other favorites inside the portals within a few feet of the fans. This really fires up the fans and pumps their adrenalin. You can actually feel the vibrations of the drums — the fans go nuts cheering with the cheerleaders.

Estimated cost of putting on a half-time show: $4,000-$5,000

Ohio Stadium joins in singing Carmen Ohio following a shutout victory over Purdue, 10-23-10

PLAY IT AGAIN, SAM

Alan A., Westport, Connecticut:

When TBDBITL played my original composition, Serenade to a Sand Dune, at halftime in the 1955 OSU game against Illinois, Woody Hayes was outraged. His team couldn't run out on the field for the second half because the fans were screaming, "play it again" over and over.

Number of TBDBITL graduates: 6,504

TBDBITL ALUMNI CLUB

Organizations are strong and remain strong for one reason: their members, past and present. Pride, tradition and excellence come from hard work, dedication and a strong sense of purpose. This dedication is not limited to current members but also to the men and women who came before — the alumni of the marching band.

The TBDBITL Alumni Club is the largest single member club within The Ohio State University Alumni Association and is a vital part of the band family. The TBDBITL Club provides tremendous support for the band in a variety of ways, volunteering time, expertise, professional skills and guidance to the staff and membership of the band as well as providing financial support to the band and its membership through scholarship funds and through the Script Ohio Club which provides financial support to maintain and purchase instruments.

Many only see the OSU Alumni Band once a year at the alumni game day reunion. Here, fans are delighted as current and alumni members march side by side in four simultaneous Script Ohio's — the Quad Script Ohio.

What fans may not realize is that the Alumni Band also has many additional performances. They have traveled the world over, delighting fans from as far away as Japan, Hawaii and Great Britain. They also perform yearly at the Buckeye Cruise for Cancer benefiting the Stefanie Spielman Fund for Breast Cancer Research at the Ohio State James Cancer Hospital and Solove Research Center. The Alumni Band is especially active in and around central Ohio with regular performances at venues including the Columbus Park of Roses Gazebo, and patriotic holiday parades in Upper Arlington and Worthington, to name just a few.

SECURITY

NO TICKET, NO ENTER

"I don't have a ticket — I'm the new football coach!"

A Redcoat, failing to recognize Brown, had halted the OSU mentor as he attempted to enter the stadium. Ultimately Brown was reduced to having to throw pebbles at the Buckeye locker room windows to get the attention of someone who would go talk to the supervisor and finally let the frustrated coach into the facility.

WHO ARE THOSE GUYS?

One of the questions I get from a lot of fans is, "What the heck is a CSC guy?" — Those guys with the yellow shirts stationed throughout the stadium. None of my fellow Ushers had a clue what CSC stood for. Google supplied the following information:

Contemporary Services Corporation (CSC) pioneered the use of peer group security and crowd management in 1967 and has since emerged as the industry leader. With more than 50 branch offices serving over 200 cities within the United States and Canada, CSC's presence in the event security industry remains unmatched. Our supervisors and event managers have received certifications through FEMA's Incident Command Systems and IAVM's Trained Crowd Manager in order to provide a safer and more inviting experience for our clients' guests.

Now you know who those guys are with the yellow CSC shirts!

Woody on Bo Schembechler: We respected one another so damn much. Now that doesn't mean I didn't get so mad at him that I wanted to kick him in the, uh, groin.

—**Woody Hayes**

LOOK OUT BELOW!

Dennen Leach has been a Red Coat for 36 years (he's hoping to make 40 years) since the fall of 1977. He spent 23 years on top of C-Deck and then moved to the Huntington Club after the remodeling of the stadium. He has been a life-long Columbus resident, and attended OSU in music education in 1949. He worked at Battelle Memorial Institute for 41 years .

My first day on the job back in 1977, I was assigned to C-deck just south of the press box when I noticed a young kid (maybe 12 or 13) holding something over the edge of the wall. On further investigation I found he was holding a thick beer mug over the side, ready to let it fall. I took it away from him and gave it to the Redcoat working in the press box and told him he needed this mug inside worse than I did on C-Deck. If he had dropped this mug it could have hit someone on the ground and possibly killed them or it could have hit the ground and blinded several with broken glass.

Dedicated, Disappointed Penn State Fans

Hugh Fraser has been a Redcoat since 2005. He grew up in Niagara Falls, N.Y., went to college at Alma College in Michigan. He later lived in Las Vegas, Los Angeles, northern New Jersey and Pittsburgh. He has lived in Columbus since 1994, and became a Buckeye fan right away. He currently works at JP Morgan/Chase. In 2008 he was on the Extra Board for Redcoats, then worked doors at the Huntington Entrance; for several years he has worked in the Press Pass booth, checking in stadium concession workers, Block O members, parking lot attendants etc.:

On October 25, 2008 I was working at gate 9 on the northwest corner of the stadium, scanning tickets about an hour and a half before kickoff, when a man and woman, obviously avid Penn State fans dressed in Penn State garb, entered. Their tickets would not scan. As we had been advised that counterfeit ticket scalpers would be out in force, I asked them how they obtained their tickets. The gentleman indicated that they had driven from Happy Valley without tickets and that he had just paid $200 each for the tickets about 50 feet from the gate.

I took them to the ticket confirmation table where it was determined that the tickets were counterfeit, and they were told they had to leave the stadium. I warned them there were likely to be other counterfeit scalpers working the area and told them it was unwise to buy tickets in the crowd.

They returned about a half hour later with another set of tickets which, just like the ones they had earlier, would not scan. They too were confirmed to be counterfeit. As he left the stadium, he was not angry, only disappointed, saying that after spending $800 trying to see his team, he'd have to be satisfied listening to the game on his car radio on the drive back to Pennsylvania. In front of an Ohio Stadium-record crowd of 105,711, the #10-ranked Nittany Lions got their first win at #3-ranked Ohio State since 1978 by defeating the Buckeyes 13-6 in a game where both offenses *were held below their season averages.*

SCAN TICKET UNIQUE TO OHIO STATE IN BIG TEN

One of the biggest changes at the gates for the Redcoats occurred in 2003 when Ohio State went to the scanning system to validate game tickets.

Football is, after all, a wonderful way to get rid of your aggressions without going to jail for it.

—Heywood Hale Brown

THINK BEFORE YOU DRINK

Gary Snyder, portal B-8 has been an Usher since 2001. He lives in Delaware, Ohio. He retired from PPG in 2005:

The most anticipated non-conference game played in Ohio Stadium in at least a decade — and maybe ever — started with flash bulbs popping and the Horseshoe-record crowd of 105,565 in a frenzy. On Saturday, September 10, 2005, the first meeting between two of college football's most storied programs, The Ohio State Buckeyes and the University of Texas Longhorns at the Shoe was a night game.

As Ushers we knew we had our work cut out for us because this was a night game and the fans had all day to get liquored up. True to form, we were alerted by some of our regulars in our section that there was an intoxicated guy, spitting, using foul language and generally being a pest to other fans. (The Usher's Manual specifies that we give a warning to any unruly fans, but cannot physically touch anyone.)

Well this guy started to harass a couple of young co-eds and was completely obnoxious to other people in the section. I went to our portal chief to explain how this fan was bothering the young ladies. He immediately went to talk with the guy and explained that he needed to calm down and quit being a jerk. Well, most drunk jerks don't have a clue how obnoxious they are, so he continued slurring his words, shouting vulgar cheers about the Longhorns and making derogatory remarks to the young girls.

Enough was enough! We discussed the situation with the highway patrol officer, Sergeant Davis, who was assigned to our section. He went to the drunk man directly through the crowd without bothering to walk to the aisle, and brought him down by a handful of the inside of his upper arm — the guy's feet never touched the ground as he was whisked down about seven rows of seats! As he passed me, the guy was pleading with Sergeant Davis not to throw him out because he had paid $400 for his ticket. Sergeant Davis replied, "Should have thought about that when you took your first drink!"

Unfortunately for the rest of the Ohio State fans who got to see the whole game, Vince Young did what star quarterbacks do, passing his team to a victory. Young threw a 24-yard go-ahead touchdown to Limas Sweed with 2:37 left and #2-ranked Texas defeated #4-ranked Ohio State 25-22.

Cause there's only one reason for doing anything that you set out to do. If you don't want to be the best, then there's no reason going out and trying to accomplish anything.

—Joe Montana

WHAT WERE THEY THINKING?

*Another beautiful day as fans poured into the stands, I direct-
ed a young couple to their seats that were situated next to the column that I lean against while watching the game. Once the game
started I assumed my position standing against the column. The
attractive young lady, in her late teens or early 20s, started a conversation with me and I could tell she had started her pre-game
partying very early. She stated that she was from out of town, and
was very excited that this was her first time to see the Buckeyes!
While her boyfriend went for snacks, she questioned me:*

"How long had I been an Usher?" (16 years.)

*"Did I get to watch the games?" (My primary objective was
to insure the fans enjoyed their visit, so after the kickoff when all
the fans had settled in their seats, I could catch most of the plays.)*

*"Did I get paid to be an Usher?" (Ushers are volunteers,
portal chiefs, supervisors and above are paid a per game stipend,
due to the extended hours and additional duties they perform.)*

*Her boyfriend returned with the snacks and they watched the
band enter the arena. I attended my duties, returned to my post
and watched the end of the first quarter. Then I noticed the couple
did not return to their seats. Not thinking anything about it, a lot
of young people go out to check messages, or text on their cell
phones, meet other friends or catch a smoke (by the way- smoking
is forbidden in the stadium — this pisses off a lot of folks).*

*When they did not return to their seats by the end of the half
I did think it was a little strange to pay all that money and not
see the game. It was not until the next game that I found out what
happened to this young couple. A Columbus police sergeant was
speaking to the officer that was assigned to our portal and mentioned they had to escort a young couple out of the stadium because they were caught in a men's room stall in a compromising
position.*

Oh well, I can understand that young people have a rush of hormones and get caught up in a moment of passion, but in the men's room of Ohio Stadium? Especially at the price they had to pay for their seats. Nothing surprises me anymore!

JERRY MARLOWE VS. OHIO STADIUM

My good buddies meet for "Boys Nite Out" every couple of months at the Old Bag of Nails in Worthington to have a few beers while we catch up on all the pertinent information. Inevitably Ohio State football comes up and Jim Schwab starts telling me about this guy from Dover, whose wife used to work with Jerry Marlowe, whose claim to fame was gate crashing the OSU Michigan games:

The fall face-off between Ohio State University and the University of Michigan has been a rivalry of legendary battles steeped in decades of tradition. Scarlet-and-gray vs. maize-and-blue. Buckeye vs. Wolverine. Woody vs. Bo. And Jerry Marlowe vs. the Ohio Stadium.

Marlowe, of Dover, a 1961 graduate of Ohio State's College of Pharmacy, has successfully entered Ohio Stadium for the Buckeyes-Wolverines game nearly 20 times without a ticket by donning an array of disguises.

Jerry has crashed the Ohio State-Michigan game as a parachutist, a concessionaire , a cheerleader, a Boy Scout, a marching band leader and Superman (for a halftime show).

Jerry said, "It all started, almost accidentally in 1954, when I was a freshman at OSU dressed in a top hat and tails, I bluffed my way past an attendant into the Michigan game (even though I had a ticket) using a bit of a British accented bluster — Tickets, tickets? Who needs tickets? Rubbish! Much to my surprise I walked right into the game."

This inspired an almost-perfect gate-crashing OSU/Michigan

*games record from 1970 to 1998. It wasn't about getting in free —
a hefty contribution to his alma mater after each stunt more than
covers the cost of a ticket. "It's the challenge of pulling a prank
that had perhaps become as traditional to Buckeye football as the
band's 'Script Ohio' formation."*

*Come 2002, however, publicity about his exploits had made
the task much tougher, and Marlowe wondered if his luck and the
university's patience were wearing thin.*

*So to bring his reign to a close in a dramatic fashion, Mar-
lowe intentionally set out to get busted at the gate. He wore an
appropriate costume — an old-fashioned, black-and-white-pris-
on-striped uniform and chains. But when he arrived too late for
a newspaper photographer to record his "capture" for posterity,
Marlowe went ahead and finagled his way into the stadium. (He
didn't stay, having already made plans to watch the game on TV
with relatives.)*

*Marlowe had to miss the 2004 game due to work, yet he's ap-
parently now back in the old spirit that got him into the stadium
as an ersatz pizza deliveryman, team doctor and a phony "NBC
Television News Referee." The "fake refs," Marlowe explained at
the gate, are officials that TV uses when they can't get a shot of a
real one on the field.*

*His favorite gambit was in 1988. He slipped into the stadium
as a hot dog vendor and, to honor a longtime college chum, Harry
Thoman, who was dying of cancer, Marlowe arranged to have the
Block O cheering section spell out "Hang on Harry" as the band
played "Hang on Sloopy."*

*Marlowe said his success lies in a talent for acting plus an
ability to tap resources for costumes, props and assisted passage
through the gate.*

*He also follows a few self-imposed rules of his game within
the game. He does not impersonate military or police personnel,
and avoids breaking any laws other than the obvious one. And
though he has utilized fake identification, he never tried to gain*

entry with a bogus ticket.

Otherwise, go for the obvious, he said. The more outlandish the better.

At the base of it was the urge, if you wanted to play football, to knock someone down, that was what the sport was all about, the will to win closely linked with contact.

—George Plimpton

BUYER BEWARE

George Montag, Usher since 1979, all in portal B-12, has witnessed a lot of changes in Security over those years:

I am not sure which year or what game this incident occurred, but as I was busily seating people in my section and the game was about to start I was alerted to a situation in row 19. Every seat in the row was occupied and 4 people were waiting outside the row to be seated. Uh oh! I thought to myself, mission control we have a problem.

I started checking each ticket until I got to seats 14-17. Those happened to be the same seat numbers that were on the tickets of the waiting foursome. It became obvious that we had 4 duplicate tickets, now my portal chief's job was to sort this out to determine whose tickets were genuine.

He escorted all eight people to the ticket services window at Section 7. After viewing all eight tickets the security officer determined that four of the tickets were counterfeit, meaning the ticketholders of the fake tickets were out of luck and either had to purchase new tickets or be escorted from the stadium. Needless to say those four individuals were very upset.

They were quizzed on where they purchased the bogus tickets. They responded "from a ticket scalper" outside the stadium for $60 a ticket — $5.00 above the standard ticket price.

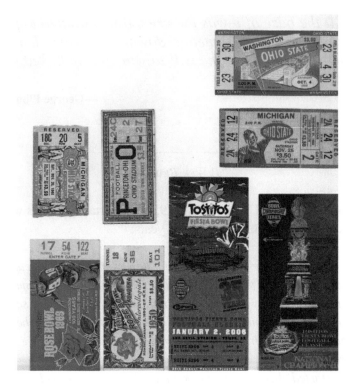

Game Tickets throughout the years

A Fan's Viewpoint

There is a Security/Authentic foil strip on all the recent tickets I have bought over the past few years. I never go to OSU games with tickets. I never have had a problem buying them from scalpers, and have never been ripped off in over 15 years of doing so. Just check for that foil strip and you will be good.

—Jason,
Grove City

CRITTERS

It's not the size of the dog in the fight, but the size of the fight in the dog.

—Archie Griffin

ROCKY

The portal chief from B-6, Gary Green, came running over to me to use my radio to call the operations office for removal of a large animal. Before I called I wanted to see what all the fuss was about, so I walked over to check out this ferocious critter.

It turned out to be a plump raccoon that had wedged its body between the two vent pipes running underneath the seats. The poor thing was scared to death after a couple of the maintenance people were prodding it with a 10 foot pole, trying to push it into a cardboard box. Rocky Raccoon did not want to have anything to do with these guys and backed further into the hole. I suggested that they leave the little guy alone and after the game, when all the people were long gone- said raccoon would come down, scavenge what he could to eat and return to his lair, or wherever raccoons call home.

GREAT RUN!

Sean F., Usher:

I have been to at least twice as many games as my 48 years, the last 15 years as an Usher. Before the track was removed my job was security near the flagpole and ramp. Between Block O, the visiting fans and the pageantry one day in 1994 a small squirrel was cheered down the field toward us. The fans' cheers confused the huddling players waiting for the third quarter to end.

I went over to the end zone and sat down to try to catch the terrified rodent. My colleagues shook their heads in disbelief. With the help of some Cheetos I lured him close enough to grab. Fan reaction was split. Half cheered my unlikely grab, the other moaned as their entertainment was ejected, gently, from the stadium.

ABOVE AND BEYOND THE CALL OF DUTY

By far, the most complaints we get concern the flying rats — or pigeons as most people call them. These guys live in the stadium, so a lot of the seats and bleachers are covered with bird poop. Fans who pay $70+ per game do not want to sit in pigeon poop, and the Ushers have to be vocal with the cleaning crews to do their job.

The first game of the year is usually the worst, even though cleaning crews are supposed to hose all seats in the stadium. My Ushers do a good job, above and beyond the call of duty, getting paper towels from the restroom and cleaning most of the seats.

Many fans don't realize the extra things that the hardworking Ushers do to make the game a pleasant experience.

WOOF

Flashback to my junior year, 1969: I can remember an old basset hound that belonged to some fraternity would show up at the games, complete with a ticket attached to his dog collar, and walk down the aisle like he owned the place. I would see the same dog at the local watering holes around campus. He was a celebrity of sorts that would look at you with those big sad eyes and beg for food — or beer. He could lap up a full bowl of beer in record time.

SOUNDED LIKE A GOOD IDEA

The Usher assigned to the field near the South Stands related this incident that occurred during the third game of the 1982 season:

Stanford was playing the Buckeyes. The game was nationally televised by ABC and John Elway was Stanford's quarterback. All of a sudden seven characters walked out of the stands dressed in gorilla costumes, which struck me as pretty funny. One of the gorillas whispered to me, "Sir, do you mind if we go down on the track to make a pyramid, get on national TV and then leave?"

Despite my better judgment, I said, "Fine, but don't cause any trouble." Well, the knuckleheads made their pyramid and got their TV time, but as they made their dismount, the crowd starting roaring behind them. The Bucks were on the 2 yard line and were getting ready to score, so the seven gorillas decided to stick around and watch the action. Bad move.

Another Usher asked them to move, and instead of leaving like they were asked, they turned to watch the score. The Usher summoned a police officer who said to one of the gorillas, "You were asked to leave."

Another of the young gorillas responded, "We are leaving."

By then the miffed officer said, "You're leaving with us." The officer marched the band of gorillas out underneath the Block O section, which immediately started booing as the officer escorted them from the field.

I learned a good lesson — always rely on your better judgment. The next game I learned that all seven of the students dressed in the gorilla costumes were bused downtown and spent a few hours in the city jail. Unfortunately, they were not on hand to see John Elway lead a comeback victory over the #11-ranked Buckeyes.

NASTY

I've noted that security around Ohio stadium is tight, and various means of patrolling the stadium are employed, including mounted police officers. Before the start of the Florida A & M game in 2013, a near monsoon was raging outside the stadium, so the mounted officers brought their horses inside the concourse to shield them from the blinding rainstorm.

The Redcoats at portal six were happy to unlock the gates to allow the large animals to stroll inside and out of the rain. I had the opportunity to meet "Nasty," an auburn beauty that allowed me stroke her neck.

7

BUCKEYE COACHES

A football coach is a person who is willing to lay down your life for the good of his team.

—author unknown

OHIO STATE HEAD COACHES

Over many months of talking with hundreds of Ushers and Redcoats, in an unscientific survey, these are the top five most popular Ohio State Coaches:

#1 - Woody Hayes
#2 - Jim Tressel
#3 - John Cooper
#4 - Earle Bruce
#5 - Urban Meyer

I know I will take some flack about this lineup and who is really #1. You have to understand the average Usher/Redcoat tenure is 17 years! In the following pages I have highlighted some of the Usher's favorite stories about these coaches and the time-honored traditions surrounding OSU football. Also, in my interviews and contacts with the coaches you will see what a deep respect they have for the Usher program and the traditions at Ohio State.

THE RUMOR MILL

Ushers come from all areas of Ohio and all walks of life, but the one thing that ties all of us together is the love and passion for Ohio State football. **Vince Miller**, an Usher for many years on D-Deck, is no exception. He said, "I love Ohio State football, as well as following the local football team Huber Heights Wayne — yes, the school that graduated Braxton Miller — and watching the team that my daughter plays on (Columbus Comets)." He officially retired from the Air Force Research Laboratory in 2010 and has done some teaching and tutoring since then:

> *In 2011 one of the season ticket holders in D-11 came up to chat, as he did most home games. He said, "Urban Meyer is going to be the next Ohio State coach." I asked how he knew this since so many rumors had been floating around. He said with a big grin, "My sister-in-law sold him a house in the Columbus area just recently." We both had a good laugh. But guess what? It came true.*

BACK HOME TO OHIO

Sometime during the morning of November 28, 2011, Ohio native Urban Meyer returned home. It was the moment the 47-year-old Meyer, born in Toledo, raised in Ashtabula with degrees from the University of Cincinnati and The Ohio State University, signed a six-year agreement to become the 24th head coach in the storied history of Ohio State football.

"I am honored and humbled by the opportunity to return to Ohio State," said Meyer. "This University and the state of Ohio have enormous meaning to me. My duty is to ensure that Ohio State's football program reflects and enhances the academic mission of the institution. I am part of it, I believe in it, and I will live it."

It was during his time as a Buckeye — Ohio State won a Big Ten title

in 1986 and 1987 was Bruce's final season as coach — that he forged a relationship with Bruce that has only been strengthened through the tests of time and change.

"My relationship with him [Earle] is extremely close, second only to my father," Meyer said during the news conference to announce his hiring at Ohio State...17 days after his father, Bud, passed away.

"Every step of my career, every part of my family life, Coach Bruce has always been there. So close that he was gracious enough to speak at my father's funeral."

Coach Meyer comments about the Usher program, "Thank you for your many years of service. I am always in awe on game day. We truly have the best run stadium in the country and it is only possible by the many hours of time, dedication and hard work. Go Bucks!"

Urban Frank Meyer, 49, hired in November 2011.

Three rules for coaching:
1. Surround yourself with people who can't live without football.
2. Recognize winners. They come in all forms.
3. Have a plan for everything.

—Bear Bryant

Coach Meyer commented after a game in September 2012, "I expect a stadium to be an inferno, I expect players to be diving over each other to hit quarterbacks, I expect the offense to score a multitude of points and celebrating in the end zone."

Meyer expects the crowd of 106,000 to be more involved. At the same time, he recognizes his team needs to be more intense in order to light a fire under the fans!

"It's a journey, it's a marathon to get it where we want it," he said of his program. I think that stadium ought to be absolutely electric. "But we need to play better. You want to get a stadium going? Go hit a quarterback. You want to really get the stadium (going)? Put a hand on a punt. That's when people come out of their seats."

OSU PLAYERS PRACTICE IN SWEATS-
OUTSIDE THE BLACKWELL-MORNING OF THE 2013 INDIANA GAME

Every year the Ushers in Portal B-8 have our traditional tailgate before we head over to the stadium. Before the Indiana game in 2013 we set up on the sixth floor of the Lane Ave parking garage and we were treated to an impromptu practice by the bucks.

QUICK CALS

Wisconsin has "Jump Around", and now Ohio State has "Quick Cals." Urban Meyer and OSU strength coach Mickey Marotti created the new Ohio Stadium pregame activity which was debuted prior to the season opener September 1, 2012, against Miami (Ohio). Here's how it works: 23 minutes before every home kickoff, in the south end zone, the players do Quick Cals — think pre-game exercises — and ask for student participation.

Quick Cals give the OSU students sitting in the south end zone a chance to feel like a football player, at least for a minute. "We started a new tradition, to show the relationship between our student body, the best student body in America, and our football team," Meyer says.

Coach Jim Tressel Leads Team onto the Field Following the Traditional Skull Session.

COACH JIM TRESSEL

In the summer of 2007 I was walking down the hallway at Westerville North High School when one of the staff members ran up to me yelling, "Coach! Coach! May I have your autograph?" I stopped, turned around and looked at the excited guy; then we both realized he had mistaken me for Coach Jim Tressel. (A lot of my friends and relatives say I bear a passing resemblance to the Ohio State Coach.)

Once he realized his mistake, being a little embarrassed and disappointed, he apologized, saying that Coach Tressel had visited the school before on recruiting visits and he missed the opportunity to meet him. I offered him my autograph, he laughed and walked away!

When I related this story to Coach Tressel, he responded:

> *Trevor, So good to hear from you!!*
> *Sorry that folks think there is a resemblance…*
> *I am sure you are much younger than me.*

DEDICATED GROUP

Coach Tressel, an Ohio guy who understands the traditions at Ohio State, when asked to give his comments on the Usher/ Redcoat program responded:

In order for us to have THE most memorable and enjoyable experience at a college football venue, we are blessed, and we have the Ohio State Redcoats/Ushers. To be the best we must embody class, humility, customer service, and loyalty. Our Redcoats/ Ushers reflect all of that and then some. They are a dedicated group that love Ohio State Football, revere and respect the Ohio Stadium, and take terrific care of the fans who file in by the thousands to cheer on their Buckeyes. They even take great care of the opposing fans and band. Our loyal Redcoats/Ushers arrive hours before the game (rain, shine, or snow), are extremely organized, are the first to welcome the TEAM/Coaches as they arrive, and then spend the next five hours making sure that everyone that enters the stadium is safe and treated special. The Ohio State Football phenomenon would not be the same without this hard-working, unselfish, extraordinary group of people. It is not surprising that they are so willing to serve each and every fan, as many have also had the ultimate joy of serving our country. Every player and coach that has ever had the privilege of wearing the scarlet and gray owes a deep debt of gratitude to our OSU Redcoats and Ushers. GO BUCKS, JT

James Patrick "Jim" Tressel, born December 5, 1952, was hired by the Buckeyes before the 2001 season to replace John Cooper.

I sat in my reserved season ticket seat at the OSU basketball game against the hated Michigan Wolverines when Jim Tressel was introduced to the crowd and immediately served notice that he understood the importance of the Michigan rivalry. Coach Tressel commented, "You'll be proud of our young people in the classroom, in the community, and most espe-

Statue donated by Ellen & Jim Tressel,
located South of ROTC Building

cially in 310 days on the football field in Ann Arbor, Michigan," eliciting a roar from the delirious crowd!

During his tenure as Ohio State's 22nd head football coach, Tressel's teams played in three BCS National Championship Games. His 2002 squad won a national title and achieved the first 14-0 season record in major college football since Penn went 15-0 in 1897. Tressel finished his career at Ohio State with an official overall record of 94-22 (.810), including six Big Ten Conference championships, a 5-4 bowl record, a 4-3 mark in BCS bowl games, and an 8-1 record against the arch-rival Michigan Wolverines.

Tressel's eight wins against Michigan place him second in school history to Woody Hayes, who had 16. He is the only Ohio State head coach to win seven consecutive games against the Wolverines. Tressel resigned as the Ohio State football coach in May 2011 amid an NCAA investigation of rules violations during the 2010 season, which in turn led to Ohio State self-vacating the victories from its 2010 season (including the 2011 Sugar Bowl). From September 2011 until February 2012, Tressel was a consultant for the Indianapolis Colts of the NFL. He is currently serving as the President of Youngstown State University.

TRESSEL HAS SCARLET FEVER

The October 25, 2008 game was one of the biggest games of the year with #3-ranked Penn State visiting the #10-ranked Buckeyes. According to the Cleveland Plain Dealer, Ohio State coach Jim Tressel was so enthused about Saturday's game with Penn State; he dressed like an OSU Redcoat.

"We wanted to make sure we made it loud and clear that we need to be wearing red on Saturday," Tressel said. "We need to make that place a sea of red."

Tressel was so prepared he even brought along a red poncho, warning fans that with a 40 percent chance of rain for Saturday, they couldn't afford to wear a red sweatshirt then cover it up with a poncho of another color.

Unfortunately, even with over 105,000 fans creating the "Sea of Red," the Nittany Lions beat the Buckeyes 13-6.

A good football coach needs a patient wife, a loyal dog and a great quarterback – but not necessarily in that order.

—Bud Grant

JOHN COOPER

John Cooper's (1988-2000) record at Ohio State is second only to Woody Hayes. He coached more than 20 All-Americans in his OSU tenure, including Heisman Trophy winner Eddie George. He was the first coach to win Rose Bowls with both Pac-10 and Big Ten teams. In 2008, Cooper was elected to the College Football Hall of Fame.

He accepted the job as Head Coach at Ohio State on December 31, 1987. It is rumored that he became the front-runner for the head coaching position at Ohio State because of his 1987 Rose Bowl victory over Michigan.

During his time in Columbus he won shared Big Ten titles in 1993, 1996, and 1998. In his 13 seasons at Ohio State Cooper compiled a 111-43-4 record, second in Ohio State history behind only Woody Hayes.

While gathering information for this book, I called Coach Cooper's house on a Wednesday and spoke with Mrs. Cooper. She said that John was out of town on business for the Cincinnati Bengals, but assured me that she would have John call me as soon as he returned. True to her word, Coach Cooper called me when he returned from his trip — 9:30 on a Fri-

Coach Cooper, Trevor Zahara

day night. He agreed to set up an interview the following week.

Q: What was it like to lead the Ohio State Buckeyes onto the field?

Coach Cooper: As noted in my bio I have probably coached in as many different conference games, bowl games and stadiums as any other college coach. When you lead the team down the ramp and onto the field with 100,000+ screaming fans, there is no greater setting for football and absolutely no better feeling. Ohio Stadium is The Best Stadium in the world and The Ohio State University is the best coaching position in the world!

I have had the honor of leading the best bunch of college players in the country, including: 1995 Heisman Trophy winner Eddie George; 1995 Fred Biletnikoff award winner Terry Glenn; 1996 Outland Trophy winner Orlando Pace; 1998 Jim Thorpe Award winner Antoine Winfield; Alonzo Spellman; Robert Smith; Dan Wilkinson; Joey Galloway; Rickey Dudley; Mike Vrabel; Korey Stringer; David Boston; Shawn Springs; Ahmed Plummer; Na'il Diggs; Nate Clements; and Ryan Pickett as well as many others.

I always lead my team onto the field and remembered joking to the players, if anybody passes me, there goes your scholarship!

While entering the stadium I would always take the time to wave to my wife and daughter. My son John was by my side for all 12 years as the carrier of my headphone cord. He loved it, and we debated on who had the greatest job in the world!

Q: Traditions are important parts of Ohio State football. Following Woody and Earle must have been difficult acts to follow?

Coach Cooper: I love everything about Ohio State football, Senior Tackle, those great cinnamon rolls at pre-game, running out on the field with the team, the terrific fans—what's not to like?

Q: The Ushers voted you as third best coach at Ohio State — quite an honor?

Coach Cooper: First of all, I have great respect for all the hardworking Ushers who volunteer their time to insure that all our great fans experience a safe and exciting time at the game. In my 13 years coaching I never had a "bad word" with any of the Ushers and felt tremendous support, for which I am forever grateful.

I appreciate their vote of confidence for me, but heck, there were some tremendous coaches at Ohio State. Woody was an idol of mine, I pale in comparison. Earle was an excellent coach and personal friend. I thought Coach Tressel was a great, great football coach, and I still think he is, I hated to see him go out the way he did. Jim is a good friend of mine.

Q: All of the coaches you mentioned were either fired or retired under duress. It had to be tough on you?

Coach Cooper: It comes with the territory. As I mentioned in my press conference, upon being hired in 1987, I came to Ohio State to win the National Championship, and my one regret was not fulfilling that dream for the great Buckeye fans.

Cooper could not lead the Buckeyes to a national title — its last one was in 1968 — but he came close. In 1995, the Buckeyes won their first 11 games before losing at Michigan, 31-23. Five weeks later, Ohio State lost to Tennessee 20-14 in the Florida Citrus Bowl.

The 1996 team won its first 10 games and was ranked #2 when it fell to #21-ranked Michigan, 13-9. That team rebounded to edge out Arizona State 20-17 in the Rose Bowl in the final seconds. His team hoisted him on its shoulders and carried him off the field.

Ranked #1 in the preseason, the 1998 team stayed atop the polls until November 7, when it lost to 17-point underdog Michigan State. The Buckeyes won their last three games, including victories over Michigan and against Texas A & M in the Sugar Bowl, to again finish #2 in the final rankings.

Q: Over 50% of the Ushers served in the military, did you have that honor?

> *Coach Cooper: Thank all the Ushers for their service to our country. Yes, I had the honor of serving our country in the Army for 2 years.*

Q: When you first came to Ohio State some of the fans considered you an "outsider," you spoke with that Tennessee drawl and didn't grow up in Ohio. Why have you made Columbus your home and do you consider yourself a Buckeye?

> *Coach Cooper: Yes, I do talk a little funny, but I am proud of my upbringing in Tennessee. But what's not to like about Colum-bus? I have my family, including my wonderful grandkids. Every morning I get up early, read the Columbus Dispatch, then I get in the car and go get my lovely wife of 56 years her morning cup of coffee.*
>
> *I get to play golf at Scioto Country Club with my good friends and Muirfield is right up the street.*
>
> *I love Ohio and Coach Meyer is kind enough to give me office space at Ohio State. **Yes, I am a BUCKEYE!***

LATER LIFE AND HONORS

Cooper was inducted into the Rose Bowl Hall of Fame on December 30, 2012. Cooper remains the only coach to lead Big Ten and Pac-12 schools to Rose Bowl Game victories.

I've always tried to coach people the way I would like to be coached; positively and encouragingly rather than with criticism and fear ... I've tried to be as fair as possible.

—Tony Dungy

EARLE BRUCE

Earle Bruce (born March 8, 1931). He served as the head coach at the University of Tampa (1972),Iowa State University (1973-1978),Ohio State University (1979-1987),University of Northern Iowa (1988), and Colorado State University (1989-1992), compiling a career college football record of 154-90-2.

At Ohio State, Bruce was the successor to the legendary Woody Hayes, and won four Big Ten Conference titles. He was inducted into the College Football Hall of Fame as a coach in 2002. Bruce returned to coaching in 2003 to helm the Iowa Barnstormers of the Arena Football League for a season and also guided the Columbus Destroyers the following year.

After Woody Hayes was fired from Ohio State, Bruce accepted the head coaching position. The first year, Ohio State went undefeated in the regular season and played in the Rose Bowl, losing the game and the National Championship by a single point.

SANTA'S HERE!

In a recent interview with Coach Bruce I asked him about his relationship with the Usher Program:

Coach Bruce: *I have very fond memories of the Redcoats. When I became Head Coach for the Buckeyes the Holidays were a special time for my family. My wife Jean made sure that all the coaches and married player's kids had presents for Christmas; she would start her shopping early to make sure she was ready for the big day. My main responsibility was to make sure Santa Claus was there to hand out all the gifts. I recruited a very robust and energetic Redcoat to fill the role. He did such a terrific job that every year I was here he was welcomed back; In fact, some of the other coaches followed my Christmas tradition.*

Q. What was your fondest memory of your time at OSU?

Coach Bruce: *Oh Wow! Where do I start? There were so many. When I was recruited by Coach Fesler to play football for the Buckeyes, freshmen were not permitted to play their first year, so I sat in the stands watching as the band marched down the field. The hair on the back of my neck stood up as the drum major flipped his baton over the goal post. I was hooked on Buckeye traditions*

As a Coach and ever since, Senior Tackle has been very special to me.

(A last practice of the year tradition since 1913 where the seniors hit the blocking sled one final time. For many years it was held following the last practice prior to the season finale with Michigan. But depending upon the Buckeyes' bowl obligation, it has sometimes been moved to the last home practice before the team departs for its bowl obligation.)

And of course, who can forget those wonderful cinnamon rolls at breakfast at OSU Golf Course.

Coach Earle Bruce, Trevor Zahara

TOUGHNESS

Urban Meyer, in 2013 Big Ten Coaches conference, said that after an Ohio State loss in his first season as an assistant with the program in 1986, Hayes, who had been fired after the 1978 season, questioned the toughness of the coaching staff.

Fair warning, there is a lot about this joke you might find offensive.

"So I guess Ohio State had lost the bowl game, so Earle Bruce brings in Woody Hayes," Meyer said. "I had been there just a week and I'm thinking, 'Holy, this is Coach Hayes.' I'm sitting in the back. Coach Hayes was not healthy at the time, but stands up and starts laying into the coaching staff about toughness. That we have no toughness in the program. That's why we lost the game. On and on and screaming, this old guy pounding the table. He says, 'We have no toughness, and the reason is because you're not

tough. No one on this staff is tough enough, and that's a problem.'

"He reaches down and grabs this box, slides the top and there was something in the box moving around. He reaches in and he pulls out this turtle. He reaches down, this turtle's snapping and he says, 'I'm going to show you toughness.' He unzips his pants and takes out whatever he takes out. The turtle reaches up and snaps at him. You see the veins and the sweat (on Hayes). He screams at the coaches, 'That's toughness! That's f'n toughness!' He reaches down, pokes the turtle right in the eye and it falls off. He wipes the sweat off his forehead and says, 'That's the problem. We don't have anybody in this room tough enough to do that right there.'

"(One assistant) raises his hand and says, 'Coach, I'd do this. Just promise not to poke me in the eye.'"

Today, Bruce works as an Ohio State football analyst for WTVN 610AM in Columbus as well as serving as an analyst for ONN on their OSU programming.

WOODY HAYES

"I've had smarter people around me all my life, but I haven't run into one yet that can outwork me. And if they can't outwork you, then smarts aren't going to do them much good. That's just the way it is. And if you believe that and live by it, you'd be surprised at how much fun you can have."

There are many reasons why Woody was voted the all time favorite coach of the Ushers. I received dozens of stories, quotes and personal anecdotes from my fellow Ushers. During his 28 seasons as the Head Coach of the Ohio State Buckeyes program, Hayes' teams won five National Championships (1954, 1957, 1961, 1968 and 1970), captured 13 Big Ten Conference titles, and amassed a record of 205-61-10.

In his second year with the Miami Redskins, Hayes led the 1950 squad to an appearance in the Salad Bowl, where they defeated Arizona State University.

That success led him to accept the Ohio State head coaching position on February 18, 1951, in a controversial decision after the university rejected the applications of other more well-known coaches, including former Buckeye head coach Paul Brown, incumbent Buckeye assistant coach Harry Strobel and Missouri head Coach Don Faurot. Ohio State at the time was known as the "graveyard of coaches," and Hayes' friends were wondering why he would want the Buckeye coaching job.

"Some men wrestle alligators for a living," said an article in Look magazine. "Others umpire baseball games. Still others munch on razor blades and wash them down with fire. And there are those, the supreme daredevils, who coach football at Ohio State."

A BRUSH WITH A LEGEND

Before the 1980 game, I met Woody Hayes outside his Converse Hall office. I explained to him how I was a Buckeye condemned to living in Michigan for the previous 10 years but that I proudly flew my Block O flag despite having had an "M" mowed into my lawn. Woody grinned and replied, "It's all a lot of fun, isn't it?"

—**Bill S.,** Powell

THE SERGEANT AND THE PROFESSOR

The following story is one of the Ushers' favorites, especially those that were veterans. From-Jack Park's Football Encyclopedia:

Pat Harmon, former historian/curator at the College Football Hall of Fame, tells a story about Woody Hayes driving all night to get home from Philadelphia after the evening's last flight was canceled. Hayes was not too happy, and as he was making arrangements for a rental car, a young Air Force Sergeant named David Buller overheard Hayes and asked if he could ride with him. Hayes readily agreed as Buller explained his need to get to Dayton to make a connection to his home in Ogden, Utah.

The two drove all night, and as they reached the outskirts of Columbus about 3:00 a.m., Hayes called John Mummey, one of his assistant coaches, and asked Mummey to drive Buller on to Dayton. As Mummey started for the Dayton Airport, Buller told Mummey how impressed he was with Mr. Hayes' knowledge of history and how enlightening it was to talk with him.

With that, Mummey asked, "Do you know who you were riding with?"

"He said his name was Hayes," Buller replied, "and he sure

---

sounded like a history professor."

Mummey asked, "Are you aware this Mr. Hayes is Coach Woody Hayes of Ohio State?"

"You're kidding, THE Woody Hayes? He never once even mentioned football," the open-mouthed sergeant answered. "I can't believe it. Just wait until I tell my parents!"

Mummey took Buller on to Dayton, then headed straight back to Columbus for an 8:00 a.m. coaches meeting — and there was Woody, eager to get started after a very short night's sleep.

THREE YARDS AND A CLOUD OF DUST

Hayes' basic coaching philosophy was that "nobody could win football games unless they regarded the game positively and would agree to pay the price that success demand of a team." His conservative style of football (especially on offense) was often described as "three yards and a cloud of dust" — in other words, a "crunching, frontal assault of muscle against muscle, bone upon bone, will against will."

The basic, bread-and-butter play in Hayes' playbook was a fullback off-guard run or a tailback off-tackle play. Hayes was often quoted as saying, "Only three things can happen when you pass and two of them are bad."

In spite of this apparent willingness to avoid change, Hayes became one of the first major college head coaches to recruit African-American players, including Jim Parker, who played both offensive and defensive tackle on Hayes' first national championship team in 1954. While Hayes was not the first to recruit African-Americans to Ohio State, he was the first to recruit and start African-Americans in large numbers there and to hire African-American assistant coaches.

Another Hayes recruit, Archie Griffin, remains the only two-time Heisman Trophy winner in seven decades of selections. Altogether Hayes had 58 players earn All-Americann honors under his tutelage, many notable football coaches, such as Lou Holtz , Bill Arnsparger, Bill Mallory, Dick Crum, Bo Schembechler, Ara Parseghian, and Woody's successor, Earle Bruce, served as his assistants at various times.

Hayes would often use illustrations from historical events to make a point in his coaching and teaching. When Hayes was first hired to be the head coach at OSU, he was also made a full professor of physical education, having earned a master's degree in educational administration from Ohio State in 1948. The classes he taught on campus were usually full, and he was called "Professor Hayes" by students. Hayes also taught mandatory English and vocabulary classes to his freshman football players.

One of his students was a basketball player named Bobby Knight, who was to become a legendary basketball coach.

Coach Hayes once shared this story with Coach Knight on getting better each game during the 1952 season: "This nice old lady came up to me and asked, 'What was the score of the Illinois game?' and I said, '27-7.' Then she asked, 'What was the score of your Michigan game?' and I said, '27-7.' She commented, 'You aren't making much improvement are you?'"

Success—it's what you do with what you've got.
—**Woody Hayes**

Mind over Matter

In the 1950s and early 1960s a west field Usher remembers standing behind the home team bench and, whatever the temperature or the weather, he saw Woody wearing a short sleeved white shirt and his trademark baseball cap with the "O" emblazoned in the center of the cap.

Woody never wore a long sleeved shirt, jacket or gloves. Woody maintained, "The cold weather was all in your head. If you didn't think about it, it wouldn't bother you." He had all the coaches get their pockets —

whether in their shirts, pants, or coats—sewn shut. Finally, on the advice of trainers and doctors, he started wearing long-sleeved shirts and jackets. But he never wore stocking caps or gloves.

Between 1951 and 1968 under Hayes, the Buckeyes won 12 of 18 contests, including a 1957 victory in Michigan Stadium, the first game in the series attended by over 100,000 fans.

In 1958, Ohio State had a 20-14 lead toward the end of the game. On the final play, Michigan fullback Gene Sisinyak ran the ball from the one-yard line for what might have been a game winning touchdown, but Ohio State defensive tackle Dick Schafrath hit Sisinyak, forcing a fumble.

In the 1968 game, Ohio State won 50-14, outscoring its foe 29-0 in the second half and attempting an unsuccessful two-point conversion attempt on its final touchdown. When asked why he went for two points with an already insurmountable 50-14 lead, Woody Hayes is rumored to have said, *"Because I couldn't go for three."* The victory gave top-ranked Ohio State the Big Ten title for the first time in seven years en route to an AP National Championship.

ONE FAN'S PERSPECTIVE

It was 1968 and my family had just been relocated to Columbus, Ohio after my father returned from tours in Vietnam. I was 10 years old and had never heard of the Buckeyes (an oversight I have corrected with my own children). Woody Hayes was a big supporter of our military men and hooked my father up with four tickets to the Buckeyes game against then #1- ranked Purdue. The Buckeyes with guys like Kern, Mayes, White, Brockington, Tatum, Stillwagon, and my favorite, Jim Otis, on the field prevailed 13-0.

I became a Buckeye on that day as did my brother, sister and father as all of us received our degrees from OSU. Thank you Woody!

—**Tim K.**, Oak Hill, Virginia

1978 GATOR BOWL

Many of the present Ushers were at the 1978 Gator Bowl in Jacksonville, Florida and were shocked by the outcome. This is the story:

Ultimately, Hayes' volatile temper ended his career. On December 29, 1978, Ohio State played in the Gator Bowl against the Clemson Tigers. Late in the fourth quarter, the Buckeyes were down by two points. Freshman quarterback Art Schlichter drove the Buckeyes down the field into field goal range. On 3rd and 5 at the Clemson 24-yard line with 2:30 left and the clock running, Hayes called a pass rather than a run because Schlichter was having a great game up to that point.

The pass was intercepted by Clemson nose guard Charlie Bauman who returned it toward the OSU sideline where he was run out of bounds. After Bauman rose to his feet and looked in the direction of the OSU players, Hayes punched him in the throat, starting a bench-clearing brawl. Hayes stormed onto the field and was abusive to the referee. When one of Hayes' own players, offensive lineman Ken Fritz, tried to intervene, Hayes turned on him and had to be restrained by defensive coordinator George Hill.

The Buckeyes were assessed two 15-yard unsportsmanlike conduct penalties for Hayes' punch on Bauman and his abuse of the referee, and Hayes was ejected. Bauman was not injured by Hayes' punch, and he shrugged the incident off. Even though the game was being telecast by ABC, announcers Keith Jackson and Ara Parseghian did not comment about the punch. The incident was not in their field of view, and at that time replay footage was relayed through the studio, so they did not see the event.

After the game, OSU Athletic Director Hugh Hindman — who had played for Hayes at Miami University and had been an assistant under him for seven years — privately confronted Hayes in the Buckeye locker room. He said that he intended to tell school president Harold Enarson what happened, and strongly implied that Hayes had coached his last game at Ohio State. After a heated exchange, Hindman said he then offered Hayes a chance to resign, but Hayes refused, saying, "That would make it too easy for you. You had better go ahead and fire me." Hindman then met with Enarson at a country club near Jacksonville, and the two agreed that Hayes had to go.

The next morning Hindman told Hayes that he had been fired. A press conference was held at the hotel where the team had been staying. The team returned to Columbus around noon, and Hayes left the airport in a police car.

Enarson said that he had fired Hayes because, "There isn't a university or athletic conference in this country that would permit a coach to physically assault a college athlete."

After the incident, Hayes reflected on his career by saying, "Nobody despises to lose more than I do. That's got me into trouble over the years, but it also made a man of mediocre ability into a pretty good coach."

XEROX THAT

Coach Hayes meant a lot to our family, in fact, my wife Patti sent Woody birthday cards. When I worked for the Columbus sales branch of Xerox Corporation we had a championship year in 1981, and were attempting for a repeat for #1 branch in the country in 1982. Neil Lamey, branch manager for Xerox in Columbus, thought it would be an excellent idea to have a dynamic speaker like Woody to motivate the sales reps. So, knowing that new hire Mike Strahine was an ex-quarterback for the Buckeyes he directed Mike to go recruit Coach Hayes for the speaking engagement. Mike diligently accepted the challenge and set up the appointment with Coach Hayes at his office in the ROTC building. He explained to Coach Hayes that the Xerox Corporation would love to have Coach as a positive motivational speaker to help the local branch achieve the #1 position of the country.

Coach responded,"Xerox, isn't that a big company? I usually give back my honorarium in my speeches, but Xerox can afford it." Mike thought to himself; Oh No! I only have $500 to offer. But, no worry, Coach wrote on his schedule: Xerox May 2nd $500. On the day of the event, Mike offered to pick up Coach Hayes and drive him to the outdoor event near Dublin, Ohio, Coach decided to drive his El Camino. Mike was waiting for Coach at the turnoff to get to the outdoor pavilion as Coach drove right past him! Mike took off running after him. Finally, he got the Coach turned around, jumped in the El Camino and headed down the dirt road. Well, Coach Hayes sideswiped three cars as he was driving down that dirt road.

Mike said nothing!

Finally they got Coach to his parking space and Coach Hayes, waiting to address the audience in a few minutes, looked over to Mike and asked, "What do you want me to talk about?"

Sweat started to trickle down Mike's forehead, thinking that Coach Hayes had a prepared speech. Mike said, "Just motivate them Coach!" Coach did exactly that for the next 45 minutes, even though a pouring spring rain fell outside the huge tent. Coach Hayes did not miss a beat during that motivational speech. It wasn't until Mike went up to Coach Hayes to congratulate him on a wonderful speech that he realized that the entire backside of Coach Hayes was soaking wet from the driving rain!

After the event was over three Xerox reps got back to their cars and exclaimed, "What happened to our cars?" Nobody knows, until this day!

THE CROWD ROARS

Tom Hamilton, former sportscaster with WBNS Radio in Columbus and now the play-by-play voice of the Cleveland Indians, was the color commentator with the University of Wisconsin Football Radio Network in 1983. Tom's first game in the Ohio Stadium was the Buckeye's homecoming game that season against the Wisconsin Badgers:

> *I was doing a halftime interview, when suddenly the crowd's applause was deafening, I simply couldn't continue with the interview. We all looked out of the radio booth to see what was happening down on the field — Woody Hayes had just dotted the "i" in Script Ohio.*

LIFE AFTER COACHING

After being fired from the head coach position, Hayes assumed a position on the Navy ROTC faculty and occupied an office in the ROTC building on the second floor with a view of the field. For the remainder of his years at OSU, he continued to teach and mentor students. Woody was proud to be selected to give the commencement speech at Ohio State in March of 1986, just a year before his death. This is part of Woody's speech:

> *"Today is the greatest day of my life. I appreciate it so much being able to come here and talk to our graduating class at The Ohio State University — the great, great university that you and I love. I am so grateful and appreciative to be here today. I just can't tell you how much. I want to start with this concept: paying forward — that is the thing that you folks with your great education from here can do for the rest of your lives. Take that attitude toward life, because so seldom can we pay back those whom you owe. Your parents and other people will be gone. Emerson had something to say about that. He said you can pay back only seldom. But you can always pay forward, and must pay line for line, deed for deed, and cent for cent."*

A year later, on the morning of March 12, 1987, his wife Anne found him dead in his bed at the couple's home. He had died of an apparent heart attack, after having been in failing health for several years.

PERSONAL LIFE

Hayes was married to the former Anne Gross in 1942. Anne Hayes was a formidable and popular woman in her own right, who used to jokingly say, "Divorce Woody? Never! But there were plenty of times I wanted to murder him!"

Craig Brown, Manager of Video Services, while talking about the old two-level press box remembered fondly that there was an automated chairlift between the two levels: The lift was called, "Anne's Chair" by people working in the press box, because Anne had difficulty negotiating the stairs in her later years.

Anne was a real fan of the game, according to Joe Menzer, author of *Buckeye Madness*. For some time after Woody's passing, she still attended the home games. Before one game she was in an elevator at Ohio Stadium riding skyward along with several OSU coaches who were headed to their box perched high above the field. They wore grim faces befitting the tension that looms before each kickoff. Suddenly, Anne Hayes broke into a cheer.

"Give me an O!" she shouted.

The somber and serious coaches looked hesitantly at each other.

Then in unison, they gave her an O.

"Give me an H!" she shouted next.

And on it went, until the aging widow of Woody Hayes had coerced several very serious middle-aged men to spell out Ohio at the top of their lungs whom otherwise would have been poring over the day's game plan in their busy minds. It was time well spent. Then they filed out of the elevator, one by one, properly motivated to go make her and everyone else in the state proud.

PORTAL MEMORIES

Rick Huhn, Usher 14-B has been a fan of OSU sports since the early 1950s. He graduated from the OSU law school and was in private practice with a Columbus law firm for over 25 years. He retired about 10 years ago to do some writing. He has an interest in baseball history. Two of his baseball biographies have been published. A third book about the 1910 batting race will be published in 2014:

I'm sure almost every Ohio Stadium Usher remembers details from the first Buckeye home game he worked. My first game was the Ohio State-Oklahoma game on September 24, 1977. The game ended in dramatic, albeit disappointing fashion as the Sooners kicked a long field goal in the final seconds to bag a 29-28 victory. Our coach that day was the legendary Woody Hayes. I was assigned to portal 14-B as a substitute. I've remained there ever since, missing only two home games over the years.

The year Woody died, our portal chief was Walter Popp. He was employed by the US Postal Service, working out of the Upper Arlington branch. Woody and Anne Hayes lived in Upper Arlington, utilized the services of their local post office frequently, and came to know Walter. A season or two after Woody's death, Walter told us that he had invited Anne to act as an Honorary Usher at our portal. We all nodded and did our best to hide our skepticism. We were, therefore, totally floored when the very next week none other than Annie Hayes promptly reported for duty at 14-B. She worked with us over the next four or five home games. She showed up on time each week and was extremely outgoing and friendly.

Although she had every intention of helping us make sure the fans found their seats, she was spotted early on by friends and fans who then swarmed over her to the point she rarely had a moment to catch her breath.

It was easy to see that she was a major asset to Woody and a great ambassador for the university. Once the game started she left for her seat on the other side of the stadium. We all hoped she would return the next year, but she retired as reigning queen of the honorary Ushers at Ohio Stadium. Her presence in our section remains my fondest memory of my lengthy tenure at 14-B.

Fans

Football is not a game but a religion, a metaphysical island of fundamental truth in a highly verbalized disguised society, a throwback of 30,000 generations of anthropological time.

—Arnold Mandell

Two hours before the games begin the gates open and fans start to meander into the stadium. Why on earth do they come so early? Some have never been to an OSU game, others just want to orient themselves to their seats and find that they are the only ones in their section. They sit there for about 10 minutes and decide that they want to explore. They take pictures of the field go to the concession stand and talk to the Ushers.

They come in all categories:

Celebrity Fans. Every game the same people seem to show up on TV dressed in their OSU garb — wild outfits or distinctive dance steps — going nuts for the cameras, screaming "The Bucks Are Number One," and thrusting their index fingers at the TV Cameramen. Other fans at the stadium or the television audience form their own impressions of these rabid fans. Some are inspiring, some are endearing and some provoke folks to slap their foreheads and say, "Who are these idiots?"

Whatever category you fall into, the following are some of those passionate characters:

NEUTRON MAN

Neutron Man (1942-2004), whose real name was Orlas King, was a popular figure in the stands for 30 years. Always seated by the marching band, King would burst into his original dances whenever the Ohio State University Marching Band played the "Neutron Dance."

King grew up in Kettering, Ohio where his father was a tool and die maker. Every year he and his father would travel to Ohio Stadium to watch a Buckeyes home football game. Later King went on to play football on a scholarship at the University of Dayton.

King along with his wife Debbi started dancing at Ohio State home football games in 1973. At that time he was known as the B-Deck Dancer– seated in section 11-B. He remained the B-Deck Dancer until 1984 when the Ohio State Marching Band introduced its rendition of the Pointer Sisters' "Neutron Dance." The spectators established a connection between

2003 National Championship Game Fiesta Bowl -Neutron Man, Orlas King- Patti Zahara

the song and King and began to chant: "Neutron Man, Neutron Man." From that point forward, the Neutron Man would dance at every Ohio State home football game during the third quarter break. King eventually began to wear his scarlet and gray beret and his very own Ohio State Buckeyes jersey with "Neutron Man" printed on the back.

According to Jack Park, noted OSU historian, "When the Ohio State-Michigan contest was at Ann Arbor, King hosted a party at his home to view the game. If Ohio State won, King immediately dove into a pond in his backyard with nothing on but his Brutus Buckeye underwear. It was so cold the day of the Buckeyes' 14-9 win in 1981, King had to crack the ice before he could take a dip. When asked if this tradition could be a little hard on his health, King responded, 'The thrill of beating Michigan is so great, I don't feel a thing!'"

Until his death in 2004, King promoted and contributed to the Ohio State Marching Band and Ohio State Cheerleading programs. He helped raise money for both groups and being the owner of several restaurants, he frequently catered lunches for the students after the marching band and cheerleading tryouts. Springing from his popularity a Neutron Man Beanie Baby was even created. A portion of the money generated from sales went to a cheerleading scholarship.

If you're mad at your kid you can either raise him to be a nose tackle or send him out to play on the freeway. It's about the same.

—**Bob Golic**

SUPER FANS

Mark Pickett, Usher for five years stationed in the South Stands, has to be one of the most passionate Buckeye fans to see or know personally some of the most recognizable "Fanatics" ever to attend OSU football

games. The following are Mark's stories, along with some of his close and personal buddies:

IT'S THE BEST SEAT IN THE HOUSE

I started Ushering in 2008 on C-Deck portal 19. To stand in Ohio Stadium for the first time was like being a kid in a candy store! I learned as much about the stadium as I could as fast as I could which allowed me to help the fans with finding their seats and in some cases to take them to their seats. The first year I spent a lot of my time checking tickets at the entrance of the portal and didn't get to see much of the game. After the second or third game I brought a camera and began a nice collection of photos of fans, players, Ushers and law enforcement personnel. Whether the stadium was empty or full, I took photos. Friends who came to the game posed so I could take their picture. Later I would send them the photos or share them with other friends.

One of the coolest things I was allowed to do that most fans never get to do was to stand on the towers on top of the north end of the stadium. The honor of guarding the towers during the games goes to two deputy sheriffs for Franklin County, Jimmy

McCoy and Richard Verhoven. According to Sheriff Zach Scott, "The duo with the lofty assignment requested the position and has been assigned there for four years. They both really like working the towers even though by the end of the day their legs are tired and 'their dogs are barking!'"

By 9:30 a.m. for a noon kickoff both report for their special duty to stand watch (sitting isn't permitted) on the towers, McCoy on the northwest side of the stadium, Verhoven on the northeast. They remain there until the game ends. Then they leave the towers and clear everybody out of C-Deck.

"The two serve as key players in game day crowd control," according to Major Geoff Stobart Head of Operations for the patrol division of the sheriff's office. "Because of the position they're in they're able to see rowdy fans or people throwing things out of the stadium," Stobart said. "They can see fights down below. They can quickly identify those guys and talk to officers on the ground to help get them to the culprits."

According to 44-year-old Officer McCoy, a deputy for 18 years, "Over the past 4 years I have not had to throw out any unruly fans. There have probably been a few I've had to say something to. They do what other fans do: If the team is losing they start flipping people off. It's like come on, have a little class."

The only downside of working the tower according to McCoy is the weather. "Some days it's breezy, other days it's pretty calm. I'm always just hoping my hat doesn't blow away! The rain is the worst. I'd rather it be cold and windy than rainy. With rain I have to get my rain gear out, then I get hot and sweaty. It'll stop raining, then start raining again. I hate the rain."

Other than the weather there is no bathroom on the tower. "So if nature calls I have to phone down for relief. But I can usually hold it all game long. And I watch what I drink."

The positive is the spectacular view of the field. "You can see all the plays develop. It's great. Unfortunately I'll watch just a little of the game but I watch all the way around the tower. It's probably 2½ feet wide all the way around. I walk around look around the parking lot (outside the stadium) and make sure no one is vandalizing anything or that no suspicious packages are lying around."

All things considered, "The best part of the job is talking to the Ushers and the fans!"

BEST JOB IN THE STADIUM

In 2009 at the first game I moved down to the Southeast corner of the field and that's when the real fun began. I was in awe to be able to stand on the "holy grail" of football fields, look up into the huge empty stands. In a blink those same empty stands were packed with screaming fans. Truly a dream come true for a devoted Buckeye!

I remember the other Ushers gave me a hard time at first just because I was the new guy. Lucky for me Lou Kauffman, portal chief, took me under his wing and showed me the ropes. We have become really good friends, call each other often to just chat and catch up with what's going on in our lives.

Within a game or two I understood what my job entailed and how to interact with all the people. I was still in awe for the first few games trying to take in all the players coaches and people, many of whom later became my friends. I was not prepared for the people that flock down to get as close as they can to the field. They all try to go places where, due to NCAA regulations, they are not allowed to go.

I have had the chance to meet a lot of super fans — some very notable like Big Nut, Buckeyeman, Buck-I-Guy. I get a lot of questions about these special people so here are their stories:

BUCK-I-GUY

In South stadium it's easy to recognize the Buck-I-Guy. Behind the 10-gallon hat, 6-foot-cape, painted-red mustache, under-eye stickers, sunglasses, gloves and custom Ohio State outfit is a family man who has used his opportunity for fame to give back to the community.

John Chubb, also known as Buck-I-Guy, has become one of the most recognizable faces in the South Stands. A lifelong fan of the Buckeyes, Chubb, 49, grew up in Columbus' north end. He is married with three children and has a career as a computer supply salesman.

Although Chubb has been going to OSU football games for years, he has not always been in the limelight. He said things started to change after an incident in 2005. On November 6, 2005 Chubb and his son Tremaine had a life-changing experience. They were the first people to respond to a car accident that left two people trapped inside a burning car.

Chubb and his son had been to the OSU football game on Saturday and were on their way to a Browns football game in Cleveland when a car passed them and went out of control. It flipped several times, "Dukes-of-Hazzard style," Chubb said. As fire came

out of the air ducts of the car, Tremaine Chubb broke out the passenger side window and freed the passenger who had been thrown to the floor, Chubb said.

John Chubb backed away from the trapped driver of the vehicle because she was grabbing at him and the car was

on fire. He told his son he would try one more time to free her and his son's reply was, "Are you sure? Because it's about to go, Dad." John Chubb said he freed the driver shortly before the car exploded in flames. The driver and passenger both survived.

Shortly after that John Chubb began to get the publicity that has made him so recognizable. "When the accident happened Buck-I-Guy was around and I don't know if this is divine intervention or good karma but it all took off after the accident," Chubb said.

Since then the Buck-I-Guy has spent a lot of time making appearances at community events. He has spoken at fundraisers for autism and diabetes while doing work with "Walk for the Cure" and the Stefanie Spielman Breast Cancer Foundation. He has spoken at retirement communities and also spends time reading to underprivileged children.

"It stems from Coach Woody Hayes always talking about paying forward, this is something that has stuck with me throughout my life. I try to stay community-minded," Chubb said.

John Chubb The Buck-I-Guy has been featured on ESPN's "College Game Day," ABC, NBC, The Big Ten Network and the Jay Leno Show. His pictures have also been included in the Wall Street Journal, Columbus Monthly, The Athlon Sports Big Ten 2009 Preview and other publications.

Chubb goes to every home and away game dressed up in full outfit to represent the Buckeyes. He even transformed a 1970 Chevy Impala into the "Buck-I-Guy Mobile." The car took him 10 years to totally restore and customize. It is a convertible with a custom Buckeye interior, custom tires axles and footballs with the letter "B" on the wheels. He drives it to the home games and local events.

"A lot of people think that he does it all for the publicity and the show but he's just a passionate guy who is genuinely in love with the Buckeyes," said Dee Miller, a former OSU football player. "He will invite me over for cookouts and we will talk about life in general whether it is about obstacles that I'm facing or troubles in my life," Miller said. "I'm fortunate enough to see him as more than just the Buck-I-Guy."

The Buck-I-Guy is a good representative of the tradition and a good guy who goes to all the games and leads the cheers!

OHIO STATE SUPER FAN BUCKEYEMAN

One of the most colorful and easily recognizable fans who always fires up the crowd around him in the South Stands is the "Buckeyeman." There are Buckeye sports fanatics and then there are Buckeye fanatics. Larry Lokai known to many as Buckeyeman, is both.

Lokai, an Urbana resident and Ohio State alumnus, collects and donates thousands of buckeyes from buckeye trees around Ohio each year in addition to being one of the Buckeyes' most rabid and recognizable fans.

Lokai attended his first OSU football game when he was a freshman in 1962. He was a member of Block O during his junior and senior years and earned a degree in science in 1967 and returned to earn his master's degree in 1973.

It would take 25 years for Lokai, now a retired educator, to become Buckeyeman. In 1998 he joined the animal sciences department at OSU as an adjunct faculty member and attended every Buckeye home game. However he didn't have tickets to the home Michigan game. His son got him a last-second ticket but it wasn't in preferred seating.

"I was stuck right in the Michigan section in the middle. I wore a jersey and my 'skunk wig,'" Lokai said. "This is how Buckeye man officially became Buckeyeman. Neutron Man danced all

the time. He's passed away now but we used to do a lot of things together. Then Brutus Buckeye was the team mascot. I thought I would combine those names."

Since then, with his trademark scarlet and gray wig, painted face and overloaded buckeye necklaces he's become a celebrity fan. Lokai began stocking up on the wigs, developing a routine and attending as many games as possible. He has been to every home game since 1999 and went to 70 straight games overall before breaking the streak.

Being a celebrity fan has its perks. "I had a press pass to be right with the team on the field before the National Championship Game in 2002; I got to rush out on the field with the players after the game. It was unreal, pandemonium."

Once Lokai started to become a popular fan he started collecting buckeyes from about 100 buckeye trees. He picks them up with a special "nut wizard tool" then dries them on drying racks he built. He stores them in buckets that hold 1,000 buckeyes each and then donates them to fans, students and cheerleaders. He also provides enough buckeyes for the entire freshman class to receive one at first-year orientation.

"It's been a really nice thing," said Jenny Osborn assistant director in undergraduate admissions and first year experience. "That is 8,000-plus buckeyes each year which is an amazing amount."

Lokai gives tens of thousands more to the university each year for OUAB and student projects. "I get a lot of gratification out of it. It comes out of my pocket but that's my way of paying forward to the university."

Lokai also makes and gives out thousands of buckeye necklaces each year. Many wonder about all the necklaces he wears on Saturdays and at appearances. It is indeed an exact science: he wears seven necklaces for the football team's seven national titles with 104 total buckeyes on the necklaces for each of the times OSU has played Michigan.

Lokai wakes up at 4 a.m. to paint his face and get ready to make his rounds through the tailgaters and attend alumni functions around Ohio Stadium. "I try to walk into a place and light it up with positive energy. I look for the most people wherever I go and I always bring buckeyes."

Fan Feedback

Hi Mark. I was at the game yesterday with my little girl and wanted to thank you for everything you did for her! She said she had the "best day ever" and you were a huge part of it for getting Brutus and the Buckeyeman to come see her. Thank you so much for everything! GO BUCKS!!

—**Stacey Casebolt Sparrow**

Enthusiast Big Nut: 'Just a fan'

Another one of the super fans that gets everyone in our section excited for the game is the "Big Nut." Jon Peters finds a way to take his Buckeye pride a step farther to stand out. He's the one you see at the games with his face painted half scarlet, half gray wearing a large assortment of Buckeye memorabilia and a jersey with the words "Big Nut."

Jon comments: "I don't like being around stuffy fans. I don't like fans who sit on their hands. So my tickets are in a section with some students and other fans that are crazy like me. We are absolutely nuts about the Buckeyes. I like to see people smiling and having fun. If the Big Nut had a mission statement it would be to act as the 12th man in the stands to get the crowd fired up because the players feed off the fans in the stands. That's the most im-

portant thing. I like putting a smile on their faces and getting the crowd fired up. It takes forever to get this stuff off but it's all worth it. I don't feel like I'm special, just a fan," Peters said. "The only thing that would possibly make me a bigger Buckeye fan would be if I had a bigger waistline."

Peters has appeared during commercial breaks on the Big Ten Network and ESPN and was even mentioned during Jon Gruden's "QB camp with Terrelle Pryor."

His attendance at home and away games doesn't stem from the fact that he graduated from OSU. He actually attended Terra Community College in his hometown of Fremont, Ohio. "I guess I'll go to my Buckeye grave disappointed in the fact that I never had the chance to get a diploma from The Ohio State University," he said.

Peters started the Big Nut era in 1995 in a competition at a local high school fundraiser in Fremont for the Ohio State-Michigan game. For a best dressed contest he decked himself out in Buckeye gear to "beat the older women." He thought painting his entire face might help him win.

People didn't start noticing Big Nut until the 2003 Tostitos Fiesta Bowl in Arizona where OSU won the 2002 BCS National Championship Game. Peters was at a pep rally the day before when his wife, Terese Peters, painted his face and legs. He said people started coming up to him and asking to take pictures with their groups.

The camera crew got a shot of Big Nut that ended up being both on television and on the national championship game DVD. He has been dressing up for all home games and as many away games as possible ever since.

Jon also is noted for passing out the Buckeye necklaces. "My wife and I make close to 1,000 of those necklaces each year and we give them all away. The only exception is when we sell them as a fundraiser for the schools. My wife and I collect all of the buckeyes ourselves — we probably picked up 15,000 of them this year. They come from property where my great-grandfather planted the buckeye trees."

He pays for all his tickets and sits in his assigned seat. This is his second year receiving tickets through the Buckeye Club and his fifth year with season tickets. For three years he received tickets through a personal friend he said. He said he works out a deal with "a guy he knows" when he gets tickets in the South Stands at football games which he prefers because "the students are a lot more active." He said his often-front-row seat isn't because of wanting TV time, but so he can sit when he wants and still see the game.

Tim Collins, a third-year in psychology student and Block O president said he sees Peters as an icon for his dedication. "Especially at away games he provides a sense of comfort and you think 'The Buckeye nation is here'" Collins said.

Jon Peters hasn't always been received well by opposing fans. He recalled an instance at a night game at Penn State where an opposing fan tackled him. "I heard somebody yelling 'hut-hut' as I walked toward the stadium. I looked over and there was a kid in the three-point-stance and he just takes off running. I'm a big guy and I usually have a couple of escorts with me, but this college kid came up behind me and knocked me to the ground. They had been partying all day so he was probably drunk. I had knee replacement surgery that summer so I was concerned about how my knee would be but some Penn State fans helped me up and apologized for the incident."

Living two hours away means it takes "Big Nut" four hours to be completely dressed painted and in Columbus. In addition to his attire he has other Buckeye-inspired items including a Block O-engraved dental crown.

Big Nut has partnered with the OSU Alumni Association for fundraisers and has even started his own Big Nut Scholarship Foundation for a senior in Fremont to attend Ohio State. "Mrs. Nut and I started the Big Nut Scholarship fund," he said. He and his committee gave away two $500 scholarships last year; this year he plans on passing out even more. "I am now adding two more," including one to any school in Sandusky County that has the best qualified individual.

"Buckeye Nation is a wonderful thing," said Big Nut. "This really is not about me being the Big Nut. It is about all of Buckeye Nation being Big Nuts about their team. I have gained so many wonderful friends both young and old because of this. I can't believe how amazing OSU fans really are."

The Buckeye, as the true Ohio State fan knows, is more than a bitter nut to chew. It's a tough nut to crack!

FAN-A-TICS HALL OF FAME AS SEEN BY USHERS IN SOUTH STADIUM:

BRUTUS BUCKEYE

Brutus Buckeye is the athletics mascot of The Ohio State University. Brutus is a student dressed in Buckeye colors with a headpiece resembling the fruit of Ohio's official tree, the buckeye. Brutus has appeared since 1965 with periodic design and wardrobe updates.

Ohio State students Ray Bourhis and Sally Huber decided Ohio State needed a mascot in 1965 and convinced the athletic council to study the matter. At the time mascots were generally animals brought into the stadium or arena. A buck deer was contemplated but rejected in favor of a buckeye. A simple paper-mâché buckeye was constructed by students worn over the head and torso. Brutus made its first appearance at the Minnesota vs. Ohio State homecoming game on October 30, 1965.

The heavy paper-mâché head was soon replaced by a fiberglass shell. On November 21, 1965 the Columbus Dispatch reported that judges picked Brutus Buckeye to be the new mascot's name after a campus-wide "Name the Buckeye" contest. The winning name was the idea of then Ohio State student Kerry J. Reed. Block O agreed to care for Brutus. Brutus wears a Block O hat, a scarlet and gray shirt emblazoned "Brutus" with a"00,"

Brutus and Young Fan at Eastern Michigan Game 2010

red pants with an OSU towel hanging over the front, and high white socks with black shoes. Both male and female students serve as Brutus Buckeye, generally two to five students per year.

Brutus & Entire Cheerleading Squad 2013

2010 TACKLING

Mark Pickett, Usher, with **Lou Kauffman:**

According to the Usher Manual and OSU Security no individuals are allowed on the field without proper field credentials.

On September 18, 2010 the Ohio University Bobcats played the Buckeyes in Ohio Stadium. The OU mascot Brandon Hanning, dressed as Rufus the Bobcat, did not have the proper field credentials and was refused entry by Usher Mark Pickett. The OU Mascot created quite a stir.

Portal chief Lou Kauffman entered the fracas asking, "What's going on?"

I said, "This guy didn't have a pass to be on the field so I told him to leave." Lou agreed so the OU Mascot left. A few minutes before the game he came up to Lou and me and showed us his pass and was admitted to the field

A few minutes later as the Buckeyes were running onto the field, the OU mascot saw Ohio State mascot Brutus Buckeye leading the team and charged onto the field. Hanning sideswiped Brutus who got back to his feet and continued his sprint toward the end zone. Hanning then ran after Brutus, jumped on his back and began hitting the mascot in the head. Hanning was pulled aside by security who told him to stop. Neither mascot was harmed. After the game Hanning was terminated from his position as OU's mascot and was banned from attending OU's home athletic events.

Later Hanning explained, "It was actually my whole plan to tackle Brutus when I tried out to be mascot." When asked if the attack on Brutus was the first mascot brawl he had been in he replied with, "Before this I actually got in a fight with the Buffalo mascot. He's a bull. I started it. I was thinking I should go ahead and try tackling another mascot. I brought a red square cape thing like in a bullfight. He was just playing around acting like he was charging me. I tackled him and put him on the ground. It was pretty funny. No one got upset"

When they heard what happened Lou and I looked at each other and said, "Someone messed up on this one," and laughed out loud!

Lord Chaz

Lord Chaz *aka* **Charles Henry Howell IV** *is a former Ohio State student/rock musician who finally found his niche in the Big Easy back in 1990- when he established one of the first ghost/vampire tours in this famously haunted city. Oh, and he is very proud to be part of three generations of Ohio Stadium Ushers; his dad and grandfather started as Ushers in 1960 and he started in 1988.*

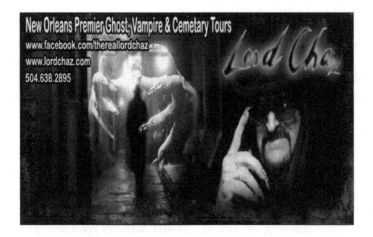

Lord Chaz's, Three Lords Entertainment is the premiere historical tour company in the Greater New Orleans area, and special-
izes in ghost and vampire tours, but also performs cemetery tours, art
and architecture tours, and other historical and theatrical events.

*Today his "Vampire Street Theater" tour is one of the highest-
rated walking tours in New Orleans.*

*"You're from Columbus? Oh you'll want to talk to Lord Chaz.
That's where he grew up."*

*But a Buckeye vampire? Now that's the kind of thing that gets
the blood pumping so to speak.*

*Lord Chaz is a large man with long, straight black hair, a
black top hat, a long black cloak and three-inch black enameled
fingernails. Imagine the unholy offspring of Severus Snape and
Meat Loaf.*

"O-H," he said.

"I-O," I responded. It seemed the thing to do.

*"We've gotten the Buckeyes down here a couple of times," he
noted. "The folks down here love it when the Buckeyes come. The
fans really come down and support the team and spend money."*

The only downside?

Ohio State has lost the last nine times they've played bowl

Charles Henry Howell III and Charles Henry Howell IV at 2011 Sugar Bowl

games against teams from the Southeastern Conference including the 2008 BCS title game here to nearby Louisiana State University. "I gotta live with all these SEC fans," said Lord Chaz. "Well maybe not 'live.'"

A terrific storyteller, Lord Chaz leads his two-hour tour through the French Quarter as he describes quite entertainingly some of the most heinous crimes of the city as well as the chilling reports of haunting that have followed. The true stories include tales of a mysterious "sultan" buried alive, a convent with an attic filled with coffins and a would-be Romeo gutted during his surreptitious attempt to woo a young Southern belle. And Lord Chaz claimed to have dozens of such stories to choose from. He also engages in a bit of street theater "stopping" his heart and performing other breathtaking (blood-letting?) feats.

As mentioned, Charles Henry Howell III and his dad were Ushers in 3-B since 1960. We would park our car in the Neil Avenue lot and walk to the stadium. Dad had suffered with heart problems, and he would get these angina attacks on the way to the game, but he would never complain. He would just "pop" a couple of nitro-glycerin pills and continue on to the stadium. He commented, "If the Good Lord wants to take me—so be it—but I ain't missing the game."

OHIO STATE FANS #1

Professors Lewis and Tripathi at Emory University who study sports marketing through advanced analytics are conducting research on the "best" *fan bases* in college football. Their findings reveal that Ohio State is the cream of the Big Ten's crop, followed by second-place Penn State. Michigan rounds out the top three.

MARTY

Carl Yarmark has been an Usher at C-26 for 39 years:

"Marty," as she likes to be called, attended her first Buckeye game with her grandfather in 1932 as a 3-year-old. In 1935 she began attending every home game with her grandfather who would carry her in. During the depression children who were carried into the stadium would be given free admission to Buckeye games. When Marty became too big to be carried, the Redcoats and Ushers would turn a blind eye allowing her to continue attending games gratis.

During these years Marty was regaled with stories of the Buckeyes and her great uncle Josephus H. Tilton, captain of the 1900 football team. She heard many times that the forward pass was illegal and that football was strictly a running and kicking game. She learned that the offense was given three downs to make five yards, and that any player except the center and quarter-back could end up carrying the ball. A touchdown was scored when a runner carried the ball across the other team's end line and "touched" the ball "down" — back then it was worth five points. "It is a much different game we watch today," she says.

As a student at OSU, Marty attended all of the games, sitting in the stands while her husband-to-be was on the field marching with TBDBITL. Following graduation from OSU they were mar-ried in 1950 and together remained lifelong OSU game attendees, followers and supporters of the Buckeyes. Marty can still recall the cold and snow of the famous 1950 Snow Bowl Game.

Marty and her husband have occupied their same seats in sec-tion 26-C including the 28 seasons I have been assigned there. In February 2010, she called me to inform our section 26-C crew that her beloved husband and our friend had passed away. When Marty arrived for the first game in 2010, a dozen red roses, com-pliments of her "26-C family" were resting on her seat in remem-brance of her husband and as a warm "welcome back." That season of 2010 Marty attended every game — home and away — following and supporting her beloved Buckeyes.

Marty believes that in all these years of cheering-on the Buck-eyes she has probably missed only 10 or 11 games.

End Note: Marty called me early in March 2013 to inform all of her "26-C family" she would not be returning in the fall. The added expense of the new ticket policy, the traffic and parking and the inevitable accumulation of years were catching up with her. She just wanted us to know how much she would miss those happy reunions with all the crew of 26-C which took place for so many years on the first Saturday of each September.

Be assured, dear Marty, that we too will be missing you!

THE PERFECT FAN

Greg Graham, *OSU grad and Vietnam Veteran; portal chief, C-29 has been an Usher since 2003.*

I brag about having the longest tenured fan in our section, John Crawford, 82. His attendance streak extended to 71 years after the Buffalo game. He has been to every home game since the Bucks beat the Illini on November 13, 1943. When people ask John why, John replies, "It just got to be a habit I guess! The streak began when I was 12 and my father took me to my first game. I was hooked ever since. I found ways to get into the stadium as a vendor selling Coke, then as a student and finally as an OSU cheerleader.

"It has not always been easy to keep up the streak. I have been sick as a dog at one game, another I could hardly walk up the stairs due to my bad knees (I had two knee replacements dur-

29 –C: Tony Mullins, Don Mullins, Terry Lamb, John Crawford, Greg Graham, Larry Miller

ing the offseason). The most harrowing time was the weekend of my nephew's wedding back in 1992. A local television station got word of my plight and agreed to pick me up outside the stadium and fly me to the airport in their helicopter so I could catch my flight to New Jersey. Mission accomplished!"

John has had different seats within the stadium but claims he likes his place in section 29-C in the shade of the tower blocking the wind. The Indiana game was John's 441th home game. He still gets tears in his eyes during Carmen Ohio and always wears his lucky Buckeye socks to the games.

BLOCK O

Adam Demchak, 2013 OSU graduate, an avid member of Block O and founder of Block O Gymnastics, he served on the Executive Board for the Block:

I love Ohio State and consider it to be a blessing. I attend both home and away football games and have not missed a game other than California in the last three years. I trademark the saying "Go Bucks — All Day — Everyday." A true Buckeye exhibits the great values of this university throughout their life, not just on game day. "Pay it Forward" is more than a saying it's what Buckeyes do!!

Q: What is the craziest thing that happened on your watch??
A: The Wisconsin game during the Fickell Era was by far the craziest thing I have been a part of on the Block. Ohio State was an underdog going into this night game in the Shoe but pulled off the 33-29 win on the last Saturday in October.

After the game finished students began rushing the field from South Stands AA-Deck which is easy due to its direct proximity to the field. For those unfamiliar, Block O South is section 39-A of the stadium. The front of the section features a stage and a plexi-glass retaining wall. This stage is where our officers direct the section and lead cheers. Guests have also frequently visited and would speak from this area. Many students who have never been down in this area don't realize that jumping from the stage to the AA-Deck is a good 10 foot drop or more. When students began rushing the field after the Wisconsin win, I was on the stage. I attempted to direct students down the staircases. We are responsible for their safety, and ours. However 32,000 students against me did not turn out to be a positive experience.

Students continued to push forward down the block, pinning me against the plexi-glass barrier. Upon reaching the front and realizing they couldn't jump (I had been yelling this the entire time) they would pivot off of me and shove their way to the stairs where our section Ushers were pinned against the top of the stair-well. Needless to say I did not rush the field that night. However I was able to take pictures of myself and fellow Usher friends in the empty section with the flooded field behind us. These pictures are still some of my favorite pictures from my game days as a student. The next morning I woke up severely bruised and in pain, but wouldn't have traded the win or photos for the world.

Q: Talk to me about your Block O Experience...

A: My Block O experience began at Buckeye Kickoff 2011. As a transfer student into Ohio State after graduating from Columbus State I was looking for ways to get involved. As a sports major I automatically gravitated toward Block O. My first day with the officers I was the only general student who came and volunteered to help set up for the event.

Being the new guy, I ended up doing all of the heavy lifting which included bringing a large stage from the Huntington Club Ballroom down the elevator in pieces and reassembling in on the A-Deck concourse underneath the stands. While officers looked on I attempted to prove my dedication this group, however at this point I was exhausted and wasn't sure if it was really worth my time.

As the event kicked off I was able to spend time with the officers rather than as a general attendant — a reward for my earlier work. Helping backstage at the event I was able to meet Ohio State personalities such as Dr. Gee and TBDBITL Director Dr. Waters.

The conclusion of this event confirmed my developing love for Block O and helped me find a home here on campus. As the band played the chimes of Carmen Ohio, I stood with the officers of this great organization after only knowing them for a few hours and sang Carmen Ohio along with the student body. I will never forget that moment. I was a member of Buckeye Nation, a student at Ohio State and a member of the great Block "O." I would go on that year to win both the "Blockie of the Year" (most dedicated member) and the "Clancy Isaac Award" (leadership, spirit and dedication to the Block).

Q: What does Block O mean to you?

A: Block O has been the center of my world for the last four years culminating in a 13- page term paper on its history. My passion for the Block and its principles runs deep and I work daily to uphold them. As an alumnus I am still actively involved in the Block and its operations.

Block O means being a part of something so much bigger than you. Where else in the world can you unite to celebrate people, tradition and excellence with roughly 100,000 of your best friends? I've made my college memories on the Block, met my lifelong friends on the Block. The Block will always be a major part of my life.

Q: How is your rapport with the Ushers?

A: Over time I have made friends with several of the Ushers in and around Block O. I am proud to call each my friend and work alongside them. Many people don't know this, but our Ushers are considered members of Block O and we recognize them every year with Block O Usher pins that they wear on their jackets.

The Ushers are very accommodating of our needs and allow us to run our own section. I am always able to escort the painted kids down into the AA-Deck in order to obtain pictures near the field for our historian. In addition the Ushers always support our "Block O Bouncers" and their decisions on removal of students from the section. When individuals misbehave the Ushers are always there to lend a hand.

WHAT ARE THEY THINKING?

No matter the weather, they always show up. The five or six mostly young, energetic and possibly well lubricated arrive with

brightly colored scarlet and gray-painted bare-bellies. The number is determined by what they want to spell — Go Bucks! — Which requires seven or eight depending on if someone wants to be the exclamation point. BUCKEYES! Requires nine bodies. It would be boring to have a stadium full of people who were just passively watching the game so these young folks strip down to their shorts (lately females are not excluded, they wear a small top) and paint themselves from head to toe.

When asked what type of paint they use a fan responds, "Tempera paint is best. Be sure to use the non-toxic water-based product. Paint will flow easily without chipping and it's washable. It makes for easier clean-up after the game." To apply she says take your time. "Don't get it around your mouth or eyes."

I remember the Michigan game in 2012 was the coldest weather of the season. I had on six layers of clothing, long underwear and the thickest down jacket I could fit under my Usher's jacket. I would look down and see these nine scantily clad bodies going nuts and cheering their heads off. I thought to myself they have to be a little crazy but hey, it's still all in good fun.

CROWD SURFING

Brutus often visits our section to "Brutus Crowd Surf." Students pass Brutus up the section and place him on the B-Deck concourse. This is a tradition that occurs every game day. Many don't know this but the pushups Brutus performs at each game (one for every point the Buckeyes score) was originally a Block O tradition. The Block still keeps the "official" count during this fun tradition. We occasionally make Brutus do extra work as we count 1-1-1-1 for each pushup.

Both the cheerleaders and the dance team frequent our section. The dance squad often stands directly in the front of the

section on kickoff. Some of my favorite memories from cheer and dance interactions include alumni visits. Each year around homecoming when Ohio State hosts "Alumni Cheer Day" various cheerleaders come to Block O during television timeouts and teach us the popular Block O cheers of their respective decades. I love immersing myself in this living history of the Block!

The Band sits in AA-Deck directly in front of our section and frequently turn and play directly to our section. Individual rows have been known to come into the aisles surrounding the Block and give us our own private concert.

Even if I didn't go to The Ohio State University I'd still be an OSU fan. It's OSU football, then golf, then women. And God. God is up there too.

—Unknown OSU Fan

THE WESTERNERS

Carl Yarmark has been an Usher for 39 years at 26-C:

It was the first game of the season in 1997 and we knew we had some "first timers" in the stadium. First timers usually arrive early and take lots of pictures of everything — including the Ushers.

Dressed in ten-gallon-hats and western garb we figured they were not from central Ohio. Since the Buckeyes were playing Wyoming for their home opener we deduced they probably followed the "cowboys." In visiting with the newbies we learned they have traveled from Phoenix and were supporters of the Buckeyes. Questioning what had brought them all this way since we did not play Arizona until later in the season, they indicated that they were relatives of one of the Buckeye players and had the same last name, Germaine. (Joe Germaine was MVP of the 1997 Rose Bowl win over Arizona State.)

They returned for several other games that season having seats in various areas of the Shoe always stopping by to say hi to the crew of 26-C.

MEMORABLE MOMENTS

Dean P., a fan, Stamford, Connecticut:

Let me first say that there have been many great moments in Ohio Stadium I have had the privilege of experiencing — from being in school when Archie played to watching the band roll out Script Ohio every time I get back to the stadium. However, without question my most memorable moment came on my birthday in 1977. It was my last fall as a full-time student and I had a great

---

seat in A-Deck somewhere close to the 40-yard line. OSU was playing Oklahoma. Woody vs. Barry (Switzer) and the Buckeyes staged one of the most hard-fought mash-mouth comebacks I have ever seen only to lose in the final seconds by two points after an Oklahoma field goal.

Needless to say the crowd was stunned but that wasn't what made the moment. What did was that almost to a person, everyone in that stadium knew they had just witnessed one of the greatest football games ever played. No one left the stadium for at least 10 minutes after the game. There was actually applause not cheering or frustrated screaming but applause from a truly impressed and appreciative crowd.

This game is still shown on ESPN Classic from time to time and if you have never watched it you should. Despite OSU's loss it was one for the ages and a moment I will never forget.

At the base of it was the urge. If you wanted to play football, to knock someone down, that was what the sport was all about: the will to win closely linked with contact.

—George Plimpton

MATURE FANS

Older folks need to make sure they find their seats before the crowds arrive. Sometimes they find themselves in the upper levels of seating and it can be a chore to navigate them to their seats. Often, if a bathroom break is required, down they will go.

Wheelchairs, walkers and seat backs are forbidden in the regular seating. Disabled seating is available at various locations throughout the stadium for those who request it ahead of time —

the portal chief is responsible for those who don't.

As one old fellow was struggling to climb the stairs to the 31st row I asked if he would be more comfortable in the wheel-chair section. With tears in his eyes he swallowed his pride and accepted my offer. I walked down to guest services with this his son and exchanged the tickets, then called on my radio to request the wheelchair service to escort our guest to his new seats by the band. After they were settled into their seats I paid them a visit to see if everything was copacetic. They could not thank me enough.

All in a day's work for a portal chief!

DANCE THE NIGHT AWAY

My name is Elizabeth Vincent (aka Liz to those who know me). I was born in Columbus, raised in Cambridge, OH until I was 16 when my Mom moved us back to Grandview where I graduated from high school. We didn't have a lot of money so I didn't go to college until later,(but not OSU)and never made it to a degree. I have two boys that are now in their 40s and I am very proud of the way they turned out. I enjoy singing in a German singing group, like watching NASCAR and most of all getting into the games at OSU and working with a great group of co-workers.

I started as an Usher in 1982 in the disabled section 22A Field Seats on the track as it was known then. During my early days I had the opportunity to meet several celebrities, namely Jimmy Crum, who worked at Channel 4 announcing sports and Greg Lashutka, the color announcer who later became the Mayor of Columbus. Greg's father, step-mother, and his father's nurse sat in the disabled section, so I got to know them as well. I even got to dance with Mayor Lashutka at Oktoberfest one year!

WATCH WHERE YOU STEP

I was almost run over by several football players because the only place for us to sit was on the track, but it was worth it because of the wonderful people I had the opportunity to meet. I got to work closely with the disabled people who sat in our section. They were very special to me and they were always so nice.

When they moved us to "South Stands" as it was known, (before it became south stadium) I became an assistant portal chief, later I was promoted to Supervisor, giving me the opportunity to work the sidelines for the OSU team. I was fortunate to meet several former players, including Rex Kern and his wife, Archie Griffin and Eddie George. I love my jobs in the past and look forward to my jobs in the future. I became an Usher so I could get into the games for free, but my overall experience, working with and helping people has been a dream come true! I only hope I live a long life so I can continue to grow in friendships that I have formed over the years and experiences that came my way. As always, GO BUCKS!

COMRADES IN ARMS

Our wonderful Ushers (and one cute cop) at 2012 Akron game. They couldn't believe it when I told them I would send this! Photo by fan, Jill Carsonie.

ALL TIME BASKETBALL GREAT

Another benefit of being an Usher is having an opportunity to see different celebrities at the stadium. Before the 2013 Wisconsin game, LeBron James, donning a black short-sleeve shirt, a black cap and jeans, led the team down the steps outside the Blackwell Hotel to the arena for the team's traditional Skull Session pep rally. Head coach Urban Meyer introduced James, who was greeted with mostly cheers, but a few noticeable boos. "He's one of, arguably, the greatest champions, greatest competitors and most importantly, a Buckeye," Meyer said as he presented James to the crowd.

"I promise, I say this all the time—if I had one year of college, I would have ended up here," James said. "No matter where I go in the world, no matter where it is, I will always rock Ohio State colors."

LeBron James, next to OSU offensive lineman Andrew Norwell, high-fived fans as he walked through the crowd on the way to the pregame Skull Session on Saturday before the Wisconsin game. Doug Lesmerises

That's the message the four-time NBA Most Valuable Player delivered to a frenzied St. John Arena that was filled to capacity with the Buckeyes faithful and the Ohio State Marching Band about two hours prior to the 8 p.m. ET kickoff against Wisconsin.

Meyer praised James—who reached out to the university for the opportunity—

> *"I love athletes that handle their business," said Meyer, who added that he met James when he was a student at St. Vincent-St. Mary High School. "To have him come and be gracious with our team, visit our team; speak to our team ... He loves Ohio State. And he's made that clear several times to me throughout the year."*

Usher on the field received an up-front view of LeBron, the nine-time NBA All-Star, playing catch with his son on the field before the Buckeyes emerged from the locker room to warm up. An Usher commented, "He has a great arm and with his height would have made a great quarterback for the Bucks!"

LeBron James throwing the football to his son before Wisconsin game 2013

THE SHOE

If you can believe it, the mind can achieve it.
—Ronnie Lott

The last 16 years I have had the distinct privilege of "going to work" in one of the most recognizable structures in the world! Ohio Stadium, nestled snugly on the banks of the Olentangy River, is the home of the Ohio State Buckeye football team and our workplace. The stadium was added to the National Register of Historic Places by the National Park Service on March 22, 1974.

With a capacity of 106,708, it is the fourth largest football stadium in the United States and the seventh largest non-racing stadium in the world. The interesting fact about the capacity of this marvelous stadium is there are only 102,429 actual seats for the fans or the paying public. The other 4,279 include everyone who walks through the gates: Ushers, vendors, security, press, and referees— even the teams and coaches.

IF YOU BUILD IT THEY WILL COME

Gary Stoll, Sr. ran track at Central High School. His brother was a center on the football team, blocking for Hop Cassidy! Gary was in the Navy during the Korean conflict and spent time in Cuba. He has been an Usher since 2000 in section 17-D:

Being an Usher in this fabulous stadium has special meaning

to me and my family. My grandfather, Pearle Trimmer, born in the 1890s, was a carpenter. He helped make the forms for the cement blocks of the OSU stadium in 1921-1922. I can remember his stories of this tremendous arena that they were building on the banks of the Olentangy River.

Built in 1922 at a cost of $1.3 million and refurbished in 2001 for slightly more than $194 million, the horseshoe-shaped stadium is a monument to college football. It is popularly known as "The Horseshoe" or "Shoe" because of its open south end, and is one of the most recognizable landmarks in all of college athletics. As part of the renovation, the once-portable South Stands became a permanent fixture, now known by all the Ushers who work there as South Stadium!

Since the opening game against Ohio Wesleyan on October 7, 1922 more than 37 million fans have streamed through the stadium's portals. The fun and exciting part of gathering information for this book was talking to and answering questions from or about some of the more colorful of these fans. From 1951 to 1973, the Buckeyes led the nation in attendance 21 times, including the 14 consecutive years from 1958 to 1971. Since 1949, Ohio State has never been lower than fourth nationally in average home *game attendance.*

Unique in its double-deck horseshoe design, Ohio Stadium is both intimate and intimidating. The closeness of the seating provides a definite home-field advantage for the Buckeyes, allowing fans to view the game from unobstructed vantage points. As part of the renovation, there are now 81 hospitality suites and 2,625 club seats on the west side of the stadium. All the seats are good, including the 17,000 in the new, permanent South Stands.

ATHLETIC DIRECTOR'S HOSPITALITY SUITE

Prior to the construction of Ohio Stadium, the Buckeyes played their games at Ohio Field. The demand for a new stadium came about during the "Harley Years" (1916-1919) when Charles "Chic" Harley became the Buckeyes first three-time All-American.

With the echoes of Harley's legendary feats ringing throughout the state, local businessmen set about raising money for a new

stadium. They did so quickly, raising almost all of the $1.3 million through private donations, and construction began in 1920. Skeptics scoffed at the thought of a 66,000-seat venue, but they were quickly quieted when an overflow crowd of 71,138 showed up for the dedication game against Michigan on Oct. 21, 1922.

STANDING ROOM ONLY

Fans have asked Ushers why standing room only seats are not issued for big games like Michigan, Texas, and Wisconsin? I contacted OSU Archives and got the following answer: Although its essential character has been preserved, Ohio Stadium has undergone profound changes, adjusting to the changing needs of its fandom. An infamous Michigan game in 1926 led to the first of many modifications. In front of a standing-room-only crowd, leading 10-0 after one quarter, the Buckeyes failed to stop Michigan's passing game, looking, as the Makio later said, "Almost as helpless as London during a German Zeppelin raid."

Michigan led 17-10 with two minutes to play when Ohio State scored

Inside OSU Locker Room-Quote from Charles "Chic" Harley

on a 12-yard run — and missed the extra point. Michigan ran out the clock and 90,000 Ohio State fans rioted, storming the field, throwing glass bottles, breaking arms and legs. The university thereafter banned standing-room-only; the policy remained in place nearly 50 years.

Ohio Stadium's distinctive horseshoe shape has been the subject of ongoing dispute for as long as demand for seats has outpaced supply. Original subscribers to the Stadium Fund were given a 10-year option on two seats for $100, or on four seats for $1,000. This led to the perception of a permanent arrangement among the 13,000 original subscribers. H.D. Smith's design allowed for temporary bleachers and standing room that would bring maximum seating capacity up from 63,000 to 82,000. With the ban on standing-room, the temporary bleachers erected for big games, like Michigan, became semi-permanent, installed for the duration of football season.

Jumbotron

September 7th, San Diego State Aztecs - Bob Vargo, Usher B-8 greeted three of the cutest little Buckeye fans, all dressed in their Ohio State cheerleading outfits, to our section; escorted by their parents, they all went up to the last row of section B. The little cheerleaders were having a ball cheering for the Bucks, and even though they knew little about football they were having a blast. By the end of the third quarter the Bucks were blowing out the Aztecs, and on this hot day fans started leaving the stadium and Bob pointed out to me that there were five empty seats in the front row. I asked the parents if they would like to watch the rest of the game in those front row seats. I showed them to their new seats and the three little girls squealed in delight. They could actually see the scoreboard, Brutus and the Ohio State Cheerleaders. They left the stadium that day with memories of a lifetime.

The scoreboard the little girls viewed was the HD Panasonic Jumbotron, added in 2012, which sits atop the south end zone, replacing the 30' by 90' scoreboard that had been in use for the previous 11 seasons. The televisions at concession stands have also been replaced with HD monitors.

Don Patko, Associate Athletic Director of Facilities Management, said the improvements were necessary and well worth the cost: "It was time for the video board to be replaced. The usual life for a scoreboard is 12 to 15 years, and the last one was 12 years old. Everybody that has an HDTV at home knows that it provides better clarity. The new board also allows you to have better viewing angles. The entire industry is moving toward HD, and we feel that we have one of the best systems out there."

REPLAY THAT

The year 2013 marked the 30th anniversary of the Ohio State Scoreboard Animation staff. In that time there have been 130 students who have created a few thousand animations for the university. Many of these students have landed their dream jobs as a result of being part of this unique and talented group.

The OSU Scoreboard Animation staff hires new students yearly. The crew in charge of Ohio Stadium's scoreboard isn't on the sidelines on football Saturdays. They are across the street in a darkened room in the basement of the Schottenstein Center, surrounded by computer monitors and control buttons connected to the Shoe via underground fiber-optic cables. This remote room in the Schott serves as the command center of the scoreboard operation.

More than five hours before a home game, the production staff and camera operators arrive to set up equipment and review a "script" for the game. By the time the stadium gates open to the public, four student videographers and four assistants have made their way there, leaving seven co-workers to monitor video screens. The control room crew takes the scoreboard live with player-introduction videos and footage of team warm-ups.

"Once the game starts, we're pretty involved," said Brown. "Everybody's got a job to do. We have to pay attention when most people (watching at home) are going to the fridge. It's really strange; I haven't been inside the stadium during a game since 1999!" Besides delivering game video and graphics to the scoreboard, the crew supplies material during band performances, timeouts, announcements and recognitions — all of which might be more chaotic than the play itself.

"If something goes wrong, it can get pretty tense," said full-time intern Craig Velliquette. "You go have a beer afterward." Among his co-workers

Craig Brown, Manager, Animation and Scoreboard Staff,
works under low light in the basement of the Schottenstein Center, where the Ohio Stadium scoreboard is controlled.

are seven full-time employees and about 30 students, including sports fans
with limited video production backgrounds and technology experts with
little interest in football.

"Rare is the university that allows students to produce scoreboard fod-
der," said Craig Brown, noting that many schools outsource the job to
professionals. The upside, though, is the teaching tool that the work represents. "It's not going to be perfectly polished every time, but they (the
students) are getting something out of it," Brown said. "They can have
absolutely no experience and by the time they leave, some are experts."

The six or so people who make up the athletic department's video
services crew will watch the game through video cameras on the field, directing the cameramen and cuing up the appropriate computer animations
from across Lane Avenue. Video services intern Ken Hathaway calls it a
"fun dance," and it's something the crew has been doing for a while but
few people know about.

Most of the video services staff are passionate Ohio State fans, including plenty of students who are interested in getting video and editing experience. It's a strange way to experience the game, Hathaway said, but he wouldn't have it any other way.

"You know you watched the whole game, but you sometimes don't feel like you watched the whole game. We only see what our cameras give us, so a lot of times, we're like, 'What's going on? What's the crowd saying?'" said Hathaway, who started with the crew in 2006 as a student and has since graduated. "It's quiet, for the most part, because you have to be able to hear if the directors are calling for something."

The program is centered on students learning. "When students first come in, typically they're a little awestruck because there are 100,000 people, and you're on the field at a place where you've always wanted to be," Hathaway said. "We have to say, 'All right, don't forget where you're at and don't forget your work, stay focused,' that kind of thing."

Students usually begin with "running the grip," or pulling the cables behind one of the four student cameramen on the field. As the season continues they learn by example. More advanced members of the crew usually end up working the buttons and levers back at the Schottenstein Center.

"Everybody wants to do the camera, because the camera's the kind of glory thing," Hathaway said. And students who are interested in directing can often move up to being a cameraman. But running the camera is a little more difficult than just pointing it in the right direction.

"You don't want to push the wrong buttons, do the wrong thing and have it broadcast in front of 100,000 people," Hathaway said.

Although they can't hear the roar of the crowd from the basement of the Schott, the staff hears about it later, usually from school officials after the game and sometimes just by panning the cameras over the audience.

Tense plays, it seems, are even tenser when you're in charge of the replay. Most fans assume that the replays they see on the scoreboard originate from the production crews of ABC, ESPN or whatever TV station is broadcasting the game, and wonder why certain controversial calls are not viewed on the scoreboard. According to Matt Fox, Video Services, "Almost all the replays, 99%, are filmed by the three student cameramen and, with a delay of less than one-tenth of a second, are viewed on the scoreboard. Rarely do they show a broadcast replay on the scoreboard.".

Before any scoreboard replay draws oohs or boos inside the stadium, the game footage that provides the pictures will take a brief detour. According to Fox, a small production crew will quickly view film from three cameras shooting the action on the football field and one "fan camera," decide which to share, then, via fiber-optic cables, send the choice back to the crowd in the Shoe. That is why we sometimes don't show that controversial call that viewers see on national broadcasts. The officials in the press box do not have access to our replays, so we don't want to run the risk of showing up the referee's official call.

SNAFUS INSIDE THE STADIUM

Most of the time things run smoothly during production, but when something does go wrong 100,000 people notice. For instance, "During the Illinois game all the stadium scoreboards, and even the backups, went dark from the band entrance until the coin toss. Sweat started to trickle down the forehead, but we did not panic and with the issue resolved, we were back in action!" Craig Brown recalled.

Downtime is scarce for crew members stationed in the Shoe. Lugging a 40-pound camera between the sidelines and the stands can be quite stressful. One young student cameraman did not eat

anything one morning and passed out while filming the action. A nearby Usher quickly summoned first aid and soon she was back in action after consuming a granola bar and a bottle of water!

Craig shared an insider prank with the graphics crew back when the old scoreboard was in place. When the new scoreboard was activated for the first game of the season, the "spotters" in the press box were horrified when the brand new screen lit up with black spots, and cracks. Before further panic ensued, Craig removed the "fake broken screen graphic" from the scoreboard while the crew back at the Schott "laughed our rear ends off."

VIEW FROM THE PRESS BOX

Working from the press box, three students maintain the small scoreboard at the north end of the stadium and the scrolling boards on the east and west sides, flashing announcements or keeping visual pace with the crowd as it cheers "O-H! I-O!"

A full-time video-services employee and two university officials oversee their work, simultaneously talking with 10 to 15 people via headsets (the Schott staff, the public-address announcer and the sound technicians, among others) to facilitate cooperation.

The press box crew can look out at the big board through an open, floor-to-ceiling glass window that almost merges with the crowd. "This is a thrill for me," said Tyler Conley, a sports-management major working on the smaller scoreboards. "I grew up a Buckeye fan, and now I'm up here behind the scenes." The post might make the Schott crew members a little envious—some have worked every football game for years, never once seeing the action in the stadium. The way Conley figures it, though; he could still be working in maintenance at the Schott, a job he held before joining the board crew.

"Now I get paid to do something I enjoy."

Rock the Stadium

A recent question brought up by the Ushers and the fans is "Why is the music so loud?"

When Coach Urban Meyer and the team enter into the stadium the scoreboard immediately blasts out favorite tunes as the players walk across the field. It is an adrenalin boost! But it is ear-splitting for the hundreds of Ushers scattered throughout the stadium. A few of the Ushers have apps on their smart phones that record the decibel levels of the music and reported complaints to command in the press box. Perhaps the feedback helped, the sound was adjusted as the season progressed. This is the official lowdown from the Meyer Sound website, on the fantastic sound system:

> *The Ohio State Buckeyes football team finished an incredible undefeated regular season with a boost from its new Meyer Sound LEO linear large-scale sound reinforcement system. In this first permanent LEO installation in the world, the sound system filled the vast 105,000-seat Ohio Stadium with crisp voice announcements and fan-pumping music over the loud, energetic crowd for all eight home games.*
>
> *"The LEO system sounds great, covers very well and gets loud," says Wayne Stephens, electronics superintendent for Ohio State Athletics. "With an excited crowd of over 105,000, the noise here gets pretty intense. But with LEO we can stay well above them without pushing the system."*

Finally during the Usher supervisor's meeting before the Penn State night game in 2013, Mike Penner, Associate Athletic Director of Event Management, spilled the beans about the level of noise in the stadium. "The coaches and team wants Ohio Stadium to be an intimidating place to play for our competitors and consequently very loud on the field. Well, the stadium's sound system is directed toward the fans in the seats for maximum effect, not down on the field. Therefore, the coaches are screaming for it to be loud on the field, while the fans in the stands are submitted to ear-splitting noise. The answer was to install additional speakers on the field to direct the sound and allow the stadium sound to be lowered." Now you know!

FACE LIFT FOR THE SHOE

In 1999, the stadium underwent a 3-year facelift that was completed in time for the season opener against Akron in 2001. An advantage of becoming an Usher is the opportunity of touring all the fantastic venues of the stadium. The Varsity O Club at the northwest corner is remarkable. The Joan Zeig Steinbrenner Band Center is amazing. The Recruit Room is impressive. The Huntington Club suites are gorgeous. Except for the walkway outside the Huntington suites where the stadium's original arched concrete wall forms a nice backdrop for all of that partying, the only interior reminders of why this place is special are the murals and photos that adorn the walls.

As a result of that renovation, the stadium is completely up to code in terms of disability seating. Additionally, aisles have been widened, rails have been added and lighting has been installed in the concourses. There are also many more restrooms and concession stands on all levels which is great for the Ushers because that is the #1 question asked by the fans!

New stadium lighting has been installed for the 2014 season, previous to that temporary lighting had to be installed for every night game.

PROHIBITED BEHAVIOR

How often do you have to throw someone out of the stadium? This is a question the Ushers hear often from fans. The question was answered by James Ericson, Assistant Director, Event Management, Ohio State Athletics.

Not very often. We give the fans a lot of leeway before they are escorted out of the stadium. Usually, the determining factor is fan safety. I can recall one instance where a fan was inebriated and out of control. He started pulling off the seat back chairs and flinging them into the stands. Police officers and stadium officials removed this individual from the stadium. But for the most part our fans are there to have a good time and enjoy a terrific football game.

The official stand of prohibited behavior includes, but is not limited to: throwing objects of any kind; demonstrating unruly behavior; attempting to enter the field of play; engaging in behavior that endangers the safety of student athletes, coaches, officials or other guests; attempting to climb the goal posts; removing Ohio Stadium turf; and/or taunting event staff, visiting teams and/or public safety officials.

Consequences for guests exhibiting prohibited behavior may include, but are not limited to: loss of ticket buying privileges, ejection from the stadium, and/or arrest. The University reserves the right to enforce, within the sole discretion of the University, prohibited behaviors based on the interests of public safety, operational or staffing considerations or any other consideration.

James finished by saying, "Don't say you were not warned! Have a great time and, Go Bucks!"

SEATBACK CHAIRS

Speaking of seatback chairs, Ushers get a lot of questions and a lot of

grief about them. They are available to be rented in advance of game day on a season basis only. Seat cushions are allowed to be brought into the stadium, only by guests demonstrating specific medical needs for personal seatback chairs; they may enter the stadium with a doctor's note at Gates 13, 16, 23 and 26 only.

GREAT TRADITIONS

Ohio Stadium is listed in the National Registry of Historic Places. Anyone who has seen a game in the giant horseshoe understands why. There are few athletic experiences that are more enjoyable!

Ohio State heads into the 2014 season with a string of 83 consecutive crowds of 100,000 or larger in Ohio Stadium. A stadium this rich in history has plenty of long-standing traditions.

After the 2013 victory over Indiana, I had the opportunity to take the winding staircase up to the Bell Tower to witness the ringing of the Victory Bell by the members of Alpha Phi Omega, a tradition that began after the

Bucks beat California October 2, 1954. Reputedly the ringing can be heard five miles away "on a calm day."

Located 150 feet high in the southeast tower of Ohio Stadium, the bell was a gift of the classes of 1943, 1944 and 1945, and weighs 2,420 pounds. The bell is rung for 15 minutes following a victory and for 30 minutes following a victory over Michigan.

A DORM—WHERE?

One of the B-Deck west Ushers who wishes to stay anonymous tells about his days as a graduate student back in 2007:

I was living in the lap of poverty back in those days, but I dearly loved to watch at least one OSU game a year in person. I was bound and determined to attend the Purdue game on October 14th, my birthday weekend. Purdue was rated as #2 in the nation and the tickets were too expensive for my blood. I don't remember the exact details, but the night started with draft beer at the Varsity Club. My buddies took me out for a few beers and introduced me to a guy who lived in the stadium. I could not believe he lived in the stadium. How lucky can you get?

I explained my plight. I really needed to see the Buckeye game the next day! So I spent the night sleeping on the floor in the Scholarship dorms. I woke up the next day with a splitting headache from overindulging, but knowing that I was actually inside of the stadium during game day. Through a series of twists and turns I entered the stands, excited that I soon would be seeing the Buckeyes playing the Boilermakers. I am forever grateful to the fellow who risked being kicked out of the dorm for helping me see my beloved Buckeyes.

Maybe it would ease his mind to know that after gradsizable donation to the scholarship fund.

HOME SWEET HOME IN THE SHOE

In 1975, the program and the stadium dormitory were expanded several times. The university completed a multi-million dollar renovation in the mid-1980s resulting in a residence hall that housed approximately 360 students. The Shoe housed only men until 1975, when the program expanded and the majority of residents voted to add women. Some opposed the idea, wanting to preserve the all-boys club and its antics. Students in the all-male era hosted an annual *Playboy* party in the press box, recruiting women from other dorms to dress as bunnies. Later, the event became the more politically correct Escapade, a semi-formal dance still conducted there.

Some students used to joke that the stadium dorm was a fraternity and sorority for those who couldn't afford to join one. The stadium provided plenty of party opportunities, especially when 18-year-olds could buy kegs of "3.2 beer."

STADIUM SCHOLARSHIP ALUMNI SOCIETY

The "Stadiumites" built such lasting friendships that the 70-member Stadium Scholarship Alumni Society, thought to be the only OSU alumni group centered on a dorm, began meetings in the 1960s and continues them today. As students, we lived in Ohio Stadium, on the west side, south of the band room. We were not athletes. We completed 8 to 10 hours of work in exchange for a discount on our room and board. The work included cafeteria duty, cleaning the dorm, and helping out in the library and music room housed in the dorm.

FAVORITE OHIO STATE MEMORIES

Sunbathing on C-Deck and coming down to breakfast—especially on the weekends—in my robe and slippers. **Barbara K.**, 1979, 1990 JD

Playing flag football in Ohio Stadium under the lights. **Rita, 1984**

It was pretty amazing to sit up on the towers and to ring the victory bell. **Kristy**, 1982, 1984 MA

I can say that I scored a touchdown in Ohio Stadium, it was just at 1:30 in the morning. **Tom H.**, Arlington, Va., 1962-1966

10

THE GAME

OHIO STADIUM
NOV. 13, 1926
Univ. of Michigan VS. Ohio State —
PAID ATTENDANCE - 90,411

All the Ushers get very excited, every second year, for the Michigan-Ohio State football rivalry. Known as The Game by fans, it is a game played annually between the Wolverines and the Buckeyes. It has attracted national interest over the last four decades as most of the games have determined the Big Ten conference title and the resulting Rose Bowl match-ups, and many have influenced the outcome of the national college football championship.

In 2000 The Game was ranked by ESPN as the greatest North American sports rivalry. The annual match-up between the two Midwest state schools has been held at the end of the regular season since 1935 (with exceptions in 1942, 1986, and 1998). Since 1918, the site has alternated between Columbus and Ann Arbor; Michigan hosts it in odd years and Ohio State in even ones. It has been played in Ohio Stadium since 1922 and Michigan Stadium since 1927. Through 2010, the Ohio State and Michigan game determined the Big Ten championship on 22 different occasions and the conference title 27 times.

All of us have different feelings and traditions for The Game. Here are some of those perspectives: Build up for the game starts early in the week!

LOOK OUT BELOW

Max Mason Miller, OSU, 2010.

The first time I heard the tradition of jumping into Mirror Lake to help the Buckeyes take down that school up north I was skeptical. November and swimming just don't go together in the Buckeye state. But as an 18-year-old college freshman I was easily convinced when my friends informed me we would need to drink plenty of booze to get our bodies prepared for the shock of the plunge. Combine that with some scantily clad college coeds and a future member of the Mirror Lake Swim Team was born.

I lived in Morrison Tower, just a short freezing sprint away from Mirror Lake, so my place became the pre-game headquarters for a couple of my buddies. Doing our best to prepare for the jump, we loaded up on cheap booze. Once the flip-flops were duct-taped on and the clothing was ready to get soaked or ruined we were ready for action.

The best part about the Mirror Lake jump is actually the approach. As soon as we left the dorm and headed down Neil Avenue you could hear the buzz of the crowd. I realized then that you're a part of something that only a select group of the population can appreciate and even fewer that would participate in. I also realized then I was slightly crazy for what I was about to do, but that was secondary.

Random high-fives aren't optional. Chants of "We Don't Give a Damn for the Whole State of Michigan" are necessary. We

The Mirror Lake jump at Ohio State is a 20+ year tradition in which students jump into the lake during the week leading up to the Michigan game.

laughed and yelled and made our way through the crowd until we could make out the edge of Mirror Lake. The area around the lake was packed with a sea of people. Some were coming, some were going. Other smart people just came down to watch the madness.

We were all there for one reason though. We would do whatever it takes to ensure we beat that team up north. If that meant jumping in a lake in November, so be it. Like the ESPN ad says, it's only weird if it doesn't work. We screamed some vulgarities at Michigan, took a deep breath, and made the leap.

LONG DRIVE CONTEST

Dave Mumma, South Stadium portal chief, had been an Usher since the mid-1980s:

When my job transferred me to Georgia I thought my Ushering days were over. I left in February and most of my Usher buddies bid me a fond farewell. But over the summer I got to thinking how much I was going to miss seeing the Bucks play in Ohio Stadium. I was already tired of hearing about the Georgia Bulldogs and Georgia Tech. I decided I still wanted to be an Usher and I began to drive the 600 miles for each home game.

People ask me why? I either tell them "if you have to ask, you are obviously not one of the Buckeye Nation" or "I do it for the big money!" (Ushers are volunteers and supervisors get paid about $50 per game.)

The Michigan game is special to me and I would drive twice as far to be at the game. I remember one game, before the stadium was renovated; my job was at the visiting locker room before the game. At halftime and after the game, we would take nylon ropes and run them from the field back to the locker room so the team could get on and off the field. Michigan hadn't yet come out of the locker room. I noticed an ABC cameraman standing there, and he started to walk back between the ropes toward the locker room.

I yelled to him, "You'd better not stand there."

He said, "No, no I'm fine. I've been doing this for many years."

I said, "Well, I'm just warning you. This Michigan game is different than other games."

He said, "OK, I'll be fine."

Wouldn't you know it — Michigan came charging out onto the field and just ran right over him. His television camera went airborne and he went down on the ground.

After the game, my family and friends asked, "Did you see the guy who was standing right there? He busted his camera. He was hobbling around the rest of the game. They gave him another camera."

The Michigan game is different!

ALMA MATER

I was blown away by the number of Ushers that have attended and or graduated from OSU. The traditions are extremely important to all of us, especially the alumni. Before the start of every home game the band plays Carmen Ohio and after the game the Coach leads the team in singing the alma mater. This is how it originated:

The inaugural meeting between Ohio State and Michigan at Ann Arbor in 1897 resulted in a lopsided victory for Michigan with the Wolverines posting a 34-0 win over the Buckeyes. The first game foretold a long Michigan winning streak, with Michigan winning or tying every match from 1897 to 1912, compiling a 12-0-2 record before the contest was postponed for several years.

The Ohio State Alma Mater "Carmen Ohio" was written on the train ride home to Columbus following the 1902 contest, which saw Ohio State losing to Michigan 86-0. The lyrics and melody (Spanish Chant) have remained largely unchanged since its conception.

CARMEN OHIO

Oh come let's sing Ohio's praise
And songs to Alma Mater raise
While our hearts rebounding thrill
With joy which death alone can still
Summer's heat or winter's cold
The seasons pass the years will roll
Time and change will surely (truly) show
How firm thy friendship ... OHIO!

A GAME OF INCHES

A 1950s fan's perspective, **Daniel C.**, Columbus:

In 1954, when I was 15, the undefeated Buckeyes hosted Michigan. The Wolverines received the kickoff and drove the length of the field for a touchdown — a grim start for the Buckeyes.

Later in the game, the Wolverines had driven to the 1-yard line for a first down. They had four downs to get one yard. Led by the great Jim Parker, the Ohio State defense held Michigan on the 1-foot line. Then, behind a great line and with a backfield of Howard Cassady, Bobby Watkins, Hubert Bobo and quarterback Dave Leggett, the Buckeyes drove 99 yards and 2 feet to score.

They went on to win the game and the National Championship.

SNOW BOWL

One of the more famous games in the rivalry is the 1950 contest, colloquially known as the Snow Bowl. Eighth-ranked Ohio State, coached by Wes Fesler, was scheduled to host the game on November 25 in Columbus amidst one of the worst blizzards on Ohio record.

The Buckeyes, who led the Big Ten, were granted the option to cancel the game against Michigan which would have, by default, given the Buckeyes the Big Ten title outright and won them a trip to Pasadena for the Rose Bowl. Ohio State refused, and the game was set to be played.

Amid howling snow and wind, in what was probably the most literal example of a "field position" game, the teams exchanged 45 punts, often on first down, in hopes that the other team would fumble the ball near or into their own end zone. Ohio State's Vic Janowicz, who would claim the Heisman Trophy that year, punted 21 times for 685 yards and also kicked a field goal in the first quarter for the Buckeyes' only points.

Michigan capitalized on two blocked punts, booting one out of the back of the end zone for a safety and recovering another one in the end zone for a touchdown just before halftime. Despite failing to gain a single first down or complete a single forward pass, Michigan gained a 9-3 victory, securing the Big Ten title and a Rose Bowl berth.

MOMENTS OF REFLECTION BY THE FANS!

Dr. Joseph R., Wichita, Kansas:

In the late 1930s, OSU had "high school day," when students got special privileges. My first game was a cold, wet day in 1939, I believe, and OSU was playing Northwestern, perfect football weather. There were a lot of empty seats then.

The most memorable game was the "blizzard bowl" in 1950, Buckeyes vs. Wolverines! Snow was coming down so thick, the field was hardly visible. They tried to cover the field with a tarp before game time but they couldn't get all of it removed.

The players slipped and slid helplessly. All they could do was try to kick field goals. All-American Vic Janowicz was the quarterback. The Wolverines blocked a punt and recovered in the end zone for the only touchdown, a tragic loss for OSU. It was so cold, my roommate and I left in the middle of the 3rd quarter. Cars were stranded all over the parking lot. Classes were canceled the next week.

Coach Wesley Fesler resigned after the game.

Heavy criticism of Fesler's play calling led to his resignation and the hiring of Woody Hayes as his successor.

SNOW BOWL MEMORIES

Albert Y., Hilliard:

In November 1950, some fraternity brothers and I had gone home to Steubenville for Thanksgiving and returned via the train to Union Station on North High Street. The trip, usually three hours long, took six that morning. Then the buses on High Street couldn't negotiate the hill, so we had to walk to campus.

The guys at our house, Alpha Phi Delta, had lunch; then we headed out for the game. By that time, the snow was knee-deep. The game was delayed, and students were called out to help clean the field so that markers could be seen.

I don't remember much about the game. I left, freezing, at halftime.

Richard M. Wittig, Berea:

I was an occupational-therapy student in 1950. My folks had come from Milwaukee to visit my wife and me and their newborn grandson. I took my kid brother to the game. We sat in the stands wrapped in an Army surplus comforter. We had good seats, about the center of the field, but couldn't see the scoreboard at the end of the field through the heavy snow.

The game was a tough one to lose.

With no classes the next day, some students hung a huge pa-per-mâché figure of a Michigan player (left from homecoming) on the stoplight at the High Street entrance to the campus and were throwing snowballs at it. The police arrived, only to have the air in their car tires released.

My parents decided to head home even though the state po-lice told them they wouldn't be able to get out of the county. Four hours later we received a call from my folks. They had arrived in Springfield, Ohio, and were lucky to get what might have been the last available hotel room for the night.

John K., Lakeland, Florida:

I played in the marching band for five years.

The most memorable game was in 1950, when due to the snow we didn't do the ramp entrance, did do the halftime show — and then immediately went home.

URBAN LEGEND

Lou Spiezio has been an Usher since 1989:

This will be my 24th season as an Usher. I currently work on the wheelchair crew (east). I'm originally from Youngstown, Ohio; I moved to Columbus in 1976. I now reside in Lewis Center. I am an avid Muskie fisherman and have won a couple of State tournaments. I own a small machining, welding and fabrication business, Lewis Center Manufacturing.

I have been to every Big Ten stadium for Buckeye games at least once and most major bowl games; including the fateful Gator bowl which resulted in Woody's demise.

I can tell you from experience that we at Ohio Stadium have by far the best Usher crew. Ushers are nearly non-existent at many

of the other venues and difficult to find.

I was at the Ohio State Michigan game several years ago, the stadium was full and rockin', but I no-

ticed an empty seat in my section. I couldn't understand how this was possible so I went up to the guy sitting next to the empty seat and asked him if he knew why there would be an empty seat for such a big game. He replied that it had been his wife's seat but she had passed away. I offered my condolences and asked why he didn't offer the ticket to a friend or a relative. "I did" he replied, "but they all went to the funeral." Go Bucks!

John Campbell has been responsible for sideline communications for 36 years—his responsibilities include making sure the coaches' headphones and players' phones are working properly both on the field and in the pressbox.

I am also there to assist the visiting team communications. The crew includes three in pressbox and three on each sideline. In the old times we had to have more people to untangle the cords, but now all the phones are wireless.

This is my Michigan story: The Buckeye's coach's booth in the pressbox and the visiting team's booths are side by side. When Bo Schembechler retired from coaching he would attend the games and sit in the visiting team's pressbox. Bo was a very excitable guy, so whenever the Wolverines would make a great play he would bang on the walls and yell, "Hey guys, what the (expletive) do you think of that play?" and then laugh like crazy. The Buckeye coaches got tired of hearing Bo, so when our guys make a great play, the banging, hollering and laughter came from our side!

My most stressful time came during the Purdue game in 2001, Coach Tressel's first year. I had to be at stadium 4 hours before kickoff and found that the communications systems were not working from the field to the pressbox. Our team finally discovered that a squirrel had eaten through the copper telephone cables, they loved to munch on the cables. The sideline headphones would not work and Coach Dantonio (1st year defensive coordinator) was calling me every 15 minutes to find out if the headsets were work-

ing. I was really starting to sweat 40 minutes before kick-off, when my stellar crew finally fixed the problem!

Most of the communications guys throughout the country know each other, because we all work together, but the Purdue guys accused us of sabotage that day when their communications weren't working. When we got their system working, they apologized and everyone was happy.

One last story about Bo:

When Bo was coaching he was worried about us listening in to conversations to the press box and would contact the local telephone company to install his own phones.

I have to constantly monitor online to make sure the phones are working properly; I hear some heated conversations and sometimes some salty language. But we are constantly vigilant to maintain confidentiality and security for both sides. Problems usually occurred and Coach Schembechler would end up using our phones anyway.

THE TEN-YEAR WAR:
HAYES VS. BO SCHEMBECHLER (1969–1978)

Wolverines coach Bump Elliot resigned after the 1968 loss and Michigan hired Miami(Ohio) head coach Bo Schembechler, who had previously been an assistant at Ohio State under Hayes, to revitalize its football program. On November 22, 1969, Hayes led his top-ranked Buckeyes into Michigan Stadium to face Schembechler's Wolverines in the first matchup between two coaches who would come to define the rivalry between the two programs.

The contest was the first in the famous "Ten-Year War" between Hayes and Schembechler, which pitted some of OSU's and UM's strongest teams against one another. Ohio State and Michigan were both ranked in the top five of the AP Poll four times between 1970 and 1975 before their matchup.

MOMENTS OF REFLECTION

Jeff E., Columbus:

1970 Michigan: The Buckeyes were driving and something happened that I don't believe happened before and hasn't happened since. We were ahead 13-9. Time out. The normal Block O to freshman South Stands OH-IO cheer was performed, usually three times, then a big cheer. However, this time Block O said OH- a 5th time, then a 6th, and a 7th. The entire stadium, 88,000 strong, were ALL shouting OH, IO.

As the teams walked back onto the field, I watched as several Michigan players looked up into the stands, bewildered by the noise and enthusiasm. It was then that they were beaten. Leo Hayden scored, and it was a sweet 20-9 victory.

The Wolverines entered every game during those years undefeated and won only once, a 10-7 victory in Ann Arbor on November 20, 1971. The Michigan graduating class of 1975 shared or won the Big Ten championship every season, yet went to the Rose Bowl only once, in 1972. They only lost or tied with Ohio State during the regular season in that period.

A MEMORABLE FIRST

Don S., Columbus:

I'll never forget the first time I walked into the Horseshoe, wide-eyed and scared to death that I'd be handcuffed and taken away, and then I'd miss the greatest college football rivalry in history.

It was 1972, and I had no game ticket. Back then, though, Ohio Stadium housed some student dormitories. This was before the renovation; luxury suites hadn't been invented. I was fortunate to have a good friend living in the stadium dorms. His room was about the size of a broom closet, but there was a big benefit: Once in the stadium dorms, you were in the stadium. After the Friday night "Beat Michigan" parade down High Street we raced back to the dorms to beat the deadline when the stadium gates were chained shut to lock out potential trespassers. On Saturday morning, we walked through the portal headed for our anonymous seats in the student section. My thoughts and my heart were racing: Blend in! Act cool! Don't make eye contact with the Ushers, the police or even band members!

The strategy worked. I had a great view of the game that day — a traditional hard-fought battle won 14-11 by the Buckeyes.

Woody coined the phrases "that state up north" and "that team up north," so he would not have to say the word "Michigan." He was famous for his intense hatred of all things Michigan and according to legend, once refused to get gas in an empty tank, saying: "No, GD-it! We do NOT pull in and fill up. And I'll tell you exactly why we don't. It's because I don't buy one "GD" drop of gas in the state of Michigan! We'll coast and PUSH this "GD" car to the Ohio line before I give this state a nickel of my money!"

FACTOIDS

During the Ten-Year War, Ohio State and Michigan shared the Big Ten title six times. Between 1976 and 1978, Michigan won the game each year and Ohio State failed to score a touchdown in each of those contests.

Woody Hayes' firing at the end of the 1978 season ended the "War."

The 1978 game was won by Michigan 14-3, giving Schembechler a record of 5-4-1 against Hayes. At the end of the Hayes tenure the series stood at 42-28-5.

THE WAR'S AFTERMATH

Earle Bruce took over for Hayes and led the Buckeyes to a 5-4 record against Schembechler's Wolverines between 1979 and 1987, perhaps the most balanced stretch of the rivalry, during which neither team won more than two consecutive games.

In 1987 Bruce was fired the week before the Michigan game due to a poor season record, but was allowed to coach anyway, and the inspired Buckeyes (each wearing a sweatband labeled "Earle") won an upset over the heavily favored Wolverines. After the game, Bo Schembechler told Bruce, "I always mind losing to Ohio State but I didn't mind so much today." After 1987, the series stood at 46–33–5 in favor of Michigan.

GOLDEN DAY

The 2002 game was a classic, Michigan was rated #12 and OSU #2. I was so confident that the Buckeyes would win; I stopped at the Longaberger Alumni Center before the game and signed up for the alumni tour for the National Championship. After getting to the stadium, early arrivals started entering our portal and two of the ushers were excitingly talking with a fan dressed in a Varsity O sweater. He was showing them his necklace-a pair of Golden Pants-signature of a win over Michigan. The following details this OSU tradition:

In 1934, Francis Schmidt came on as the head coach for Ohio

State. The team had lost nine of the previous 12 Michigan-OSU contests, and when a reporter asked Schmidt if Ohio State could beat Michigan that year, he replied, "Of course we can win, Michigan puts their pants on one leg at a time just like we do." The Buckeyes thereupon ran off four straight shutout victories against Michigan, outscoring the Wolverines 112-0 from 1934 to 1937.

Schmidt's quote spawned an OSU tradition — since 1934, every Ohio State player receives a gold pants pendant after a victory against Michigan.

GOLD PANTS CLUB

Before a crowd of 105,000 OSU beat Michigan 14-9. OSU was headed to the National Championship game against Miami!

ONE BIG HAPPY FAMILY

Eric M., Westerville:

After the game in 2002 my sister Karen and I jumped onto the field. My sister then jumped onto the back of No. 7 Chris Gamble.

He didn't seem to mind. When hints of pepper spray hit us, we became separated in the chaos. I wouldn't see her again for two or three hours.

I grabbed a piece of end zone turf and left the stadium alone. I waited patiently back at my car, not knowing where she was. Once reunited, she told me she had been cordoned off with the OSU football team and their families and the next thing she knew, she was herded under the seats and into the locker room.

She got some big hugs, lots of autographs and memories that will last a lifetime!

HIS LUCKY NUMBER

Robert S., Columbus:

Thirteen seniors led the Buckeyes to their 13th regular-season win in 2002, and I watched the final minutes from the front row of section 19AA. When play ended in glorious victory, fans all around began hopping over a fence onto the field. Our friendly Ushers were requesting not to do so! Unaware of the stairs nearby, I, too, jumped over. When I stood up after landing, my left ankle seemed unsteady and my white sock had turned red. Emergency technicians wrapped it, and a stretcher whisked me across the field to the 20, the 10, the 5, the end zone, past the flagpole and up the band ramp. The pitter-patter of stretcher-bearer shoes climbing up the ramp and their pleas to "Make a hole" were drowned out by the clatter and din of hobnail boots and wild, vocal fans descending. Missing the post-game Carmen Ohio hurt most of all.

Once outside the north entrance of Ohio Stadium, I enjoyed a leisurely ambulance ride to the Ohio State University Medical Center where the ankle was repaired with 13 stainless-steel screws, one for each game of the season.

Was it a lucky omen?

The Buckeyes next beat Miami to win the National Champion-ship, and in June my kids both graduated from Ohio State — on Friday the 13th.

James Laurinaitis attempts to tackle Brandon Minor.

TRESSEL VS. MICHIGAN

Coach	Win	Loss	Pct	GB	Home	Road	Streak
Tressel	9	1	.900		5-0	4-1	Won 7
Ohio State	9	1	.900	--	5-0	4-1	Won 7
Rodriguez	0	3	.000		0-1	0-2	Lost 3
Carr	1	6	.143		1-3	0-3	Lost 4
Michigan	1	9	.100	8.0	1-4	0-5	Lost 7

GAME OF THE CENTURY

MICHIGAN Wolverines	OHIO STATE BUCKEYES
(11–0)	(11–0)
39	**42**
Head Coach: Lloyd Carr	Head Coach: Jim Tressel

	1	2	3	4	Total
Michigan	7	7	10	15	39
Ohio State	7	21	7	7	42

One of the most exciting games that I have attended in my 17 years as an Usher occurred on November 18, 2006, Ohio State and Michigan met for their annual showdown, each carrying an 11-0 record. The day before the epic match up, legendary Michigan coach Bo Schembechler died. For the first time in the history of the rivalry, the two rivals faced off while holding the top two spots in the Bowl Championship Series rankings. Ohio State won the game by a score of 42–39 and became the outright Big Ten champion, earning the right to play for a National Championship at the BCS National Championship in Glendale, Arizona. Michigan struck first blood with a touchdown run by junior running back Mike Hart, but the Buckeyes then scored 21 unanswered points, and at halftime they were up 28-14. However, the Wolverines weren't ready to back down. Thanks to an interception and a fumble recovery by junior defensive tackle Alan Branch, Michigan made it 35-31 Ohio State with 14 minutes to go in the fourth quarter. But after appearing to have forced Ohio State into a fourth down situation with six minutes to go, junior outside linebacker Shawn Crable was called for roughing the quarterback, giving the Buckeyes a fresh set of downs.

Ohio State quarterback Troy Smith then passed to Brian Robiskie for a touchdown, increasing the Buckeyes' lead to 42-31 with five minutes remaining in the game. The Wolverines still had fight in them, and after Ohio State was called for pass interference on a failed 4th down attempt, giving Michigan an automatic 1st down, junior quarterback Chad Henne found senior tight end Tyler Ecker for a 16-yard touchdown with two minutes to go to cutting the OSU lead to 42-37.

Senior wide receiver Steve Breaston caught the two-point conversion to bring the Wolverines within a field goal. Michigan needed to recover the ensuing onside kick, but failed to do so. The Buckeyes ran out the clock for the victory and a trip to the BCS National Championship game.

Terrelle Pryor (right) eludes Brandon Graham with a stiff arm.

2012 – Zach Boren sacks QB Devin Gardner, momentarily standing over him like the famous photo of Muhammad Ali standing over a knocked out Sonny Liston!

MOMENTS OF REFLECTION

Juan A., Columbus:

A friend scheduled her bachelorette party on the same day as the Michigan game in 2006. My roommate, who had a ticket to the game, had to attend the party because she was a bridesmaid. She sold me her ticket, and the price I paid for it was nothing compared to what I experienced that day.

I have been to many games at the Shoe, but there was something in the air that day that I simply cannot put into words. The crowd was deafening even before TBDBITL's ramp entrance, and when Chris Wells broke free for a 50-yard touchdown, you couldn't even hear the person next to you. Running onto the field with my friend Emily when the game was over was an experience that I will never, ever forget! GO BUCKS!!!

With an undefeated season on the line, Ohio State stood up against Michigan in the Horseshoe Saturday, 26-21.

Photo courtesy of OSU Website

One Usher's Recollections

Football is not a contact sport. It's a collision sport.
Dancing is a good example of a contact sport.
—**Duffy Daugherty**

Trevor Zahara, the author, portal chief B-8: As I mentioned in the prologue, my good friend Jim, other ushers and I would spend hours reminiscing about our Ohio State adventures; I cannot highlight all the adventures of my peers, but I can relate to the reader what Ohio has meant to me and my family. These are my stories:

1966-71-THE COLLEGE YEARS

I was a small-town, 17-year-old from Bucyrus, Ohio thrust into the big city life of Columbus, a freshman at The Ohio State University and I was out of my mind with excitement. During orientation, after all the intros, speeches and class scheduling crap, my foremost concern was how do I get my football tickets? I was directed to French Field House where the cattle call was in place and the rest of my 10,000 classmates were battling for their football tickets. Being freshman, we had the opportunity to buy the suckiest seats; therefore I was intrigued by the rah-rah antics of the Block O folks beseeching us to join the fun and excitement of their group. I thought to myself, "What the hell, this might be interesting," so I joined up.

For those unenlightened, Block O is an Ohio State student organization and also serves as the official student cheering section of the Buckeyes. Founded in 1938 by OSU cheerleader Clancy Isaac, Block O has grown to become the largest student organization on campus.

OHIO AND THE OH-IO CHEER
WERE ALSO STARTED BY CLANCY ISAAC

Now that you know the history and the purpose of Block O, I can tell you that my excitement for the 1966 season was dampened by a losing season and a 4-5 record. Chants of "Goodbye Woody" were heard around the stadium, but buoyed by my fellow Block O'ers, and a lot of 3.2 beer, we cheered our hearts out and hoped for a better outcome in 1967.

Things did get better and so was the team's record of 6-3. By the mid-point of the 1967 season, Woody Hayes was on shaky ground as OSU's football coach. The decision by the school's Faculty Council to deny his 1961 Big 10 championship team a Rose Bowl trip had seriously hindered recruiting that decade. And after suffering a 4-5 season in 1966, Hayes' 1967 group had come out of the gate 2-3, including a 41-6 beating at the hands of Purdue and a 17-13 loss to Illinois — the Bucks' second straight loss to the Illini.

> *To play OSU, ya gotta be good. To score on OSU, ya gotta be lucky. To beat OSU, ya gotta be kiddin'!*
> **—Rex Kern**

No one could have forecast it then, but that loss to Illinois would be the last time Ohio State would taste defeat until November 22, 1969 in Ann Arbor. The 1967 team got the ball rolling by winning their last four, and waiting in the wings as freshmen (who were ineligible for varsity games) was arguably the greatest recruiting class in Ohio State history. Collectively, they would come to be known as the "Super Sophs," and in 1968 a dozen of them would eventually crack the starting lineups. But Ohio State regrouped and finished the 1967 season by winning their last 5 games, including a 24-14 win over Michigan.

Meanwhile, Hayes' latest recruiting class was highly regarded, and they would be expected to contribute mightily to the team when they became eligible to play as sophomores in 1968. The Super Sophs included starting quarterback Rex Kern, backs Leo Hayden, Larry Zelina, and John Brockington, and ends Jan White and Bruce Jankowski on offense. Defensive backs Jack Tatum, Mike Sensibaugh, and Tim Anderson became instant starters along with nose-tackle Jim Stillwagon. After taking care of business in their first two games, the Buckeyes were itching to get a measure of revenge over Purdue for the previous season's humiliation.

Then the miracle turn-around happened for the Super Sophs during my junior year. Suppose you are an Ohio State team that is ranked #4 in the country and you are about to start the Big Ten season with a home game. You are coming off two impressive out-of-conference wins and your margin of victory in both games was in double digits (the Bucks withstood a 76-pass barrage by SMU to win their opener, and then dispatched Oregon). You would probably feel pretty good about your chances, right?

Well in 1968 this was the case, yet the Buckeyes were 13-point underdogs going into the game because the team they were playing was #1-ranked Purdue. Purdue had started the season at the top of the rankings, and there was good reason for that—their offense was led by All-American quarterback Mike Phipps and two-way halfback Leroy Keyes. They also had powerful offensive and defensive lines. Purdue had slaughtered the Buckeyes 41-6 in Columbus the previous season.

To start the game, OSU took over after receiving the kickoff and immediately started running a no-huddle offense. Hayes had felt that the Purdue linemen were slow and out of shape, so he wanted the offense to move at a quick pace to keep them moving. They would call three plays in the initial huddle and then run them consecutively without huddling.

On the first drive, the Buckeyes moved relentlessly down the field as Brockington repeatedly gashed the Purdue defense with his hard running style. But the drive stalled at the Purdue 4-yard line, and then OSU missed the field goal. Other drives in the first half would end in similar fashion, but the defense was giving Purdue all they could handle.

Tatum focused on stopping Keyes and wherever the star halfback tried to go, "The Assassin" was waiting for him. The entire first half was a defensive struggle that ended in a 0-0 tie. OSU had controlled the tempo and had numerous opportunities, but they were unable to punch it in or even convert a field goal.

The Buckeyes were much more opportunistic in the second half. Purdue started with the ball, but on their 4th play from scrimmage Phipps would make a critical error. The previous play, Tatum had jumped an out pattern and nearly intercepted the ball. On the next play, Tatum and fellow defensive back Ted Provost switched assignments, and Phipps read it as a change in coverage. He attempted the same out pattern as before, but this time Provost jumped the route and made the interception. He returned it 35 yards for the touchdown and Ohio State was suddenly holding a 6-0 lead (after a missed PAT).

Later that same quarter, Phipps would compound his error with another interception as the future Cleveland Browns quarterback would be picked by Stillwagon. Unfortunately for the Buckeyes, Rex Kern would be injured on a quarterback keeper to the right sideline, forcing Hayes to go with little-used senior backup Bill Long. Ohio State had the ball at the Purdue 14-yard line, and Hayes had always been averse to passing. But he crossed up the defense by calling a pass play. Seeing all of his options covered, Long tucked the ball and ran through the confused defense and into the end zone. After the successful PAT kick, OSU held a 13-0 lead. The defense continued to thwart the Boilermakers on offense, and Ohio State held on for an improbable 13-0 victory.

The Bucks moved up to #2 in the AP poll after derailing the Boilers, and justified the ranking by routing Northwestern 45-21 the next week. The 4-0 start had all been accomplished within the friendly confines of Ohio Stadium, and now the Buckeyes would take their overall 8-game winning streak into Champaign for Illinois' homecoming game.

The Illini were winless to this point of the season, and it showed as the Buckeyes steamrolled to a 24-0 halftime lead. Jim Roman got OSU on the board with a 21-yard field goal in the first quarter, then in period two fullback Jim Otis had scampers of 31 and 17 on a drive that he capped off with a one-yard plunge over the right side. Later, quarterback Rex Kern sneaked right up the middle for an 11-yard touchdown to make it 17-0, OSU. The yardage continued to come in chunks as Kern passed to wing-back Larry Zelina for 10 and tight end Jan White for 23 on a march that he would cap with his second touchdown of the day — a 15-yard option keeper over the left side.

Things had come easily to Ohio State in the first half as 17 first downs, 294 yards and 24 points would attest. At halftime middle guard Jim Still-wagon was basically informed he was done for the day, and as he told former Columbus Dispatch writer Paul Hornung in the book *Woody Hayes — A Reflection*, Hayes used the halftime to pontificate about Abraham Lincoln since they were in Illinois, "The Land of Lincoln."

"Woody came into the dressing room and started talking about Lincoln...Here we were...in the middle of a Big Ten game—and he was talking about Lincoln. We went out in the second half and almost got our a##es beat."

Ohio State was actually fortunate to that point that the offense had brought their "A" game. Linebacker and captain Dirk Worden was out, corner Mike Polaski and end Mark Debevc hadn't even made the trip; corner Tim Anderson had gone out in the second quarter with a back injury and Jack Tatum hadn't played yet with an ankle injury he suffered the week before against Northwestern. The patchwork defense had held Illinois to only 3 first downs and 84 total yards in the first half but the dam was about to break.

Illinois started the third quarter with a spread offense. Their offensive tackle lined up further away from the guard and a slot back filled the gap behind them. The Illini ran their backs out of this look to the tune of 177 yards in the second half. A Rex Kern interception set up a short scoring drive for the Orange and Blue that Richard Johnson finished with a 2-yard touchdown run. Johnson also scooted for the 2-point conversion to make it 24-8. On Illinois' next drive they converted a pair of fourth-down plays and hit pay dirt as quarterback Robert Naponic went over from 2 yards away. Naponic added another 2-point conversion and after three quarters it was suddenly 24-16, Buckeyes.

Late in the fourth quarter the Illini pulled even as a drive that was aided by an OSU personal foul penalty was topped off on a short run by backup fullback Ken Bargo. Amazingly, Bargo did the honors on a 2-point run and in a comeback that probably had Lincoln rolling in his grave the game was now tied at 24. In 159 previous games under Woody Hayes only 13 opponents had scored 24 or more points on Ohio State, and what's worse is OSU had lost every one of them. Now, after Jim Otis fumbled and recovered Illinois' ensuing kickoff on his own 26, the Bucks had 4:38 left to salvage their 4-0 start.

Rex Kern scrambled for 8 and Zelina picked up 2 to give Ohio State a first down at their own 36. On the next play Kern was dropped for a loss of 6 and, just to throw more gas on the fire, Rex had to leave the game with a head injury.

Ron Maciejowski came on and revved up the dormant OSU offense, dialing up Zelina for 10 and then racing for 12 yards and a first down on the Illini 48. The back-to-back quick strikes had the Illinois "D" confounded and they lined up for the next snap without formally huddling. Wingback Larry Zelina got lost down the middle and Maciejowski hit him with a perfect toss at the 27 which Zelina then took all the way to the Illini 4. Without question, in this magical season of 1968 the 44-yard pass play would shine brightly by year's end.

From here it was Jim Otis' turn and the junior plowed over two plays later from the 2. Roman's point after touchdown made it 31-24 with 1:30 to go. Illinois had made hay with their running attack in the second half but now had to go to the air. Safety Mike Sensibaugh just missed a diving interception but on the very next play the Illini went in his direction again and this time Sensibaugh picked it off to seal the deal.

Illinois would finish the 1968 season at 1-9, but for 30 minutes had given the Bucks all they could handle. Maciejowski would earn the nickname "Super Sub" for his heroic efforts down the stretch in relief of Rex Kern and OSU would continue on their way to a National Championship. In the book *Ohio State '68: All The Way to the Top*, Mike Polaski admitted that the tight Illinois win, "Might have been the best thing for us, because if there'd been a blowout there it might've led to big-headedness down the road."

Believe it or not, Ohio State's 1968 win over Illinois was the first time in school history that a football game had ended 31-24. And remarkably enough, it has only happened one time since — on a glorious Friday night in January 2003 under the desert skies of Tempe, Arizona where the Buckeyes climbed to the top of the college football mountain for the first time since ... you know!

After close calls with Michigan State and Iowa the 8-0 Buckeyes met the Michigan Wolverines on November 23, 1968, in front of what was, at the time, the largest crowd to ever fill Ohio Stadium (85,371). Ohio State was ranked number 1; Michigan was ranked number 4. Michigan scored first to lead 7-0 in the first quarter. Ohio State followed with its own touchdown. Both teams scored at the end of the half, and the score at halftime was 21-14 for Ohio State.

But in the second half the Buckeyes, hammering a sagging Michigan defense with their power running game, took charge and began to dominate. The score became 27-14, then 30-14, then 37-14, then 44-14. With 1:23 remaining, Jim Otis barged over for his fourth touchdown of the afternoon, hurling the ball into the joyous mass in the stands behind the

north end zone. It was now 50-14.

But Woody wasn't through. Just as he had done in 1961, he ordered up a two-point conversion attempt, which, in this case, failed. When asked why he'd gone for two with such an enormous lead, Woody gave his famous reply: "Because I couldn't go for three."

The final score was Ohio State 50, Michigan 14.

The 1968 Ohio State Buckeye football team was considered one of the strongest in OSU history, fielding 11 All-Americans and six first-round NFL draft picks. With quarterback Rex Ken and running back Jim Otis leading a powerful OSU offense and Jack Tatum on defense, Woody Hayes' Buckeyes capped an undefeated season with a dominating 50-14 victory over archrival Michigan and a come-from-behind 27-16 victory over Southern California in the 1969 Rose Bowl to secure the national title.

This was also the year Woody Hayes dumped his program's red helmets and brought in the now-iconic silver headgear. With the new garb, Hayes instituted a new policy: Individual players' contributions — those that helped the team win but might otherwise go unnoticed by traditional statistics, like a key block on a touchdown run — would be rewarded with a small buckeye leaf sticker. (It's now trademarked by the university.)

1969-1970 SEASON — A SENIOR AT LAST!

My senior year was crazy busy with 18 credit hours of class and a part time bartender job that kept me on my toes all year. But the advantage of being a senior was that I had great seats in the student section of 9-A. Ohio State's 1969 football team was dubbed by the media as the "greatest college football team of all time," with a handful of proven All-Big Ten players and All-Americans, such as quarterback Rex Kern, running backs Larry Zelina, Jim Otis and John Brockington, wide receivers Jan White and Bruce Jankowski, middle guard Jim Stillwagon and defensive star Jack Tatum.

The 1969 edition of the Michigan-Ohio State rivalry is considered one of the most memorable games of the series as well as one of the biggest upsets in college football history. The Buckeyes went into the game as the top-ranked team in the country, with a 22-game winning streak under the direction of Woody Hayes. They were also defending national champions. The Wolverines went into the game under their new coach, Bo Schembechler, who was trying to redefine a college football power that had fallen on hard times. Ohio State was playing for its second straight national title, Michigan was playing for the Rose Bowl, and the championship of the Big Ten Conference was on the line. The game was witnessed by a (then) stadium-record crowd of 103,588 at Michigan Stadium in Ann Arbor. And so began the combative stretch of the rivalry that became known informally as The Ten Year War.

Leading up to the Buckeyes' meeting with Michigan, Ohio State had never trailed in a game during the 1969 season, and no team had scored more than 21 points on them all season (Michigan State in a 54-21 loss). Ohio State had not scored fewer than 34 points in any game — their closest margin of victory was 27 points in a 34-7 win over Minnesota.

Michigan was in the process of rebuilding after a period of mediocrity that saw them go to only one Rose Bowl between 1951 and 1968. The program, known for its winning traditions under Fielding H. Yost and Fritz Crisler, seemed to have lost its way. Schembechler was hired before the 1969 season after six successful seasons as head coach of his alma mater,

Rex Kern: Hall of Fame Material

Miami University of Ohio, where he'd won two MAC titles.

The team began the season with an unassuming 3-2 record, including a loss to in-state rival Michigan State. But they did get a key 30-21 win vs. #9-ranked Purdue in October that was crucial; had they lost that game, Purdue would have gone to the Rose Bowl (Ohio State could not go due to the Big Ten's "no repeat" rule). They would go on to win their next four straight, with a team including quarterback Don Moorhead, fullback Garvie Craw, wingback John Gabler, tailbacks Glenn Doughty and Billy Taylor, offensive lineman Dan Dierdorf and defensive stars Barry Pierson, Thom Darden, Cecil Pryor and Henry Hill.

When Schembechler was hired, he set the team goal — beat Ohio State. One advantage Schembechler had was that he had played for Woody Hayes at Miami, and then coached with him at Ohio State, so he patterned his team after Hayes' 1969 behemoth. There was also a revenge factor from the 1968 game when Ohio State trounced Michigan 50-14, including going for two after their last touchdown in the game's final moments. **After the game, when reporters asked Woody Hayes why he went for two, Hayes replied, "Because I couldn't go for three!"**

Ohio State was favored by 17 points going into Michigan Stadium. The Buckeyes knew a victory would give them their second consecutive National Championship because they could not go to a bowl game. Michigan was playing for a share of the conference championship. To motivate his team, Schembechler had the number "50" displayed everywhere in the

Michigan locker room and taped to every player's practice uniform.

SENIOR+

Who would have thunk it? Not only did I survive my senior year of college, I had the distinct advantage of another two quarters of classes at my beloved university. Wow! I could actually take some courses that I would enjoy, and let my hair and beard grow because I was through with my ROTC commitment. But, most important, I could get another year of season football tickets — with the "kicker" a home Michigan game.

The Bucks were stocked with excellent players and were slated to contend for the Big Ten title. I was excited about the first game of the season in my great seats in section A-7 with all my senior buddies. Top-ranked Ohio State rolled up 513 yards of offense and scored touchdowns off five Texas A & M turnovers in a 56-13 rout. Fullback John Brockington scored twice and six other players accounted for touchdowns. The Buckeyes' defense forced three fumbles and an interception which led to four scores in an eight-minute span in the third quarter even though Woody Hayes pulled the starters a little after halftime.

The Buckeyes compiled a 9-0 regular season record to attain a #2 ranking. The Bucks won the Big Ten Conference title and a berth in the 1971 Rose Bowl against the Stanford Indians, ranked #12 and champions of the Pac-8.

> *The only meaningful statistic is number of games won.*
>
> **—Woody Hayes**

After winning the first seven games, the Bucks won a hard-fought victory over Purdue with a fourth quarter winning field goal. President Richard Nixon called to congratulate Woody Hayes after the game, and then asked to speak to Fred Schram, who made the game-winning field goal. Fullback John Brockington carried the ball 24 times for 138 yards and Leo Hayden added 64 yards on 16 carries.

LET THE FUN BEGIN!

The pre-season was now "in the books" and it was Michigan week!

I had threatened to take my boa constrictor, RainBoa, to the Michigan game, but either I was not drunk enough or my roommates talked me out of it. RainBoa actually belonged to my next door neighbor when we lived in a duplex on 7th Avenue, near High Street. Jim was a part-time student and worked for the railroad, so he was gone a lot and left the care of Rain-Boa to me and my roommates. RainBoa lived in a hollowed out TV in our living room, required little care, and ate only once every couple of weeks. Feeding time was an event that usually involved a party.

Jim had the bright idea that we could have a huge Michigan game party if we knocked a hole in the basement wall between our two apartments. As I mentioned, Jim was a railroader and his roommate was an ironworker, so between them they had an abundance of tools, including a sledgehammer.

Down went the wall, complete with day glow paint around the edges. The party room was complete; black light was in place, now all we needed was a whole mess of people. That is where RainBoa comes in — feeding time required a trip to the pet store to obtain a delicious white rat. Word went out that the party was on for Friday night. Despite the fact this was long before any social media, internet or cell phones, by 9:00 p.m. there were over 100 people in our two apartments, with the overflow into the front lawn. The crowd was chanting, "Feeding time, feeding time," so I opened the doors to RainBoa's lair and, holding the rat by its long tail, flung it into the lair. Girls starting screaming as RainBoa quickly struck and snapped his powerful jaws around the rat's head and wrapped his

4-foot-long body around the rat. After the rat expired the snake started to constrict and swallowed the rat whole!

Needless to say, the crowd, including yours truly, was now whipped into an alcoholic frenzy. In my inebriated state I was cajoled into removing RainBoa from his cage, to the hoots and hollers of the crowd — probably not the brightest idea in my 21 years.

The snake became very agitated, and then two not-so-wholesome things happened in succession. First, the half-digested rat was immediately expelled to the disgust of the crowd and secondly, RainBoa extended his body away from mine and struck me in the neck and cheek with his sharp fangs.

Trying to explain that to the emergency room nurses at 2 a.m., I received my tetanus shot, as well as a stern lecture from the doctor to use some of my college smarts in the future. Oh, and as I exited he also yelled GO BUCKS! BEAT THE BLUE!

Trevor Zahara & RainBoa

GAME DAY

So it's the morning of The Big Game, my roommates and I are still half in the bag with gigantic hangovers pounding our heads; what's a guy to do at 9:00 a.m. to prepare for a 1:00 game? Yep, Strohs and Jack Daniel shots! We pooled all our hard-earned money to go first class. After the first beer we were cranking up the sounds, well on our way to cheer on our Bucks!

As we headed out the door, neighbor Jim was in charge of our last bottle of Beam and, being the knucklehead he was, he dropped the ¾-full bottle on the concrete porch. Not to be beaten down, we quickly ran back in the house and grabbed a couple of t-shirts and a pair of underwear (clean!), sopped up the alcohol and strained it through the underwear into another bottle. Another one of those not so bright college moments! Next we hit the "North Berg" where another old buddy was bartending. The place was jammed, so we slammed a couple of pitchers of beer then went off to finish the pre-game at the Varsity Club.

We were ready for the game. We headed across the St John parking lot, singing at the top of our lungs, "We don't give a damn for the whole state of Michigan!" As we approached the entrance gate we strategized on how we were going to sneak the scavenged bottle of Beam into the game. I couldn't carry it because I had six cans of Strohs hidden in my bomber flight jacket. So Jim slipped it down the back of his jeans into his under-wear (not the same underwear we strained the booze through).

Well we got to the gate; I started to hand the Redcoat my ticket and one of the beers slid out of my coat — BUSTED! So I had to hand over my booty and pitch it into the waste basket before I entered the stadium. As I was causing all the commotion, Jim walked through with the Beam bottle.

We got to our seats in section 9-A in time for the kickoff. We were having a great time and by third quarter had polished off the Beam within four cups of Coke. Then Jim, having had many beers and much Beam and Coke, urgently had to go to the bathroom. He didn't want to miss any of the game and he knew the lines to the men's room would be huge, so he had the bright idea (yes, another one) to pee into the empty Beam bottle.

We all stood around him to give him cover, but after having all those beers and Beam, Jim's aim wasn't so hot. He overshot the bottle and hit the white fur coat of the lady sitting in front of us. She was so involved in the game she didn't realize what had happened. I felt really bad to think what that poor lady did when she got home and saw the back of her beautiful coat.

While all this was going on, the #5-ranked Bucks whipped the #4-ranked Blue 20-9. Now on to the Rose Bowl!

ROAD TRIP

What the hell, we thought, this is our last year of college; let's go out with a bang—off to the Rose Bowl! As we were brainstorming how to make this happen with a limited budget, my neighbor Jim said he knew a guy who had a car who would volunteer to drive if we would help pay for gas. The trip was on. Then Jim dropped the bomb: his dad had always wanted to go to a Rose Bowl and offered to pay for half of the gas if he could ride along. This made five of us in a 1965 Plymouth Roadrunner. As Elwood of Blues Brothers fame said, "Its 2,000 miles to Pasadena—we have half pack of cigarettes, a six pack of beer, a full tank of gas and we have our sunglasses on, it's dark — hit it!"

Needless to say, we had our moments on the 2,000-mile trip. As we traveled along the highway near Albuquerque, New Mexico the temperature dropped to 36 degrees below zero and the Roadrunner's defroster could not keep the windshield free of frost, so we decided to stop and take a break. We pulled into a local watering hole. The locals did not cater to outsiders, especially ones with long hair and beards. As we walked into the bar, every head in the place turned and watched us.

My buddies ordered beers and I went to the men's room. When I returned, I took up a bar stool next to one of the locals and he commented to Jim, "Is your girlfriend going to have a beer too?" Meaning me! I took offense to that statement and before I could say something stupid, my ironworker buddy Ed came over and stood beside me. Now, Ed was 6'4" and weighed 250, so he commanded a presence in the room. Ed calmly said we didn't want to have any trouble and offered to buy a round of drinks. The local guy smiled and opened up his jacket coat to show a gun in a holster. Boy was I glad Ed was an ironworker. He immediately started up a boisterous conversation with the locals and after a couple of brews we were on our way.

Next stop was the Grand Canyon and a quick stop to take some photos. Jim thought it would be really funny to have his photo taken on the other side of the safety guard rail — doing a head stand! All I could think of was Jim bouncing off the walls on his way to the bottom of the canyon, his dad going completely psycho on us and missing the Rose Bowl. But Jim got his photo and we rolled on to our next stop, Las Vegas. We were awestruck as we approached the city and saw all the lights and the glitter.

As we were driving down the strip we decided to stop at the Flamingo, which was advertising steaks for $5.99 and mugs of beer for a buck. We were famished and headed for the bar. After downing the steaks and a few beers we wandered into the casino. Wow! All these slot machines chattering and clouds of smoke filled the air, again we were awestruck. I stopped at a craps table and all these people were hooting and hollering, as a Texan, wearing this big cowboy hat, was on a hot streak rolling the dice.

He said something funny and I started to laugh. The large Texan immediately stopped with the dice in his hands, turned toward me with a scowl on his face and said to me in a booming voice, "What's so goddamn funny? You a member of the lost generation? Whatcha want me to do — Ride Ya, Rope Ya or Whoop Ya?" Obviously, my long hair and beard got me in trouble again. I just turned away, found my friends and got the hell out of Dodge!

We got back in the Roadrunner and headed off to my Cousin Shelly's house in Manhattan Beach, just outside of Los Angeles. Shelly was a stewardess for United Airlines and offered to let us stay at her beautiful beach house. Right then and there she became my favorite cousin. We found out that a couple of her neighbors were one of the Beach Boys and another was one of the Smother Brothers. But all this took a back seat to the Rose Bowl game on the following day.

We woke up early on New Year's Day to take advantage of all the Rose Bowl festivities. The day became even more exciting when top- ranked and defending national champion Texas was upset 24-11 in the Cotton Bowl in Dallas, Texas by #6-ranked Notre Dame, ending the Longhorns' 30-game winning streak.

Heavily-favored Ohio State could claim their second national title in three years that afternoon with a Rose Bowl victory over Stanford. Stanford (8-3) was led by quarterback Jim Plunkett, the 1970 Heisman Trophy winner. The Indians had climbed to a 6-0 conference record and 8-1 overall, but lost their final two regular season games, to Sugar Bowl-bound Air Force and arch-rival California. Stanford lost earlier in the season at home to Purdue, a team OSU had defeated on the road.

Arriving at the famous Rose Bowl, we parked the car a few miles away from the stadium and hoofed it the rest of the way. We found our way to our seats, wineskins in hand, ready for the game to begin.

The Buckeyes led Stanford by four points after three quarters, but were outscored 14-0 in the fourth quarter and lost 27-17. Later that night, #3-ranked Nebraska won the Orange Bowl 17-12 over #5-ranked LSU in Miami to claim the top spot in the AP.

With Jim Plunkett fashioning an explosive aerial bombardment and a clutch second half defense making the big plays, Stanford exploded for a stunning 27-17 victory over mighty Ohio State before 103,839 spectators and a national television audience in the 57th Rose Bowl game.

We were bummed out and headed for the exit, minus my wineskin. It was empty anyway and I threw it toward the field when Stanford scored their last touchdown. Somehow Jim and I got separated from our other buddies, so we headed for the highway. Pasadena was not noted for its transportation system, so we started to hitchhike in the direction all the cars were going. A long while later three Latinos picked us up in this really cool Chevy that had lifters on the front end that made it spring off the ground. They asked us where we were going and we said, "Manhattan Beach." Replying something in Spanish we could not understand, they wanted to know if we played pool.

So we stopped at a local pool hall, where the driver put on an exhibition of the Chevy's bouncing capabilities to an appreciative crowd gathered outside. We shot a few games of pool and drank many beers with our new found friends, after which we were off to Shelly's beach house. My cousin was relieved that we made it back unharmed! The next day we said our goodbyes and were off for the long drive home, disappointed by the loss to Stanford, but excited for the memories.

ROTC

Before I detail my graduation and post grad days, I would be remiss not to discuss an important part of my maturation period at Ohio State, as

Reserved Officer Training Candidate (ROTC). OSU being a Land Grant College meant that all enrolled male students were required to take two years of military training. I chose the Army, to follow in the footsteps of my dad and uncle, both of whom served during WW II.

"Rotcy," as most students pronounced it, was a two-hour credit course, one in classroom and one in drill training. The classroom contained military stuff conducted by an Army officer, "Hurrah," and all that crap! It was honestly kind of cool, because these guys had actually been in combat. Remember, this was in the 1960s and the Vietnam War was in full swing. One of these "swinging Richards" came in one day and put the fear of God into us, saying that if we didn't apply ourselves and take this shit seriously that we would find ourselves in the "friggin' jungles of South Vietnam" (and he didn't say "friggin'!").

Since I had a draft number of lucky seven, I had no choice but to get my shit together and do as the man said. For those too young to know what the hell a draft number means, let me explain. In the 1960s all 18-year-old men were required to report to the Selective Service Bureau to get their draft cards, which the hippies immediately burned. The rest of us poor suckers had numerous options:

Join the military

Get a 4-F exemption

Go to college and maintain a 2.0 average

We poor sons-a-bitches who had low draft numbers were going to be drafted in the military. Hurrah! Remember when I said earlier that my draft number was lucky 7? The lower your draft number the greater your chance was of being drafted. At #7, I was a dead ass cinch to be humping those rice paddies.

So being a ROTC schmuck muck was not a bad deal. I had to really apply myself to get the Gestapo off my back. Therefore, I immediately got a job as a bartender — a great way to apply yourself in college! I worked five nights a week at the Draught House, which was the first nightclub near campus that had a dance floor with all the psychedelic lights so popular during the drug-crazed 60s. The club used to pack in over 2,500 college aged kids per night, dancing to bands like the James Gang, Lighthouse,

Bob Seger and the Silver Bullet Band — meaning I would usually not get home until 3:00 a.m.

This seemed like a wonderful way for a knuckle-headed 21 year old kid to spend his evenings, but it was tough to get up and go to an 8:00 a.m. class. And, luck of the draw — during my senior year that class happened to be ROTC. I was comatose for most of those classes, but my instructor, Sergeant Hardass (not his real name), had no mercy. Being a hardened veteran he knew all the signs of a classic hangover and loved to mess with me by calling me to the front of the room to discuss all kinds of military strategies.

Fortunately, I secretly loved my military classes and actually read and studied my class material, so as hard as my instructor tried to screw with me, I came up with the correct answers. I remember him telling me, "Cadet Zahara, you have more balls than a bowling alley." I guess that summed up my time in ROTC.

I actually graduated in winter quarter 1971 and was sworn into the Army during the commencement ceremonies at St. John Arena. I had to wear my Army Dress Greens uniform under my graduation gown. After the graduation I was officially a 2nd Lieutenant in the Army. A long-standing tradition was to give a silver dollar to the first non-commissioned officer that salutes you. As I walked out of St. John, Sergeant Hardass was waiting for me. Grinning from ear to ear, he gave me my first salute and I reluctantly handed him my silver dollar. I was now officially Trevor J. Zahara, 2nd Lieutenant, US Army—Lord have Mercy!

I have to admit that the ROTC education helped me develop the discipline that allowed me to be successful in my adult life. I would highly recommend the ROTC program to those thinking about an education at OSU.

FLAG RAISING

One of my big regrets while in ROTC was not being part of the flag raising detail. At football games the ROTC programs have the honor of raising the flag up the 150 foot pole. Participants on the flag raising detail get into the games for free and have some of the best seats in the house right on the field. It is quite an honor! This is one of those stories:

Photo From the Troy Daily News, 12/20/2010, by **David Fong**, Executive Editor:

Troy High School graduate Alex Baker, a junior Air Force ROTC student at The Ohio State University, stands on the field before the Ohio State-Marshall football game. Baker was one of the ROTC students at Ohio State who helped raise the flag during the national anthem before football games the past two years.

Proud Buckeye, proud American
Troy grad raises flag before OSU games

When I called David Fong, Executive Editor of the Troy Daily News to get his permission to print the previous photo about Baker, he not only gave me the okay, he told me that he was a graduate of OSU and had worked with the OSU newspaper, The Lantern. He also said that Alex was a good friend and he would e-mail him that evening and let him know that I was working on a book and would love to have his feedback on the article.

Lt. Alex Baker and I exchanged emails and he was gracious enough to send me his personal thoughts on his experience raising the American flag at the OSU game.
Alex E. Baker, 2Lt, USAF:

> _Before each home game we have about 10 slots to fill to be a part of the ROTC flag detail at The Horseshoe. Each branch gets ten slots (30 total) and one has an extra for a flag detail commander. The list is first come, first serve. I had season tickets for each of my four years here, which were 2008, '09, '10, and '11. I am a diehard Buckeye fan and I knew what an incredible honor and privilege it would be to raise our nation's flag in front of 105,000+ people on a Saturday before a football game in Ohio Stadium. So once my sophomore year, and twice my junior year, I volunteered to be on the flag detail. They were experiences I am so thankful for and which I will never forget._
>
> _Four or 5 hours before kickoff we would meet for flag detail practice, typically in civilian attire. For the noon games, 7:00 a.m. was early and usually chilly, but it didn't matter because we were all excited for the game and for the honor of raising the flag. We would run through the commands, facing movements and such several times in the parking lot then would march over to The Shoe. We'd enter through the North Rotunda — just like game time, then go down the same ramp that the band comes down and_

march to our places east of the flag pole while the flag bearer held the flag at the end of the detail furthest away from the flagpole. The Army and Air force cadets are to the east of the flag pole in their own formation and the Navy midshipmen and Marine Corps cadets would be to the north of the flagpole ready to pull the rope. We would practice until we were satisfied with our performance, then leave until two hours before game time.

When game time comes it's electric. Woody Hayes Drive is amass with people milling all around, music playing and thousands of tailgaters everywhere and we're in uniform. We'd meet in the same spot outside Converse Hall where we practiced earlier, but now it's the real deal. Ohio state troopers escort us into The Shoe, which was really cool because you know that they are escorting you for what precious nylon you are holding and what it represents rather than escorting us just as cadets.

I'll never forget the announcers on the AT&T stage who, on a loud microphone, said "Let's hear it for the men and women of our armed forces!" I always had to fight back tears when they said that because of how much it humbled me that these people would scream as loud as they would at the game for us carrying our nation's flag and for what we had signed up to do.

The troopers would lead us down the brick pathway leading to the North Rotunda blowing their whistles and clearing people out of the way so we didn't have to break our strides while marching. We marched through the Rotunda and as we went down the ramp, the people inside The Shoe who could see us would cheer and yell for us as we passed. Then we'd march to our places and just wait at ease for about an hour before kickoff and watch people fill in the stands. I always felt bad for the flag bearer because he had to hold it for such a long time and if you have ever seen it, you can imagine why. It's a massive flag in size and it's made of thick nylon as well.

About 10 minutes before game time, we are commanded back to attention and given the proper commands to prepare to unfurl the flag. It is not the easiest thing in the world to hear the detail commander because it is already a little loud when we start the process. The unfurling of the flag can make one nervous in practice because you don't want to look dumb and let your section of it slip out of your hands or something when you have 30-some people around, let alone 105,000. When it's time to set up and unfurl it, you grab your section and hold on for dear life as the Army cadet across from you runs away with his/her side of the flag until it runs out of slack. It feels great when it's unfurled and people start cheering. Then the side opposite the field of blue is lifted up just so the first three cadets are no longer holding it. This is where the detail commander waits for the band to start playing the Star Spangled Banner.

When the drum roll starts, that's when the commander knows to give the command "Colors." Then the Navy and Marines start pulling the rope and the Army and Air Force cadets let go of the flag as it starts to rise in front of them. They face the flag and salute as the national anthem plays. It is really moving to hear over 100,000 people singing the national anthem. When it's at the top of the flagpole, the Navy cadet positioned on the ramp that is keeping the rope tight yells "gangway!" runs down to the pole, stops his momentum with his foot as he risks maybe not life but limb, and he and another midshipman tie the slack and upon finishing, render salutes. THAT is the sexy position on the detail — the one all the crowd is watching. Once it's up and the music stops, we are commanded to march into the stands where we get to sit almost right on the field.

It is great sitting there. We get a free drink and a free personal pizza, Brutus comes and takes pictures with us. We're so close to the action, another cadet friend of mine and I met former Coach John Cooper. I even got to do an O-H-I-O pose with two other cadets and President Gee one time.

Whenever Ohio State scores, all the cadets have to run down to the area just north of the north end zone and do however many pushups we have scored up to that point. The games for which I volunteered were decently high scoring games, where we ended up scoring 30 some or 40 some points. I'm just glad I didn't volunteer for the game where we played Eastern Michigan and scored 72 points!

The flag coming down part can be nerve-racking, especially on windy days. By the time the flag comes down, the stands are mostly empty. As it starts lowering, we are at attention and saluting. Then, when it starts to come into view for those closest to it, the cadets cut their salutes and start running — and I mean RUN-NING — into the stands to catch it before any part of it touches the ground. I have never been on a detail in which we ever let it touch the ground and I'm proud of that. We then get back to our places north and east of the flag and unfurl the flag, then fold it back up, get back into formation, and march back up the ramp and through the Rotunda to go back to Converse, and the day is over.

I have always been very patriotic and it is truly an honor to be able to raise our nation's flag in front of 105,000 at Ohio Stadium. I am currently at Ohio State right now on an assistance program while I wait for pilot training to start next month in Oklahoma. Recently a kid walked in asking about ROTC. He was into football and I told him about the flag raisings and how awesome they were. I hope everybody who does it has the same overwhelming feelings I had when we passed the AT&T stage and heard all those people were cheering for us, what we were doing, and for our nation's flag and what it stands for.

Good luck and Godspeed, Alex. Our country's future is in good hands!

The time you give a man something he doesn't earn, you cheapen him. Our kids earn what they get, and that includes respect.

—Woody Hayes

1st Lieutenant Trevor Zahara,
Hialeah Compound –Pusan, Korea 1971

YOU'RE IN THE ARMY NOW!

So, I was sworn into the Army as a 2nd Lieutenant and my first duty station was Ft. Gordon, Georgia. Then, two weeks before Christmas 1971, I left for Seoul, Korea. When I landed, I met with a staff sergeant who was manning a small crew of administration people processing the newbies. He asked where I wanted to go. "I guess home is out of the question!" I answered. He sent me to Hialeah Compound in Pusan, where I remained for 13 months.

ARMED FORCES RADIO

As I sat on my bunk at 2:30 a.m. in Pusan, Korea the radio broadcast announcer said those magic words: the #9-ranked OSU Buckeyes vs. the #3-ranked Michigan football game was minutes away from kickoff! I was immediately wide awake and ready for the Bucks to kick some heathen ass!

Back in 1972, there were no ESPN or network worldwide TV broadcasts, so I was lucky the Armed Forces Radio decided to broadcast The Game. Ohio State made two goal line stands, one in each half, to hold onto the 14-11 victory. The first came just before halftime as Dennis Franklin fumbled on fourth down at the two. In the fourth quarter, Randy Gradishar stopped Franklin on a sneak from the one. The Buckeye fans tore down the goal posts with 13 seconds remaining.

I was so psyched that I stayed up the remainder of the night to savor this hard-fought victory for my beloved Buckeyes!

You've got a goal in life. I've got a goal in life. Now all we need is a football team.

—Groucho Marx

THE BIG "X"

My career with Xerox Corporation covered 36 years of working with some of the brightest minds in the business world — executives, CEOs, business owners, teachers, governmental officials, doctors and presidents of companies. I had the opportunity to travel the world meeting the most interesting people, yet wherever I went, be it on a beach in Hawaii, a pub in London, or walking down Beale Street in Memphis wearing my OSU National 2002 Championship t-shirt, I would always hear "O-H" and of course I would respond with a resounding "I-O." I was amazed that being an OSU alum would always be a conversation starter, no matter if it was a friend or foe, especially in SEC territory.

I remember attending a University of Memphis, Tennessee game at the Liberty Bowl Memorial Stadium, again wearing all my OSU gear. People would holler, "Ain't you in the wrong stadium — yours is 1,000 miles north!" or "OSU football sucks!" But most people were friendly and cordial.

I was invited to many tailgates on the way to the game and a lot of people were interested in talking to me about OSU football. I even met the University of Memphis Athletic Director R.C. Johnson and his wife while attending one of the tailgates. He pointed out some of the U of M many game day traditions, including displaying the official mascot, Tom III, a live Bengal tiger, who I viewed through a glass cage that sat outside the stadium before every home game. The university is one of a few schools in the country that keeps a live tiger as a mascot, although the practice of live animals serving as university mascots is carried on by a number of other universities. The game was not a sellout; both Memphis and Tennessee were having a down year, so I moved from my crappy seats to the 50 yard line. No Ushers blocked my move!

Another game I attended was the University of West Virginia vs. Central Florida at Mountaineer Field in Morgantown. I was invited to the Annual Xerox Tailgate held in a huge circus-type tent in the parking lot next to the stadium. The local Xerox agents have this event every year and go all out, with a lot of food and adult beverages. In fact, some of the partiers don't even make it to the game.

I entered the game with my good buddy from Beckley, West Virginia who gets great seats because he is President of the WVU Alumni Club. He asked me to join him on the 50 yard line to watch the action. It was starting to drizzle a little, so over my ever present OSU garb I donned my recently-purchased WVU rain poncho and hat and became engrossed in the game. I didn't pay much attention to the announcer when he mentioned they were going to announce the "Fan of the Game," until I looked up at the Jumbo-tron and saw my smiling face! I was awarded a game ball, a WVU sweatshirt and a gym bag full of other WVU Swag. Of course, all the fans around me wanted to know how this guy wearing all the OSU gear could be the "Fan of The Game" in the WVU Stadium!

At halftime I walked back to the Xerox Tailgate and received a ton of grief from the West Virginia contingent that stayed in the tent to watch the game on the big TV and stay close to the adult beverages. I told them the reason I was selected fan of the game was because Kirk Herbstreit, an ex-OSU quarterback, was announcing the game on ESPN and he gave preferential treatment to OSU fans.

Tom III University of Memphis Official Mascot

NO BREW IN THE SHOE

One of the differences I noticed while attending games at other stadiums is the liberal policy of selling alcohol inside the stadiums and allowing people to leave the stadium and then return to the game. Many colleges sell alcohol at football games, but Ohio Stadium remains dry. According to

Joe Podelco / Lantern photographer Chris Poche / Design editor

Danielle Hyams of the Ohio State Lantern, "Although universities around the country have started selling beer and spirits at their football games, with West Virginia University being the most recent; it looks like OSU won't be jumping on that bandwagon any time in the near future. Despite the potential monetary benefits of beer and liquor sales, OSU officials maintain that for now, Ohio Stadium will remain dry."

> *"Historically, the issue of alcohol sales during Ohio State football games has been discussed, however, the university's current policy has been in place better than 10 years," said Liz Cook, assistant director of media relations, in an email to The Lantern. "While a few colleges and universities across the nation do sell alcohol during games, our policy has worked well for the university and our fans. We are not engaged in any discussions to change the policy."*

One of the questions I get from the fans, especially visiting fans from universities with a more liberal alcohol sale, "Where can I buy a cold beer?" It appears, based on the Lantern article that there are strong opinions on this topic:

> *"I think they should (sell beer)," said Emily Sullivan, a fourth-year in strategic communication. "I think that most other sporting events do it. If people would not act insane, it wouldn't be a bad thing."*
>
> *Sullivan said that she does not believe selling alcohol at football games would lead to increased levels of public intoxication and underage drinking.*
>
> *"If anything, students might be more controlled because they have to buy (alcoholic beverages) at the stadium," she said.*
>
> *Corey Phelps, a first-year in engineering, said the football games are already crazy, and nothing is going to change that.*
>
> *"The fans are already crazy," Phelps said. "I think it would be fun, and the school would probably get more money."*
>
> *But not everyone around campus approves of the idea.*
>
> *Former student Daniel Starek, who graduated in August of 2010 with a degree in history and currently works at Eddie George's Grille 27 as a bartender, said that selling alcohol during football games would be a "liability" and a "public image nightmare."*
>
> *"More arrests would be made after the games," Starek said. "People wouldn't go home after the game, they would stay, and instead of sobering up they would want to stay out drinking."*
>
> *OSU police chief Paul Denton said that while his department is neutral on the issue, they would be prepared to react to any decision that the university makes regarding the matter.*
>
> *"If that decision would be made to sell alcohol in the stadium during game days then we would have to add staff and evaluate the situation as necessary," he said.*
>
> *Denton added that it is not necessarily the sale of alcohol that would cause problems.*
>
> *"It's not the issue of selling alcohol. It's the behavior that results when people abuse a legal product that it becomes a police*

issue, such as underage drinking and public intoxication. We have made a lot of progress and we don't want it to go backwards," he said, referring to OSU's effort to make football games fan-friendly.

During the first three home football games against Akron, Toledo and Colorado, there have been 90 open-container citations on campus made by OSU police, according to OSU police records.

Many universities that allow the sale of alcohol have not run into any major issues.

Oliver Luck, athletic director at West Virginia University, has nothing but praise for the university's decision to sell beer at football games. On June 3, the WVU Board of Governors voted to serve alcohol at sporting events on campus.

"We made a recommendation that the board change its policy which prohibited the sale of alcohol at West Virginia University sporting events. The board agreed to do so this past spring and we have taken advantage of that at our football games and it has worked very well," Luck said.

Luck added that the introduction of alcohol has not caused any safety issues at West Virginia.

"Like most colleges and universities, there is plenty of alcohol being consumed pre-game, during the game, and post-game and I think that ultimately the decision to sell beer certainly hasn't caused any more incidents according to the police," he said. "Our security folks think it's going very well and are very happy with it. The feedback we have gotten from the police after three home games is that they reported a better atmosphere."

Currently 36 Division I programs serve alcohol during football games. In addition, four Big Ten teams serve alcohol during home football games: Wisconsin, Iowa, Illinois and Purdue.

Govan Curl Jr., a third-year in psychology, said fans are going to drink regardless, and believes OSU should serve alcohol at games.

"They are already rowdy as f**k," Curl said. "And I don't appreciate that West Virginia is ahead of us in anything."

CAN YOU GET ME A TICKET?

People are always intrigued when I mention that I have been an Usher at Ohio Stadium for 15 years and then the first question I get from a lot of these folks is, "Can you get me a ticket to the game? " or "Let me tell you about my favorite OSU football story." I love it! This is one of those tales from my friend and business colleague:

My friend **Paul Schadek** graduated from high school in 1973, went into the US Army from 1974-76, and was shipped to Germany. He attended OSU 1976-1979:

> *Actually my adventure with Trevor does not pertain to football, but I will always remember the time we went to the OSU Indiana basketball game. We went to the game without tickets and tried to buy them from scalpers. After circling the arena for the fifth time, we were about ready to give up and go watch the game at the Varsity Club. All of a sudden I looked up and Trevor was coming out of the Television Video Truck carrying some cables and other important looking equipment and walking in the building with another station worker. I could not believe my eyes, but I have heard all about Trevor's ability to gain entrance into all sorts of sold out sports venues. Trevor had prevailed once again. By the way, OSU beat the Bobby Knight-led Hoosiers!*

FLASHBACK — PENN STATE AT OHIO STATE, 1978

> *Penn State was one upset loss away from an undefeated season in 1977. When the fall of 1978 arrived, many in State College and across the nation were looking forward to another impressive season from the Nittany Lions. What they would find is a season that would go down as one of the most memorable, glorious, yet painful in Penn State football history.*

1978 gameday pictorial for Penn State vs. Ohio State.

All that, of course, would have been moot had Penn State lost its first major test of the year, a visit to the Horseshoe for a date with Woody Hayes' 6th-ranked Ohio State Buckeyes.

Penn State was #5 in the nation following two lackluster wins over Rutgers and Temple, relying heavily on special teams and the defense to carry the Nittany Lions over the finish line in both games. Ohio State, meanwhile, was playing its season opener against Penn State, and planning a few new wrinkles on both offense and defense.

Tickets were almost impossible to find, after walking around the stadium three times we were ready to throw in the towel and head over to the Varsity Club to watch the game on the tube. I said to my buddy Ed, "I really want to see this game in person, so I'm going to get into the stadium, come hell or high water!"

So I went over to the east side of the closed end of the Shoe around gate 4. After checking to see if there were any cops watching, I took off running, leaped onto the iron bars, scrambled up, grabbed the top of the pointed posts and carefully tried to pull my body over the fence, but my hand got caught and I was hanging with this metal post piercing the meaty part of my palm. OUCH!

As I was trying to unhook my hand, I heard a State Highway Patrolman yelling for me to stop! After pulling my injured hand off the barb, I landed with a thud on the inside of the stadium, gathered myself and ran like hell up the first set of stairs that I could find. I did not slow down until I was sure that I was in the clear.

From my vantage point on B-Deck I called down to my buddy Ed, "Come on in the coast is clear." So Ed took the same path over the iron fence and met me on B-Deck. We walked around to the west side of the stadium and ran into another friend of ours, Don Caldwell.

He noticed that my hand was bleeding down the left side of my body and asked, "What the hell happened to you?" After explaining to him what caused the wound, I headed to the nearest First Aid station as Don laughed his ass off. The First Aid worker was kind enough to bandage my cut without asking any embarrassing questions.

Now our quest was to find some seats and watch the game. At the 50 yard line we noticed two empty seats, so we sat down for the entire game without anyone kicking us out!

Unfortunately the rest of the day was not so advantageous. Would Hayes' offense, known for almost single-handedly inventing the "3 yards and a cloud of dust" style of football, come out with the hot-shot freshman quarterback Art Schlichter throwing early and often?

In the end, none of what Ohio State had planned would matter. Penn State came out ready to shut down the Buckeyes. By the time the final whistle sounded the Nittany Lion defense would force eight Buckeye turnovers, including four interceptions. It would be a launching pad for Penn State's historic rise to its first ever #1 ranking. For Ohio State, it would be the second time in 14 years the Nittany Lions shut out the Buckeyes on their home turf.

Author's Note: we all do things in our youth that we are not proud of; the previous story is one of those times. I regret breaking the rules and have since donated money to the university to pay for this indiscretion. Not only was this foolhardy and dangerous, it was totally against my better judgment. For the youngsters out there- NEVER ATTEMPT THIS!

How you respond to the challenge in the second half will determine what you become after the game, whether you are a winner or a loser.

— **Lou Holtz**

RELATIVES

Thanksgiving dinners take eighteen hours to prepare. They are consumed in twelve minutes. Half-times take twelve minutes. This is not coincidence.

—**Erma Bombeck**

When I decided to document the many tales of my fellow Ushers I bounced off the results to all my friends and relatives, trying desperately to elicit a positive response from them, most of the time they were extremely patient with me during our Thanksgiving/Christmas/Birthday celebrations, often telling me what a great and wondrous task I was undertaking. Then they would go back to eating their turkey and mashed potatoes.

But it also occurred to me at these celebrations the many connections, sort of like the seven steps of Kevin Bacon type deal that my family had with The Ohio State University and OSU football. I soon realized how tremendous an influence the university had on all our lives. My constant barrage of questions to my loved ones opened up a new window in my life;

it's like a light switched on in my brain to illuminate the past and explore those experiences before they are gone! This is the story of my wonderful and loving family:

My Wife. The love of my life, Patti graduated from Ohio State in 1970 with a degree in education. Since then she has been my source of inspiration. She has done a terrific job raising our twin daughters Lara and Megan. Both have moved back to Westerville where we raised them. It gives us a sense of pride that our grown daughters, now with beautiful families of their own, still want to be close and associate with Mom and Dad!

Patti has been a Buckeye fan since we both attended OSU, after graduating from Bucyrus High School in 1966 and without her it's likely my attendance at OSU would not have happened.

During my junior year in high school my guidance counselor was reviewing my-not-so-stellar academic performance. In those days I was more in tuned to having fun than to sticking my nose to the grindstone. My guidance counselor suggested I start looking at two year schools because I did not have the grades to get into OSU.

This is when Patti jumped in with both feet and said that I had to start taking my studies more seriously—and that she would be my tutor. You see, when Patti moved to Bucyrus after our freshman year, we became next door neighbors and best friends. Then we began dating, first by going to the Annual Snowball dance together. She in her lovely sparkling dress and I with my dark suit with the skinny tie, were walking together down the aisle to get to the dance floor. I so romantically said to my date, "We may as well hold hands—everyone else is." I swept her off her feet!

So after that, my academics were in Patti's capable hands. She was, of course, the National Honor Society member and I was a struggling pupil whose draft number was that unlucky 7. Well it all worked out and I got the grades, thanks to Patti's iron hand in the area of academics and we headed together as freshman at OSU in September 1966.

Daughters. One of the best days of my life occurred on December 4th, 1980, our twins, Lara and Megan, were born two months prematurely in the neo-natal intensive care unit at University Hospital. Back then it was a big risk for premature babies, but due to the great care they received from the excellent staff of doctors and nurses, they grew up to be healthy, beautiful and intelligent women. Lara graduated with her Master's degree from The Ohio State University and Megan graduated from Ohio University with her Master's degree. (OK, we can't all graduate from OSU, but Megan married Josh, who received his PHD in Molecular Biology from Ohio State!)

Mother-in-Law. Ellie Miller was very excited when she entered the Shoe on October 19th, 1985. It was her first football game in the historic stadium, the Bucks were playing the Purdue Boilermakers. She has been a lifelong fan of Ohio sports—football, the Bucks and the Browns; baseball, the Indians; basketball, the Cavs. But her viewing was usually in front of the TV in her living room in Bucyrus. Grandma Ellie, as she is called by her four sons and daughters and many grandkids and great grandkids, has been active in sports all her 91 years. Bowling was her specialty, but she was always ready to play volleyball in her son's backyard, where beer drinking, euchre playing, and kids running around like crazy always made for a great time.

Kellie was in great shape due to her active lifestyle; she was a Marine Sergeant during World War II and was even bestowed the honor of christening a new Liberty Ship, the USS Bucyrus, on October 31, 1944 in San

MR. AND MRS. GALE FEGLEY AND THEIR DAUGHTER, SGT. ELEANOR FEGLEY,
OF THE UNITED STATES MARINES
OCTOBER 31, 1944   THE PERMANENTE METALS CORPORATION   PHOTOGRAPH NO. TL-13
SHIPYARD NUMBER ONE
RICHMOND, CALIFORNIA

Diego, California. Being from Bucyrus, Ohio, she christened the ship for the second time with a bottle containing water from the Sandusky River (the official christening was done with champagne).

She said the ship was named in honor of her hometown because its citizens had bought a huge number of war bonds. "My Dad (Gale Fegley) was the head of the war bond drive, and he wanted somebody from

Bucyrus to christen the new ship. It was really a choice between me and Mary Ann Kaupt, who was a Navy WAVE. But Mary was stationed in Washington, D.C. and I was in California," Ellie said.

Her parents, two uncles and aunts were there for the ceremony, bearing a bottle of Sandusky River water provided by the late Kay Hopley of the local Women's Christian Temperance Union.

"It was very exciting and I was kind of in shock during the whole ceremony," Ellie said.

As for the water, she said, "It was kind of cloudy."

The Liberty Ship Bucyrus met the fate of all the swiftly built transports by being scrapped after the war ended, Ellie said.

Cousin. Jeanne Jacobs of Bloomington, Indiana, graduated from OSU in 1972. She double dated with Rex Kern, quarterback of the "Super Sophomore" team of 1968.

She also has two daughters, a grandson and two granddaughters (photo below) that undoubtedly will be great Buckeye fans!

Photo by Jennie Edgington -proud parent of vocal twin Buckeyes -Connor & Grant!

HONOR FLIGHT

Ellie Miller and her brother Kenny had the distinct pleasure to go to Washington, D.C. Saturday October 20, 2012 as part of Honor Flight, the program that flies World War II and Korean War veterans to see the various war memorials. People magazine published a story about the Honor Flight; they were both photographed and interviewed during the flight. There were dozens of family and well-wishers at the Columbus International Airport for both the departure and arrival of their heroes from the war and there was not a dry eye in the house as patriotic songs and wild applause echoed through the terminal.

A surprise visit by members of the OSU Marching band serenaded the veterans as they deplaned. This was a long day for the honorees, as well as those who attended the OSU-Purdue game that afternoon. The game was a double overtime thriller that was one of the most exciting games ever played at the Shoe. The 8-0 Ohio State Buckeyes tied the Purdue Boilermakers with three seconds left, then won, 29-22 in overtime on the strength of a Carlos Hyde touchdown run. The thrilling comeback win eased the sting of the loss of Braxton Miller at quarterback.

Facing an 8-point deficit with 47 seconds left, Ohio State backup quarterback Kenny Guiton drove the Buckeyes 61 yards in 44 seconds, making the score 22-20 on a two-yard pass to Chris Fields. Guiton then found Jeff Heuerman for the two-point conversion to send the game to overtime.

After their long and exhausting day, both Ellie and Kenny quipped, "What about that game!"

Dad, John J. Zahara. He never attended college but learned a lot through the time he was in the military during World War II. He was stationed at Schofield Barracks on the Island of Oahu when Pearl Harbor was bombed, contracted malaria on Guadalcanal amidst bitter fighting and then got married in Auckland, New Zealand while on R & R (Rest and Relaxation). After the war Dad was more a fan of Cleveland Browns football than he was of the Buckeyes. Back then, few OSU games were televised so we would watch all the Browns games on our little black-and-white TV set.

Morse (left) at the National WWII Memorial with vets (front to back) Kenny Fegley, his sister Ellie Miller, Sens and George Gribben Jr.

People | HEROES AMONG US

FLYING VETS TO A SPECIAL PLACE

WORLD WAR II HEROES REMEMBER

EARL MORSE, 54
Enon, Ohio

Earl Morse was a physician's assistant at a VA clinic when he asked a few WWII-era patients if they'd been to the memorial in Washington, D.C., that had opened that spring of '04. "None had, and they weren't going to—they didn't have the means," Morse says. "It broke my heart."

So Morse, a retired Air Force captain and private pilot, decided to take them there. Recruiting volunteer pilots and raising funds to rent small planes, he flew 12 vets in May '05. It would be the first of 100 flights Morse would make; his efforts vastly expanded with help from Jeff Miller, 58, a businessman who started raising funds to charter commercial flights. Joining forces, the two formed Honor Flight Network (honorflight.org), which has flown more than 100,000 vets to the site.

Last fall Charlie Sens, 89, of Marion, Ohio, cried as he laid eyes on the monument's granite pillars. "Earl did this for the lowest of the low infantrymen," says Sens, who won a Purple Heart fighting in Europe and Africa. "He did it for people like me."

By Anne Lang and Nicole Weisensee Egan

1. Kenny Fegley, 92, transported supplies in Europe. 2. Sens (right, in Italy during the war with his brother Jim, who served in the Army Air Forces). 3. Ellie Miller, 90, was a Marine mechanic in Hawaii. 4. George Gribben Jr., 88, fought in the Battle of the Bulge.

KNOW A HERO? SEND SUGGESTIONS TO HEROESAMONUS@PEOPLEMAG.COM

98 May 27, 2015 PEOPLE

Photograph by ETHAN HILL

Dad finally became a convert to OSU football when my brother and I attended Ohio State from 1962-1971. I even convinced him to attend one of the games during my senior year. I can't remember what game it was, but I do remember it was raining that day. It didn't dampen Dad's spirits as he cheered on his now-beloved Buckeyes!

I recall, in 1971 while I was stationed in Ft Gordon Georgia, that my Dad was rushed to University Hospital after passing out due to his prostate cancer. I caught a military hop and hitch-hiked from Cincinnati, arriving late in the day after traveling over 10 hours. When I walked into Dad's room he bellowed to me, "Guess who came to visit me? Woody Hayes! The great Coach talked to me about World War II and gave me this box of chocolates."

Well, I guess my visit was trumped by the wonderful man and great human being. I have never seen my Dad happier!

Brother, John W. Zahara. Attended OSU from 1962-1967, graduated with a Doctor of Optometry.

Brother-in-Law. Second oldest to my wife Patti, Mike Miller graduated OSU 1974.

Mike and wife Pam celebrate The Game every year with their famous (or infamous) Mimosa Party. It starts early in the morning when the guests start arriving with all the potluck goodies, booze and even a marching band! Mike makes the Mimosas (champagne and orange juice) while Pam readies the mounds of delicious shrimp and other scrumptious treats.

Brother-in-Law, **Gary Miller** is the youngest in my wife's family

Lara Uher, Lisa Miller, Ellie Miller, Mike Miller, Patti Zahara , Gary Miller, Michael Miller, Kathi Kilgore Mimosa Party 2009

Nicole Miller, Kathi Michael,
Michael S. Miller, Patti Zahara, Lara Uher

and the most artistic having played in a rock band most of his life. He's presently still cranking out the tunes with the classic rock group, "Sinister Midget." I know this is not the most politically correct title, but what the hell, they're rockers.

Sister-In-Law, Lisa Miller. Wife of Gary Miller, the Ohio State University Grad 1979. Previous Assistant Editor of Bucyrus Telegraph Forum. First relative to hug a US President.

Nephew Max Mason Miller is a 2010 graduate of OSU. I watched Max, a gangly middle-school kid; emerge into an outgoing star athlete at Bucyrus High School. I am fiercely proud of this outstanding young man.

After graduation from OSU Max explored a few local jobs in the Columbus area, until he realized that he needed to embrace his life and branch out. He made a decision to join the Peace Corps. This was not a surprising decision—Max had been a giving person his whole life and this

Lisa Miller at rally in Marion Ohio for President Barack Obama- Gary Miller (with O in forehead) watches, as does the Secret Service guy!

Lisa Miller, Archie Mason Griffin, Max Mason Miller - OSU
event honoring 50th year of Peace Corps

was another way to influence the lives of others.

Based on an article in the *Columbus Dispatch*, Max is in good company with his fellow OSU alumni, with 79 other graduates currently serving as volunteers. OSU ranks #9 among all universities with total number of alumni serving in the Peace Corps.

According to Carrie Hessler-Radelet, acting director of the corps, "Ohio State University has been a great and longstanding partner for the Peace Corps. They have a great recruiter there, the faculty is supportive, and the curriculum is very forward-thinking and global to prepare students." Ohio State hosted the country's first Peace Corps campus recruiter in 1974, and has continued to build its on campus office and program.

Max left for Cameroon, Africa in 2011 and returned safe and sound June 2013.

FRIENDS

When you want to win a game, you have to teach.
When you lose a game, you have to learn.

—**Tom Landry**

Once a month our poker group gets together for a fun night out. My wife and I join three other couples for dinner out, and afterwards we go to the host's house where we play dealer's choice poker — not exactly Las Vegas style poker, but we have a blast.

After the 2011 football season, the dinnertime topic often revolves around OSU football, and one hot topic was whether OSU should keep Luke Fickell as coach. The hot rumor around Columbus was that Urban Meyer would be named head coach, but our poker playing buddy, Jim, would have nothing to do with that decision declaring: "I will be a Notre Dame fan and not watch another OSU game if Luke is not hired for another year."

Not everyone in our poker group agreed with Fickell's hiring. Most of us still have a strong allegiance to Coach Tressel and will forever hold a special place in our hearts for his years as "our" coach.

Jan, one of the original members of our poker group has a special reason she looked forward to OSU football and basketball games:

During my rounds of chemotherapy at the James Cancer Hospital, for Non-Hodgkin's Lymphoma, from 1999 to 2003, I looked forward to OSU football games and basketball games with enthusiasm! Sometimes I was tired and weak but I always revitalized during an OSU game. Even when we lost, I'd be so involved with the game that I'd feel better.

There wasn't much to look forward to back then, but the games always provided an escape from what was going on with me. I have been in remission since 2014, but I'll never forget those dark times being interspersed with some great games. I believe they raised my blood cell count! Now I can watch games with no underlying worries.

In the 1960s I attended Michigan State University as an undergraduate in nursing school, but when my husband and I moved to Columbus, we quickly found ourselves Buckeyes and have remained so ever since. I attended OSU graduate school in the 1990s in early childhood education.

I've attended a few games in person. Now my favorite thing is to invite two of my grandsons over to watch a game and we scream and cheer to our heart's content. I wear my buckeye necklace during every game.

Another story from Jan:

My aunt, who died in 2012 at the age of 91, was a great fan of OSU sports. Once, a visit from Archie Griffin was arranged at the retirement center where she lived. I have a picture of her and Archie on my refrigerator because she always told me, "That was the best day of my life."

She always decorated her apartment and later her room with Buckeye paraphernalia and she watched games on her TV even when her roommate didn't like the noise. When my cousin and I moved her into the retirement center, the first thing we did was hook up the TV because there was an OSU basketball game on. People came to the door to greet my aunt and we asked them to come back after the game!

Although she never made it to an actual game, my Aunt Vinnie would be so pleased to be included in a book of OSU stories!

THANK YOU OSU

Needless to say, The Ohio State University has been an extremely important influence in my life. I am proud to "give back" to my university by volunteering over the last 17 years as an Usher at the stadium. I am sure that this "One Usher's Recollection" could be repeated 1000 fold by telling each life story of my fellow Ushers & Redcoats! The following photo shows my family and degrees from Ohio State!

Patti (Miller) Zahara B.S. '70, Trevor Zahara, B.S. '71, Evie* , Joe
Uher, B.S. 2003, Josh Arnold, Ph. D., Molecular Biology 2008, Ellie*
Lara (Zahara) Uher Master's of Social Work 2005 , Mack*, Megan (Za-
hara) Arnold B.S. & M.S. in Clinical Exercise Physiology OU ,Zoey*
*Future Buckeyes

ACKNOWLEDGMENTS

This book is dedicated to all my fellow Ushers and Redcoats who called, emailed and mailed all the interesting stories included in this Journal. I want to thank the incredible Athletic Department staff, James Erisson, Mike Penner, Ericka Hoon and the advisory committee for their support and unlimited access to my fellow Ushers and Redcoats.

I started this endeavor over 17 years ago, starting to archive these fascinating events at the famous "Horseshoe," but in all reality it incorporates decades of events. I have had the honor to compile these wonderful anecdotes from my fellow Ushers, Redcoats, media, other authors, band members, coaches, executives, friends, and especially my relatives for their understanding, putting up with my constant barrage of questions about their OSU activities.

I have listed many authors in the Bibliography, but Jack Park was extremely gracious in patiently listening and answering all my first time author questions. Jack was instrumental in getting me started in the right direction with documenting these stories.

Special thanks to my fantastic editor, Adele Stratton for taking my ideas and giving me a roadmap to organize into a readable format. Without her incredible focus I was like a ship without a rudder!

Speaking of editors, I want to personally thank The Ohio State University Lantern for their tremendous support and encouragement throughout this entire process. My first call to the editor Kristen Mitchell was very positive in directing me to her Assistant Editor for Content, Caitlin Essig. Even though Caitlin was swamped with her own work, she took the time to completely critique and edit my book. Faculty Advisor, Dan Caterinicchia was especially kind and encouraging in allowing me to use quotes and photos from the Lantern archives.

Thanks to my IT guru, Chris Michael, for fixing my myriad of computer issues.

I also leaned heavily on the internet- Wikipedia, Bucknut.com, 11 Warriors, OSU Official website- for subject matter experts concerning, fact checking, detailing game play by plays and incredible photos from Michelle Drobik, Audiovisual Archivist, Photo Archives The Ohio State University Archives and The Ohio State University website.

Special thanks go to Westerville Library staff for answering dozens of my technical questions while writing this book.

Finally, thanks to Columbus Publishing Lab for putting the finishing touches on my manuscript.

I thank the following newspapers & magazines for allowing excerpts, reprints and photos of their excellent articles:

* *The Columbus Dispatch*
* *The Ohio State University Lantern*
* *The Cleveland Plain Dealer*
* *The Toledo Blade*
* *The Troy Daily News*
* *St. Clairsville Times Leader*
* *The Daily Jeffersonian*
* *People Magazine*

BIBLIOGRAPHY

1968- David Hyde- Orange Frazer Press Wilmington, Ohio Orangefrazer.com

Ohio State Football-The Great Tradition- By Jack Park-Lexington Press

Ohio State University- Football Vault-Whitman Publishing Jack Park

The Official Ohio State –Football Encyclopedia- Jack Park-2001 Sports Publishing

The Die-Hard Fan's Guide to Buckeye Football- Mark Rea Renergy publishing

Game of my Life-Ohio State- Memorable Stories of Buckeye Football Steve Greenberg & Laura Lanese-Publishing-LLLC

I love OSU- Steve Greenberg-Dave Ratermann-Triumph Books-2011

Buckeye Madness- Joe Menzer- Simon & Schuster-2005

Heart of a Mule- The Dick Schafrath Story/Stories

What It Means To be a Buckeye- Urban Meyer/Jeff Snook-Triumph Book-2003/2012

Woody's Boys- Alan Natali-Orange Frazer Press-1995

Buckeye Dreams- The Tyler Tank Whaley Story- Ken Gordon-Blue River Press-2008

For the Love of the Buckeyes- Frederick Klein-Triumph Books-2008

Then "Tress Said To Troy" Jeff Snook-2007,

More Than A Coach What it Means to Play ForCoach, Mentor and Friend –Jim Tressel- David Lee Morgan,Jr-Triumph Books-2009

The Winner's Manual- (For The Game of Life) Jim Tressel with Chris Fabry-Tyndale House Publishers, Inc

Glory Years- Photos by Jim Davidson- Text by John Porentas- Triumph Books

Stadium Stories-Ohio State Buckeyes-Jeff Rapp- The Globe Pequ0t Press-2003

Chic –Bob Hunter with Marc Katz- Orange Frazer Press Wilmington, Ohio Orangefrazer.com

Game Changer's Triumph, David Lee Morgan,Jr.

For Buckeye Fans *Only!* Rich Wolfe Lone Wolfe Press

HUTTA
ORTHODONTIC SPECIALISTS
Distinctively Different

Trevor,

Congratulations, your drive and dedication has truly paid off. Now we are both in the business to make people smile. Best of luck on your future accomplishments a s a writer.

Sincerely,

Dr. Larry Hutta

Pictured: Dr. Hutta with former patients and Trevor's daughter's, Lara and Megan.

Dr. Larry Hutta

Diplomate, American Board of

Orthodontics

Dr. Brandon Cook

Diplomate, American Board of

Orthodontics

Congratulations Trevor and all the hard working volunteers at Ohio Stadium.

Play More....

Pay Less!

Ohio's largest golf discount program

Get The Best Deals at The Best Courses

www.TeeTimeGolfPass.com

GO BUCKEYES!

Nartker, Grunewald, Eschleman & Cooper, LLC

Certified Public Accountants

"Best of Luck with your outstanding book. You have been a longtime client and friend."

Thanks to your fellow Ushers for the tremendous job that they do at the Buckeye Football Games.

GO BUCKS!

6253 Riverside Dr., Ste. 100
Dublin, OH 43017-5034
614-793-1333
614- 793-8784 (fax)

CPSIÅ information can be obtained at www.ICGtesting.com
Printed in the USA
BVOW10s1148120415

395672BV00002B/2/P